Informed
Legislatures

Center for Science & International Affairs

John F. Kennedy School of Government, Harvard University
79 JFK Street, Cambridge MA 02138   (617) 495-1400

The Center for Science and International Affairs (CSIA) is the hub of research and teaching on international relations at Harvard's John F. Kennedy School of Government. CSIA seeks to advance the understanding of international security and environmental problems, placing special emphasis on the role of science and technology in the analysis and design of public policy. The Center seeks to anticipate emerging international problems, identify practical solutions, and encourage policymakers to act. These goals animate work in each of the Center's four major programs:

- The International Security Program (ISP) is the home of the Center's core concern with international security issues.

- The Strengthening Democratic Institutions (SDI) project works to catalyze international support for political and economic transformations in the former Soviet Union.

- The Science, Technology, and Public Policy (STPP) program emphasizes public policy issues in which understanding of science, technology, and systems of innovation is crucial.

- The Environment and Natural Resources Program (ENRP) is the locus of interdisciplinary research on environmental policy issues.

Each year CSIA hosts a multinational group of some two dozen scholars from the social, behavioral, and natural sciences. Harvard faculty members and adjunct research fellows from the Boston area participate in CSIA activities. CSIA sponsors seminars and conferences, many open to the public; maintains a substantial specialized library; and publishes a monograph series and discussion papers. The Center's International Security Program, directed by Steven E. Miller, publishes the CSIA Studies in International Security through MIT Press, and sponsors and edits the quarterly journal *International Security*.

CSIA Occasional Papers are a series of monographs sponsored by the Center for Science and International Affairs (CSIA), co-published with and available from the University Press of America (UPA). Recent books in the series include:

Lewis Branscomb and Fumio Kodama, *Japanese Innovation Strategy: Technical Support for Business Visions.*

Bruce J. Allyn, James G. Blight, and David A. Welch, eds. *Back to the Brink: Proceedings of the Moscow Conference on the Cuban Missile Crisis.*

CSIA Occasional Paper No. 11

Informed Legislatures

Coping with Science in a Democracy

Megan Jones
David H. Guston
and Lewis M. Branscomb

Center for Science and International Affairs
Harvard University

University Press of America,® Inc.
4720 Boston Way
Lanham, Maryland 20706

3 Henrietta Street
London, WC2E 8LU England

Co-published by arrangement with The Center for Science and
International Affairs, Harvard University

Library of Congress Cataloging-in-Publication Data

Jones, Megan.
Informed legislatures : coping with science in a democracy / by
Megan Jones, David H. Guston, and Lewis M. Branscomb.
p.   cm.
"Co-Published by arrangement with Center for Science and
International Affairs-Harvard University.
1. Science and state--United States. 2. Technology and state--United
States. I. Guston, David H. II. Branscomb, Lewis M. III. Harvard
University. Center for Science and International Affairs. IV. Title.
Q127.U6J65   1996   328.73 --dc20   96-8767 CIP

ISBN 0-7618-0403-X (cloth: alk. ppr.)
ISBN 0-7618-0404-8 (pbk: alk. ppr.)

Book design and desktop publishing by
Lynne Meyer-Gay

For all concerned and committed
state legislators and their staffs,
who bring complex scientific issues
into the democratic process
in the 50 states.

CONTENTS

ABOUT THE AUTHORS

Megan Jones is an associate of the Science, Technology, and Public Policy program in the Center for Science and International Affairs at the Kennedy School of Government, Harvard University, and a guest investigator of the Woods Hole Oceanographic Institution. She is a former executive director of the Massachusetts Centers of Excellence Corporation and Massachusetts representative to the Science and Technology Council of the States. She has served in administrative positions in the Executive Offices of Economic and Environmental Affairs, as legislative aide in the Massachusetts legislature, and as trustee of a state university. She is a past president of the Marine Biological Laboratory Associates, and a founder and former board member of the Woods Hole Science and Technology Education Partnership. She has served on many boards and committees in her town of Falmouth, Massachusetts, including positions as elected town meeting member for over 25 years. She is also a trustee of Falmouth Hospital, and founder and co-chair of its Women's Health Care Task Force. She is a graduate of the Kennedy School of Government and Wellesley College.

David H. Guston is assistant professor of public policy at the Bloustein School of Planning and Public Policy, Rutgers University, and an associate of the Center for Science and International Affairs at the Kennedy School of Government, Harvard University. He is co-editor of *The Fragile Contract: University Science and the Federal Government* (with K. Keniston) and author of articles on the congressional oversight of science and other topics in science policy. He also edits *Truth & Power*, a newsletter examining the role of experts in the policy process, published by the Federation of American Scientists. He has worked as a researcher at the National Academy of Sciences and the former congressional Office of Technology Assessment. Dr. Guston holds a bachelor's degree from Yale University and a Ph.D. in political science from MIT.

Lewis M. Branscomb is the Aetna Professor of Public Policy and Corporate Management at the Kennedy School of Government, Harvard University, where he directs the Science, Technology, and Public Policy program in the Center for Science and International Affairs. A physicist educated at Duke and Harvard Universities, Branscomb has served as a director of the National Bureau of Standards (now the National Institute for Standards and Technology), and as vice president and chief scientist of IBM Corporation. In 1979 Dr. Branscomb was appointed to the National Science Board and served as chairman for four years. He is a member of the State-Federal Technology Partnership Task Force, the Governor's Council on Economic Growth and Technology, and has served on the executive board of the Massachusetts Centers of Excellence Corporation. A member of the Carnegie Commission on Science, Technology and Government, and an author of several of its reports, he has also been principal investigator and an author of *Beyond Spinoff: Military and Commercial Technologies in a Changing World*, editor and an author of *Empowering Technology: Implementing a U.S. Strategy*, and author of *Confessions of a Technophile*. He is co-editor of the forthcoming *Converging Infrastructures: Intelligent Transportation Systems and the NII*.

PREFACE

In a 1822 letter, James Madison warned that "[a] people who mean to be their own governors must arm themselves with the power which knowledge brings."[1] The nation's founders had designed a governmental structure with separate legislative, executive, and judicial institutions sharing power, and a federal system in which power is shared between the national government and the many state governments. This design invited conflict among branches and levels of government. But it also invited them to bring to bear many resources to legitimate their roles and to help them be more effective, including access to the scientific and technical information that undergirds a great deal of contemporary decision making.

Much has been written about access to scientific and technical information by the branches of national government.[2] But despite the fact that state governments face many of the same technically challenging questions as the federal government, and that they are now increasingly involved in research and development projects on their own or in cooperation with the federal government,[3] very little is known about how state governments, and especially state legislatures, acquire and use technical information and analysis.[4] We designed and conducted the State Legislative Science and Technology Project in order to answer these basic questions and to explore opportunities to strengthen the capability of legislators to govern effectively when challenged by increasingly complex issues.

In phase I of the project, we surveyed the state legislatures, inquiring about their need for scientific and technical information and basic aspects of legislative organizations and resources. Interested legislators or staff from all 50 states responded with remarkably little follow-up required. This interested response encouraged us to proceed with the study and helped us to identify those people who became our primary contacts in the second phase of the project. We concluded the first phase with a workshop, held in Cambridge in December 1993, at which we discussed the findings of the survey and our plans for the second phase with attendees from 17 states. We were fortunate to have among our workshop speakers Raymond Sanchez, Speaker of the New Mexico House of Representatives, and Charles Horn, Ohio State Senator and Chairman of the Committee on Energy, Science, and Natural Resources of the National Conference of State Legislatures (NCSL).

In phase II of the project, Megan Jones and David H. Guston conducted field work in 11 states. We chose the states we visited (Florida, Georgia, Kentucky, Louisiana, Minnesota, New Mexico, New York, North Carolina, Ohio, Wisconsin, Wyoming) with attention to geographic, demographic, and economic characteristics, as well as the level of professionalization of the legislatures and the availability of interested and cooperative contacts. Within each state, we identified interviewees with the assistance of the primary contact in that state. Most often, the primary contact was the person who responded for the state in the phase I survey and/or attended the December 1993 workshop. The two researchers conducted a total of 185 interviews (66 legislators, 94 staff, 25 others), the majority of them during the spring and summer of 1994. The interview questions consisted of a combination of open-ended and numerical-response questions. The average interview lasted about 45 minutes, and each interview was recorded and later transcribed.

We concluded the second phase of the project with a second meeting in Cambridge in September 1995, at which we presented a preliminary analysis of our results to participants from most of the 11 phase II states, a number of federal agencies, and other interested organizations. Former Governor of Pennsylvania Richard Thornburgh was very generous to speak at the opening of the conference, and we thank Dr. Eric Lander, Director of the Human Genome Project, Whitehead Institute, for his provocative lecture as well.

We gratefully acknowledge the financial support of the National Science Foundation (NSF) (#SBR-93-21880) and The Carnegie Corporation of New York (#B-6000), whose Commission on Science, Technology and Government has had a major role in bringing attention to the need to improve both executive and legislative performance in dealing with science and technology. NSF also supported an undergraduate research assistant, Paul Hodgdon, who provided invaluable support, particularly in "surfing" the Internet for state legislative information. We would also like to thank NCSL for its sponsorship of the project. The Kennedy School's Taubman Center for State and Local Government Innovations Program helped to support the first workshop through its Ford Foundation Innovations Program. We would also like to thank the Center for Science and International Affairs (CSIA) at the Kennedy School for providing a hospitable institutional home for the project and the Department of Public Policy at the Bloustein School of Planning and Public Policy, Rutgers University, for supporting David Guston's participation in the project after July 1994 when he joined their faculty.

A project as large and participatory as this one naturally requires the selfless assistance of a large number of people beyond the researchers, who, for better or worse, receive some public recognition of their efforts. But because of promises of confidentiality made to our many interview subjects, we cannot recognize them by name even here. Nevertheless, we owe a debt of gratitude to the legislators, staff, and other professionals who participated in our study, and we hope that our efforts have proved at least somewhat helpful in performing their jobs to keep state legislatures informed.

There were some legislators and staff persons who provided unique assistance in facilitating our site visits and whom we can thank by name, including: Karen Stolting (Florida); Terry Minvielle, Jeannie Thomas, and Jim Kundell (Georgia); Peggy Hyland (Kentucky); Noel Hunt and Steve Perry (Louisiana); Rick Krueger and Phyllis Kahn (Minnesota); Chuck Horn (Ohio); Ray Sanchez, Gordon Meeks, and Dave Warren (New Mexico); Terry Sullivan (North Carolina); Rosemary Hinkfuss, Spencer Black, and David Stute (Wisconsin); and Richard Miller (Wyoming).

We are indebted to our advisory committee—composed of Alan Altshuler, Director of the Kennedy School's A. Alfred Taubman Center for State and Local Government; Richard Celeste, former Governor of Ohio; Rick Kreuger, former Speaker pro tem of the Minnesota House of Representatives; and Speaker Sanchez of New Mexico—for their assistance in designing the project. T. Dwight Connor of the NCSL staff deserves special thanks for his helpful counsel throughout the duration of the project. Chris Coburn at the Battelle Memorial Institute in Columbus, Ohio, provided valuable information and advice, and Alan Rosenthal of the Eagleton Institute of Politics at Rutgers University lent important expertise as well.

Teresa Johnson Lawson, senior editor at CSIA, Lynne Meyer-Gay, copy editor and desktop publisher, and Michelle Harris of University Press of America were instrumental in helping us to move our research to book form. Although Laura Wilson at CSIA joined the team only at the very end, she contributed significantly to those last important tasks. And we must single out for our greatest appreciation Veronica McClure, administrative assistant to Lewis Branscomb, who produced drafts and documents under demand-

ing timetables and served as the nerve center for a somewhat far-flung research team.

Megan Jones
Cambridge, Massachusetts

David H. Guston
New Brunswick, New Jersey

Lewis M. Branscomb
Cambridge, Massachusetts

January 1996

NOTES

1. Letter to W. T. Barry, August 4, 1822, as quoted in Elizabeth
   Frost, ed., *The Bully Pulpit: Quotations from America's Presidents* (New York: Facts on File, 1988).

2. Among recent publications, for Congress see Bruce Bimber,
   *The Politics of Expertise in Congress: The Rise and Fall of the
   Office of Technology Assessment* (Albany, N.Y.: SUNY Press,
   forthcoming); for the president, see D. Allan Bromley, *The
   President's Scientists* (New Haven, Conn.: Yale University
   Press, 1995); for the federal bureaucracy, see Sheila Jasanoff,
   The Fifth Branch: Science Advisors as Policymakers (Cam-
   bridge, Mass.: Harvard University Press, 1990) and Bruce L.
   R. Smith, *The Advisors: Scientists in the Policy Process* (Wash-
   ington, D.C.: Brookings, 1992); and for the judiciary, see
   Sheila Jasanoff, *Science at the Bar: Law Science, and Technol-
   ogy in America* (Cambridge, Mass.: Harvard University Press,
   1995).

3. Christopher Coburn, ed., *Partnerships: A Compendium of
   State and Federal Cooperative Technology Programs* (Columbus, Ohio: Battelle Memorial Institute, 1995).

4. Most prior attention to state legislatures and their access to
   technical information focuses on the State Science, Engineering and Technology (SSET) Program of the National Science
   Foundation (NSF), which in 1976 awarded $25,000 to each of
   49 state executives and 42 state legislatures to conduct
   planning studies in the provision of technical information. In
   1980, SSET provided matching funds to seven implementation projects in legislatures in Colorado, Florida, Illinois,
   Maine, New Hampshire, Puerto Rico, and Washington, but in
   1981, the incoming Reagan administration terminated the
   program. See Irwin Feller, et al., "Scientific and Technological
   Information in State Legislatures," *American Behavioral
   Scientist* 22 (January-February 1979): 417-36; Richard
   Jones, *Descriptions of State Science and Technology Offices*
   (Denver, Colo.: National Conference of State Legislatures,
   1980); and Douglas M. Sacarto, *Science and Technology in
   Legislatures: A Review of Seven SSET Implementation Projects*
   (Denver, Colo.: National Conference of State Legislatures,
   1984).

EXECUTIVE
SUMMARY

Making informed political decisions increasingly requires technical information that is normally in the hands of unelected experts. At stake in the relationship between these experts and political decision makers is a fundamental issue of the legitimacy of democratic government. Motivated by this concern, a three-phase project, funded by the National Science Foundation and the Carnegie Corporation of New York and supported by the National Conference of State Legislatures, reviewed the science and technology (S&T) policy support available to state legislatures. The project staff are: Lewis M. Branscomb (Principal Investigator), Aetna Professor of Public Policy and Corporate Management, and Director of the Kennedy School of Government (KSG) Science, Technology, and Public Policy Program; Megan Jones (Project Director), former Director of the Massachusetts Centers of Excellence Corporation; and David H. Guston (Research Consultant), Assistant Professor of Public Policy, Bloustein School of Planning and Public Policy, Rutgers University.

In phase I, the project surveyed all 50 state legislatures on their S&T policy support needs and practices. A workshop held at Harvard's Kennedy School of Government in December 1993 reviewed the findings, with invited representatives from 17 states attending. In phase II, research staff conducted 185 interviews with legislators and staff from 11 states: Florida, Georgia, Kentucky, Louisiana, Minnesota, North Carolina, New Mexico, New York, Ohio, Wisconsin, and Wyoming. A conference held at KSG in September 1995 reviewed the findings of the field work, which are summarized in this report. Phase III seeks to implement recommendations in cooperation with interested legislatures.

The project uses the term *science and technology* for any issue that requires technical information and analysis for informed legislative decision making. The interviews were analyzed according to seven criteria: (1) need for S&T policy support, (2) internal and external sources of S&T policy support, (3) characteristics of useful S&T policy support, (4) legislative use of technology, (5) technical information in a political environment, (6) legislative satisfaction with existing S&T policy support, and (7) recommendations for improvement.

Findings

1. Need for Science and Technology Policy Support

The project finds nearly unanimous agreement that state legislators need access to technical information and analysis and substantial agreement that this need has been increasing over time. The principal reasons for this perceived increase in need are the overall complexity of contemporary life, the need for technical information and analysis in important policy areas of the economy, education, and the environment, and a growing sophistication of the public and their representatives.

2. Internal and External Sources of S&T Policy Support

State legislatures have a variety of sources for S&T policy support. Internally, state legislatures make use of different staff mechanisms, including joint research offices, separate House and Senate research offices, legislative libraries, personal staff, mentor legislators, and, in the largest states, multiple specialized mechanisms. Most staff are generalists, and although many have advanced or professional degrees, few have advanced degrees in scientific or technical fields.

Externally, state legislatures make use of executive branch agencies, lobbyists, state universities, national and regional clearinghouses, federal sources, personally known (individual) sources, and in some states, specialized S&T sources, to gather technical information and analysis.

In all but three states in the sample, some form of internal staff organization is the most important source of technical information and analysis. In two states, executive agencies are the most important source.

3. Characteristics of Useful S&T Policy Support

The most important characteristics of useful technical information and analysis pertain to the sources of information rather than to the information itself. Sources have to be trustworthy and accessible. With respect to the information, the most important characteristics are accuracy, objectivity, and timeliness, followed by its presentation in a nontechnical and usable format. Technical information also has to be up-to-date and relevant, or specific to the legislative problem at hand.

The interviews suggested that trust of a source develops through repeated, high-quality interactions among people who share underlying values or interests. Trust is closely associated with process-related issues such as accessibility, timeliness, and the clear and nontechnical presentation of technical information and analysis. Although respondents appreciate a necessary role for partisan and interested information and analysis in the legislative process, they believe that sufficient nonpartisan technical sources needed to be available to help them balance the interested sources or to triangulate among them.

4. Legislative Use of Technology

The visited states were generally in the midst of many changes in the computer technology they use and how they use it. Something of a common model did exist, however, in which all staff have personal computers linked in a local area network. The variety occurred in areas such as the extension of the network to district offices, the use of computers by legislators themselves, and the degree of public access to legislative information systems. Some respondents suggest that a generational divide among legislators has produced a division between older legislators unfamiliar with new technologies and younger legislators able to take advantage of it.

Although staff (and computer-using legislators) make heavy use of internal e-mail systems, at the time of the interviews the Internet and other electronic or on-line services were not important sources of technical information and analysis because of the lack of modems, the need to go through a gatekeeper to conduct searches, or the lack of training in finding information on-line.

Legislatures face challenges in procuring new computer and information systems for themselves and for state government generally, and some legislatures developed sophisticated internal sources of expertise after having had procurement difficulties. They also face challenges posed by general issues of electronic democracy such as general privacy, security, and freedom of information, as well as particular questions about increased accessibility, increased contact, and the durability of the citizen-legislature.

5. Technical Information in a Political Environment

Technical information and analysis is only one part of legislative decision making, and respondents from across the states indicated that only rarely was it the most significant or definitive part.

Respondents agreed that the opinions of constituents are usually more important than technical information and analysis, although they did attempt to distinguish some issues and some legislative styles that gave priority to technical information. Legislators also suggested that technical information and analysis is important not only for decision making but also for enabling them to educate their constituents.

Technical information is most important at the stage of drafting legislation. It is important but slightly less so when legislators are responding to legislation introduced by their colleagues and when they are evaluating previous legislation or administrative actions. It is only somewhat important for helping legislators decide what issues are important in the short or long term, and it is not important in helping legislators decide how to vote.

Respondents agreed almost unanimously that technical information and analysis provided by staff has increased the independence, authority, or power of the legislature vis-à-vis both the executive branch and lobbyists. Nevertheless, there is still a strong undercurrent of belief that legislatures have not come far enough in their efforts to achieve equal status with the executive branch and sufficient independence from lobbyists.

The principal barriers to the provision and use of technical information and analysis in the state legislatures can be characterized as either supply-side (involving the production of information) or demand-side (involving the consumption of information). The primary supply-side barrier is that staff feel they do not have adequate time to produce information and analysis for legislative use. Other important supply-side barriers include lack of access to electronic databases, incompatibility of hardware and software among potential sources of data, uncertainty about the accuracy or credibility of data, lack of cooperation from potential sources, and the volume of potentially relevant but difficult to access information.

Time is also a principal demand-side barrier. Legislators feel time pressured and may not spend enough time to formulate correct questions and to assimilate and use information. There are also some attitudinal and intellectual barriers among legislators that prevent them from taking complete advantage of the technical information and analysis to which they have access, as well as a barrier posed by competition between interested and disinterested sources of information for the attention of legislators.

6. Legislative Satisfaction with S&T Policy Support

The average level of satisfaction among legislators with the technical information and analysis to which they have access, on a scale of 1 to 5, where 5 is "most satisfied," is 3.86. Satisfaction varied little state to state and seems to bear no direct relation to the level of professionalization in a legislature, suggesting that some equilibrium exists between the demand for technical information and the supply. Despite this expressed satisfaction, respondents also agree that legislators often do not necessarily know enough to be dissatisfied.

Specific sources of residual dissatisfaction include: a lack of adequate staff expertise in technical areas; a desire for technical information better linked to political (not partisan) information, such as district-level data; a need for more coherent and effective synthesis of technical information; better translations of technical information for the layperson; unreasonable expectations and confusion about the contribution of computers and information technology; information overload; unclear lines of communication with external sources—particularly state universities; and the inherent uncertainty of technical information.

Respondents were nearly uniform and positive in their perceptions that staff do provide accurate and unbiased information, but they were somewhat less positive (although similarly uniform) in their perceptions of the ability of staff to provide timely information and analysis and to present it in a useful format. The responses suggest that the institutional controls to ensure accuracy and lack of bias among staff members are adequate, but that a more important locus of reform might be enhancing the ability of staff to meet deadlines and produce more readable documents.

7. Recommendations

Despite the acknowledgement that change does not come easily to legislatures—for both political and financial reasons—respondents nevertheless recognized the increasing need for technical information and analysis and made a number of suggestions for improvement, including the following:

1. Improve staff expertise in scientific and technical areas by adding technically trained staff to research offices, hiring part-time experts for specific assignments, hiring technically trained staff as personal aides, and/or offering scientific and technical training to generalists currently on staff;

2. Increase computer access, use, and training for both staff and legislators;

3. Facilitate access to technical expertise at state universities and intersectoral organizations;

4. Increase the use of interns from professional societies and universities.

SUMMARY
FINDINGS

Introduction

The Center for Science and International Affairs (CSIA) at Harvard University's Kennedy School of Government has conducted a project to study the science and technology (S&T) policy support available to state legislatures and, if warranted, to explore in cooperation with interested state legislatures, alternative models for meeting their needs.

The fundamental issue at stake is the legitimacy of democratic government. If political decisions increasingly require technical information which is in the hands of unelected experts, then, in the words of James Madison, can "[a] people who mean to be their own governors arm themselves with the power which knowledge brings"?

The project received grants from the Carnegie Corporation of New York and the National Science Foundation and support from the National Conference of State Legislatures. Dr. Lewis Branscomb, Director of CSIA's Science, Technology and Public Policy (STPP) Program, served as principal investigator; Megan Jones, former Director of the Massachusetts Centers of Excellence Corporation, as project director; and David H. Guston, Assistant Professor, Bloustein School of Planning and Public Policy, Rutgers University, as chief research consultant.

The project has been divided into three phases:

Phase I surveyed all 50 state legislatures on their science and technology policy support needs and current practices, and received a 100-percent response. The survey findings were reviewed at a workshop held at the Kennedy School in December 1993, with invited representatives from 17 states attending.

Phase II was devoted to the field study of needs and practices of 11 states: Florida, Georgia, Kentucky, Louisiana, Minnesota, North Carolina, New Mexico, New York, Ohio, Wisconsin, and Wyoming. These states were selected for their political, geographic, economic, and demographic diversity as well as their interest in participating in the project. Project staff conducted 185 interviews with legislators and legislative staff, many of whom were recommended to us for their interest and experience in science and technology issues.

Project staff prepared separate state reports and a summary report based on the seven criteria for analysis listed below. Selected state legislators, staff, and other experts reviewed the reports and summary in conjunction with a conference held at the Kennedy School, September 21–22, 1995. To conclude Phase II, these findings are being distributed to all 50 legislatures.

Phase III will seek to encourage implementation of recommendations based on our findings by interested state legislatures.

Definition

For the purposes of our study, we define the term *science and technology* as referring to any issue that requires technical information and analysis for informed legislative decision making.

Criteria for Analysis

1. Need for science and technology policy support;
2. Internal and external sources of S&T policy support;
3. Characteristics of useful S&T policy support;
4. Legislative use of technology;
5. Technical information in a political environment;
6. Legislative satisfaction;
7. Recommendations.

Findings

1. Need for Science and Technology Policy Support

We did not want to assume that S&T issues are significant in the work of legislators, so we asked "Do you ever have a need for technical information?" The interviews conducted in the 11 project states produced virtually unanimous agreement that legislators need access to technical information and analysis. "Absolutely, there is a need," declared a key staff official from Ohio. "There is an overwhelming number of science and technology issues which need technical information and advice, but unfortunately we don't have it. It is a glaring weakness. Your study is something that needs to be done and we need to learn from it and make changes." "I can't think of any issues that don't require technical information and analysis," declared a Florida legislator. "I cannot think of an area where technical components would not be required involving major public policy issues," said a legislative leader from New Mexico. A member of the Kentucky Assembly observed that "there's a realization in the General Assembly among enlightened members that nothing is really more important than having good technical information. And if you have good technical information, you can control policymaking." The urgency of the problem was evident in a comment by Ohio legislators. "We have a wide range of issues from defense conversion to the impact of chickens on windshields, and we are struggling with how to get this kind of technical information," he said. In terms of low-level nuclear waste, a senator asked, "How are legislators to know what are the dangerous agents? How do we deal with them? Where do we find waste disposal sites? What are the criteria for selecting them?" In reference to tax information, a committee chair said, "We are basing decisions on things that happened 40 or 50 years ago when we were a manufacturing state. Now we're moving on to technology and we need to have a lot of updated information." One legislative leader said that in the area of telecommunications, "We need more information on distance learning and whether we should rewire every school. I'm not sure we are ready. I'm not sure that we understand what's involved. It cannot be done by a quick fix."

A technical staff expert from Wisconsin summarized the problem for legislators as one of information management. "Clearly, there is a need for a synthesizing role and a digestive role because there is no shortage of information out there, be it from interest groups or other organizations," he said. In just one example, during floor debate on pesticide regulation, a senator held up a bibliography of 60 or so studies for which there was no summary of findings and, therefore, no way to utilize the information. As more legislatures are wired into advanced information systems, "there will be even more access to unlimited sources of information and the need for analysis will become even more important."

The examples of science and technology issues before the 11 legislatures mentioned in the interviews covered a wide spectrum. Respondents reported technical issues involving economic development, environmental protection, and health care legislation in all 11 states; telecommunications and education in ten states; energy and human services in eight states; agriculture in seven states; transportation in five states; gambling and state S&T policy in four states; and political and judicial issues in three states.

The variety of issues addressed by the legislatures are the following:

Economic Development: technology transfer; defense conversion; tax reform; trade issues, including gateway to North American Free Trade Agreement (NAFTA); biotechnology development; space port development and single stage rocket technology; industrial extension service; technology incubators; mining technology; impact of technology on workers' compensation; strategic state planning and economic forecasting;

Environmental Protection: water quality and quantity management; ambient air quality; wildlife and fisheries management; wetland protection; oil field cleanup; high- and low-level radioactive waste storage/disposal; solid waste management; underground storage tank leakage; waste tire recycling; environmental trust fund; lead screening; asbestos removal; pesticide regulation; ozone layer depletion; biological diversity; land use; comparative risk assessment;

Health Care: telemedicine; cancer prevention; genetic engineering; licensing of genetic counselors; prison health; surrogate motherhood; disabilities research; medical technology development; infectious waste incineration; HIV testing; mammography equipment regulations; abortion;

Information Technology: telecommunications; information infrastructure; space science; Global Positioning System (GPS); state computer system procurement; building code reform; equity access to cable TV;

Education: R&D infrastructure; science and math K–12 education; facilities and equipment funding;

computer literacy; distance learning; equitable access to educational technology; higher education;

Energy: alternative energy sources; energy conservation; utilities regulation and deregulation; nuclear power issues; retail wheeling of electricity (opening power company transmission lines to competitors); coal technology; oil and gas exploration; power line siting; mine safety;

Human Services: welfare reform; child support enforcement; social service data transfer;

Agriculture: livestock issues; bovine growth hormone; food irradiation; tobacco farming;

Transportation: alternate modes; highway/airport construction; mass transit; high-speed rail; auto emission inspection;

Gambling: computerized state lottery; evaluation of gambling proposals; interactive gambling;

S&T Policy: state S&T policy legislation;

Political Process: redistricting; public access to legislative information; computerized constituent mailings; storage durability of computerized state records; impact of technology on constitutional rights;

Judicial Process: DNA evidence; driving while intoxicated (DWI); computer tracking; automation of court system; security technology; firearm technology.

Recent Increase in Need

The overwhelming majority of respondents in all 11 states agreed that the need for technical information and analysis has increased in recent years. There was a small minority that felt that the need has not increased. "It's always been there," a staffer from North Carolina said. In one case, a Wyoming staffer thought that with "term limits changing the caliber of legislators," the need is even "getting less." The majority, however, saw a definite increase in need and traced its roots to overall complexity of contemporary life, the "three big Es" of economy, education and the environment, and a growing sophistication of the public and their legislative representatives.

Complexity of Issues

"The general incorporation of technology in our everyday life has meant that it's a factor in a lot more decisions," explained a staffer from Florida. "The issues that Florida faces as a legislature are exceedingly complex, and traditional structures simply don't adequately address the kinds of complex problems that we have to find solutions to," added a colleague. "Biotechnology is nothing my father ever dreamed of when he was in government, whereas now it's a big deal," said a legislator from Wisconsin. Telecommunications was also mentioned as a highly complex issue about which legislators now need technical assistance in order to make informed decisions. "Legislators need to know such things as different bandwidths, what they can carry, the difference between copper wire and fiber optics, and what software technology is the best and not the one with the most political clout," explained a legislator from New Mexico.

Economy

The most important specific issue causing an increase in the need for technical information and analysis was the growing importance of technology to the state economy. "With IBM leading the way, there is an understanding that New York's economy is directly tied to technology development and that the legislature must support policies to encourage its growth," said a New York legislator. "Telecommunications, computer technology, biotechnology are all keys to New York's economic growth. For the legislature to understand and regulate those industries requires a great deal of technical skill that wasn't needed ten years ago," declared a key New York staff member.

A legislator from New Mexico commented that technology was revolutionizing his state's economy, and the legislature needed to understand the impact of such dramatic change. "Ten years ago we were still seeing ourselves as involved with an extractive and service industry, and it never dawned on us that the service industry was going to be led by technological advances. New Mexico is now being seen by the outside world as a place to come to, and companies are looking to move here. It used to be that they wanted to know if you needed a visa to get here and 'what language do you speak?'"

Respondents also referred to competition from other states and foreign countries in capturing the market for high-tech goods as increasing the need for technical legislative competence. In states with a large federal presence, the end of the Cold War and the need for defense conversion to a domestic economy were also seen as important influences.

Education

Respondents saw the issue of education reform, tied closely to the advent of new technologies for telecommunications, as a second major reason for the increasing need for technical information by legislators. A state representative from New Mexico explained that "there are kids who travel 75–80 miles one way in a school bus. We could educate them through telecommunications at half the cost. We've got to start using our imagination." A key Ohio staffer declared, "We can't expect Ohio to move forward unless we have an educated work force." The legislature has a role in "making the people understand why [education] is a priority."

Environment

Respondents cited the increasingly demanding nature of environmental problems as a third issue driving the need for greater technical competence on the part of legislators and their staffs. In particular, respondents mentioned the requirement of states to implement federal environmental protection mandates, such as the Clean Air Act, as an important component of the need for legislative expertise.

Public and Legislative Sophistication

Another frequently mentioned reason for the increase in need was the greater technical sophistication of the public. "The knowledge of citizens groups has grown, and they are holding the legislators' feet to the fire," said a staffer from Ohio. "There is a great deal of pressure on state legislatures to perform better. That inherently places a burden on the legislators, especially citizen-legislators, to become more informed and more current on technical knowledge than they were required to be in the past," said a staff member from New Mexico.

"The same answers that were good enough 10 to 15 years ago aren't good enough today, and that is pushing members up against the wall, and they are reaching out for scientific knowledge," a New York staff director explained. "Also, with the democratization of society, new constituencies are becoming increasingly active participants in the political process. Therefore, issues such as the ethical and equitable distribution or impacts of certain kinds of technology advances become very pressing and important in the legislative decision-making process."

A respondent from Wisconsin voiced a similar concern about the role of technical information in distributory politics. He observed that advocacy groups are increasingly going to the legislature with their concerns to deal with the "sins of the past," forcing legislators to have technical knowledge not only to be able to vote properly but also "to keep advocacy groups honest." He also felt that advocacy groups turned to the legislature because "it is cheaper to settle differences through the legislature instead of lobbying the executive branch or going to court."

Respondents noted the increasing sophistication of legislators themselves, which they attributed to a generational change. "The baby boom generation is generally better educated, and as a result they ask more questions. Legislators are wanting to know more details about what they are deciding on," said a staffer from Minnesota. A staffer from Florida observed that legislators now have careers that "demand they become more skilled in terms of the use of technology. They want to know 'Has this type of analysis been done? Do we have statistical information on this?'" A respondent from Louisiana mentioned that the more "educated brand of legislator is more apt to pursue 'preventative maintenance legislation' rather than react with a 'seat-of-the-pants, off-the-cuff type of approach'." A North Carolina legislator, having assumed a leadership position, now finds himself "expected to provide . . . support and background information as you propose legislation."

There was general agreement that keeping up with rapid technological change is not an easy task for legislators or their staffs. "We have created a democracy to govern our society, and the democratic process is slow to respond to change," said a technical staff expert from New Mexico. "It has been increasingly difficult for legislators and the democratic process to keep up with changes in technology. And yet, the need to upgrade the technical information and comprehension of that information is critical. I have a hard enough time keeping up with the information and that is my field." With fiscal constraints facing legislatures across the country, legislators and staff need technical information to prevent costly mistakes. As a respondent from Louisiana explained, "We can't afford to make bad decisions anymore."

2. Internal and External Sources of S&T Policy Support

Internal Sources

Reflecting their diversity, state legislatures have developed a variety of internal mechanisms to respond to the need for technical information and analysis. These include: (1) central, nonpartisan research offices, (2) nonpartisan House and Senate research offices, (3) permanent committee staff, (4) majority and minority House and Senate research offices, (5) a legislative S&T commission, (6) personal legislative staff, (7) legislative libraries, and (8) individual legislators with expertise.

Joint Legislative Research Offices

Six of the project states (Kentucky, North Carolina, New Mexico, Ohio, Wisconsin, Wyoming) rely on central, nonpartisan legislative service offices for technical information and analysis. The House and Senate leadership usually appoint directors of the central research offices who then hire the rest of the professional staff. The research offices are often the first point of contact for individual legislators seeking information as well as the source of technical support for the regular and interim committees they staff.

The first state to develop a nonpartisan, centralized policy support agency was Wisconsin. In 1901, under the leadership of Governor Robert LaFollette, Wisconsin established the Legislative Research Bureau to provide professional services to all legislators in order to help them better represent their constituents and counteract the influence of special interests. The reason for its creation "was to bring democracy into the legislative branch," explained a bureau official. "So, while our agency is strictly nonpartisan, our creation and existence were very much a political statement. It means that a representative who is an auto worker on the assembly line who comes up here will get just as good services as a rich businessman or lawyer, somebody with a lot of education or somebody with access to special interest groups." The Legislative Research Bureau still operates, primarily assisting in bill drafting, although the legislature has added two additional joint, nonpartisan policy support agencies, the Legislative Fiscal Bureau and the Legislative Council. The Legislative Fiscal Bureau provides fiscal and policy information and analysis to both individual legislators and the legislature as a whole. The Legislative Council, whose staff includes a staff scientist, was cited as the primary source of science and technology policy support. In the words of a legislator, "they make it possible for me to excel." These agencies have served as a model not only for other states but also for the Congressional Research Service, which Robert LaFollette, then U.S. Senator, was instrumental in establishing in 1914.

House and Senate Research Offices

Three states (Georgia, Louisiana, Minnesota) originally had joint, nonpartisan research offices. They are now separated into House and Senate agencies in order for each chamber to establish independent jurisdiction over its own policy support mechanisms. In Georgia, for example, where the Senate's active presiding officer is the lieutenant governor and there is a perception of an executive branch orientation, the House is particularly interested in maintaining control over its own sources of information. In spite of the separation, there is still an effort to maintain nonpartisanship, a policy originally advocated by the first director of the Wisconsin Legislative Research Bureau, Charles McCarthy. "If you have to choose between a partisan staff and none at all, choose the latter." In Minnesota, the nonpartisanship requirement of house research is so strict that no staff may have participated "in any way" in a political campaign.

Multiple Mechanisms

Only the most populous states have the resources to provide multiple, specialized mechanisms for legislative technical information and analysis. Florida, the fourth largest state, has a large and extremely differentiated staff structure. The nonpartisan, permanent professional committee staff, particularly those of the Joint Information Technology Resources Committee and the Auditing Committee, is considered by far the most important source of technical information and analysis. The staff is responsible not only to committee members but to all members in their chamber and serves at the pleasure of the chamber's leader. The Information Technology Resources Committee staff sees its role as informational, "trying to incorporate all sides of an issue and gather all the facts from the sources." It recently has been working on assessing a potential state role in developing a global positioning system for use by harbor pilots. Florida also has a Joint Legislative Management Committee that provides more centralized policy support. Under its jurisdiction is the Economic and Demographic Research Division, which is responsible for economic revenue and expenditure forecasting and provides statistical and other research support to standing committees. Historically a one-party state, Florida has had few problems with its nonpartisan structure, although it is not clear what consequences a newly competitive Republican party will have.

The New York legislature, in keeping with the state's long-time leadership position and a population third only to California and Texas, has an extremely complex system of policy support agencies. These multiple policy support agencies available to New York legislators reflect a legislature that has the largest budget and greatest number of legislative staff in the 50 states. For approximately 30 years, until the mid-1970s, New York operated a joint office of legislative research. But with the control of the two chambers now split between a Democratic Assembly and a Republican Senate, all policy support agencies (with the exception of the legislative library) fall under either Senate or Assembly majority or minority control. Majority and minority committee staff were generally seen as the most important source of technical information. A former staff member explained that the New York legislature has a great deal of partisan staffing because "neutral scientific advice is not part of the legislative culture." However, a staff official of the Senate Research Office disputed that view because of the great diversity in the Republican conference. "We would get killed from liberals on one side or conservatives on the other if we took sides," he declared.

A majority senator uses teams of staff from the Senate Program and Policy Office, the finance committee, legislative committees, and personal staff for his technical support. Also available to senators is the Senate Research Office that responds to approximately 10,000 requests a year, primarily from majority members of the Senate. To serve their approximately 300,000 constituents, "majority senators get all the resources they need," commented a former staff member.

The majority members of the Assembly receive support through the Program and Policy Office of the Speaker and the Economic Research Office of the Assembly Ways and Means Committee, although there is no counterpart to the Senate Research Office. An Assembly mechanism specifically designated to deal with technical issues is the Legislative Commission on Science and Technology, which operates under the jurisdiction of the Speaker's Program and Policy Office. Created in 1979 to support the work of committees by producing background and option papers and to respond to legislative requests for assistance on technical issues, the commission was based on the federal Technology Assessment Act which established the congressional Office of Technology Assessment, but was tailored to fit New York. It is the only legislative commission dedicated solely to science and technology that exists in the 11 project states.

The Commission on Science and Technology staff of seven has an executive director with a technical background in engineering and atmospheric physics as well as legislative staff management experience and six other professionals who hold degrees in science (4) or public policy (2) at either the master's or doctoral level. Also affiliated with the commission staff is an American Society of Mechanical Engineers (ASME) fellow and an intern. The budget of approximately $300,000 must be approved annually in the appropriations bill. The commission's technical skills are used for both short-term responses and long-term research. According to Program Development Group staff, "Ideally, if we do our job right, by the time an issue hits the front pages and a legislator needs an answer, we will have had six months worth of work anticipating it."

Staff Qualifications

The staffs of research offices, whether centralized or not, are for the most part attorneys who are often highly skilled in the legislative process and who have also acquired varying levels of technical expertise in the course of some-times-long legislative careers. In some cases, legislative staff members have advanced degrees in economics, statistics, political science, education, and public policy. Staff with strong science backgrounds, such as those serving on the New York Legislative S&T Commission or the staff scientist on the Wisconsin Legislative Council, are the exceptions.

There was a difference of opinion between those who felt that general research and analytical skills rather than specific technical credentials are the most important staff qualifications, and those who felt that a scientific background is essential to analyze and translate technical issues adequately. One technically trained staff member from Wisconsin argued for the generalist approach: "Maybe the best qualification is to take all of the 101 courses, across the board, a wide spectrum. We have had interns here that have had specialized training and came out of a doctoral program, and they have been disappointed and frustrated because there are very few issues that typically fit neat and tidy into any one discipline. If you're the Congressional Research Service, maybe you can afford that specialization. But at the state level, especially a state the size of Wisconsin, we can't afford that large a staff."

Other respondents argued for technical specialization. "The problem of a legal mind trying to translate technical information into a scientifically sound piece of legislation is very difficult," explained a Ph.D. legislator from New Mexico. A research staff member from Minnesota concurred that technical staff expertise was necessary in order "to be accurate and be able to convey information in nontechnical language, which means you have to have a lot of background to do this." Despite a good deal of in-house training and encouragement for staff to take outside courses, a staff director from Wisconsin explained, "You are not going to train an historian to be a chemist by sending him or her to a seminar on recent advances in chemical engineering or whatever, so there are limits to what you can do."

Legislative Libraries

Legislative libraries were also mentioned as important sources of information by legislators from five states (Florida, Louisiana, Minnesota, New York, Wisconsin). The libraries are not staffed with technical experts but are nevertheless "spectacular at getting information and chasing down references," said a legislator from Minnesota. The Wisconsin legislative library staff, in addition to maintaining a large reference department and responding to 2,000 requests per month for information, prepares short and long factual reports, some on technical issues that "present all sides of the issues as best we can identify them," explained a library official.

Personal Staff

Another important source of technical information and analysis can be personal staff for those legislators who are entitled to hire their own legislative aides and who are interested in technical issues. Legislators from Florida, Minnesota, New Mexico, New York, Ohio and Wisconsin referred to personal staff as important to technical policy support, and for some legislators, personal staff were considered the most important source. They are the key "because everything filters through them," said a senator from New York.

In New Mexico, a Senate chair took the unusual step of hiring a technically trained analyst to staff his conservation committee during the session. The senator considers the analyst his most valuable source of science and technology policy support and refers to him as a "trusted evaluator." The aide reads and reports on all committee bills as well as bills not referred to the committee that he feels belong there. He also sits with the chair during hearings and will negotiate between contending parties when the senator instructs him to do so. Although the aide works formally for the senator only during the session, he remains available to him during the interim period as a friend and trusted advisor and "through him and his network, we can anticipate what issues are going to be important."

In New York, new members of the Assembly are allotted one personal staff person, typically appointed for political not scientific skills. However, one legislator who himself has a scientific background hired a technically trained aide whom he considers his most important source of S&T policy support. "The day-to-day crush of citizens and lobbyists with a need for an immediate response limits my time, so the most efficient and effective way to brief me is verbally. With his strong scientific background, I know when he tells me something that it is accurate, that he has the ability to analyze technical information and boil it down to 25 words or less," he explained. "If there are topic areas outside his particular expertise, he knows how to access those people. He also anticipates issues, and while he is not as tuned in as somebody who is doing research in a field, he stays in contact with them so he keeps me informed."

Mentor Legislators

Finally, the few legislators with expertise can themselves be good sources of technical information in the opinion of respondents in five states (Minnesota, New Mexico, New York, Ohio, Wyoming). "In any legislative body, it is just a traditional way of doing business for an individual member to give great credence to another legislator whom he knows is interested in a particular subject area," said a staff member from New Mexico. "We have 112 legislators, and you find at least one or two that are experts in any field you are interested in," a New Mexico legislator explained. "The beauty of talking to your fellow or lady legislators is that they are expert in a particular field and they also understand the legislative process." Another legislator from New Mexico reported that "we are getting more people in the legislature that have technical expertise, so that resource is increasing."

A respondent from New York also agreed. "We have a number of brilliant members who, once they bite into a topic and do their research on it, become a primary source." Another added the caveat that "a lot of what legislators know comes from talking to colleagues they trust. It might be right or wrong, but when legislators develop a reputation as knowledgeable, members treat their opinion almost like gospel."

External Sources

Executive Branch

In all but a few of the states visited, the executive branch was the most important external source of technical information and analysis (being supplanted by public colleges and universities in New Mexico, for example, and by personal sources in New York). In Georgia and Louisiana, respondents saw executive branch agencies as even more important sources than any internal mechanisms.

The role of technical information in inter-branch rivalry was a constant theme among the respondents. Despite the omnipresence of executive agencies, many legislators and staff find it difficult to trust them as sources of information, placing them in the same category as lobbyists as either advocates or opponents of policies. As one staffer from New York said, "The only information from the executive branch that is useful comes through personal contacts that are trustworthy." However, staff and legislators often recognized the importance of the day-to-day experience in administering programs that contributes to the expertise of executive branch agencies.

In some states, there are agencies or committees with particular and narrow jurisdiction over science and technology policy issues, for example, the recently established Office of Technology Policy and the Governor's Advisory Council for Science and Technology in Georgia, the Governor's Technical Excellence Committee in New Mexico, and the Governor's Science and Technology Council in Ohio. These agencies or committees can become the useful focus of inter-branch communication and cooperation, especially when legislators themselves are actively involved.

Lobbyists

Lobbyists ranked highly among respondents as important sources of technical information and analysis. But respondents were also quite explicit in their skepticism of the information lobbyists provide. As one staffer from Florida put it, "Not that I don't trust their data. It's just that I would have to review their data. . . . My decisions are not based upon what data they give to me." Nevertheless, the importance of lobbyists is related to their ability to provide particularly timely and relevant information. Said one New Mexico legislator, "They get me accurate, dependable information faster than any other way." Recognizing the partial or nonobjective nature of lobbying, legislators and staff develop strategies to manage their information. As one legislator in Wyoming described, "As we leave the chambers at noon and I've got a question on a bill coming up that afternoon, I try to find a pro and a con lobbyist and say, 'Tell me why I should or shouldn't support this.' And when I get back from lunch, on my desk are the pros and cons."

State Universities

Public colleges and universities ranked fairly highly among respondents as an important source of technical information and analysis, but respondents were often nevertheless unsatisfied with the relationship between the legislature and state universities. As one staffer in Florida said, public colleges and universities "are not realizing their potential. . . . [because] they tend to deal with the esoteric aspects of research rather than the really pragmatic applied research that is needed for decision making by our legislature." More than one staffer told the joke about the legislator who ask the university professor for the time and in response gets the instructions for building a clock.

But one legislator in Kentucky lays some blame on the legislature itself for this shortcoming: "The universities have been quite helpful, but could be more helpful. But they give us everything we ask for. We're probably not sophisticated in what we ask for." In Kentucky, the Legislative Research Commission tried to augment its expertise by accessing the state university. A compendium of names and research projects at the university was compiled, but it did not prove particularly useful because either the research projects were not relevant to the legislature's questions, or interested faculty needed money.

Although legislatures occasionally make use of academic faculty in formal ways such as in hearings or study commissions, the more frequent way seems to be through informal contacts. Patterns of contact vary widely, from Wyoming where the state university is the only four-year institution and legislators call the university president directly, to Minnesota where contact is often handled through a public relations-type office at the university, to Georgia where a sophisticated set of institutions, including the Georgia Research Alliance and the Vinson Institute of Government, mediate between the legislature and the universities. In some cases, such as the New Mexico Engineering Research Institute or Wyoming's Science, Technology, and Energy Authority, the legislature has chartered organizations in universities to provide technical information and assistance to state and local government.

Such mediating institutions are important because they can depoliticize the relationship between legislatures and universities and defuse the inherent conflict of roles of the public universities as both providers of technical information and recipients of public support. But one staffer in Louisiana explained the failure of an innovation at Louisiana State University to provide a vice chancellor to coordinate and handle legislative requests: "Members [of the legislature] are never happy with having that kind of stuff screened."

National and Regional Clearinghouses

The importance of national and regional clearinghouses in providing technical information and analysis varied widely among the states, ranging from only modest importance in well-staffed legislatures such as Florida, New York, and Wisconsin, to important in less well-staffed legislatures such as Wyoming and Louisiana. The National Conference of State Legislatures (NCSL) was the most prominent of the clearinghouses, but other important regional clearinghouses included the Southern Regional Education Board (SREB) and the Regional Energy Council. The American Legislative Exchange Council, a conservative clearinghouse, was also mentioned. The clearinghouse function is vital for some states, as one staffer in Kentucky said, to get them "pointed in the right direction." These organizations also help standardize policy data and provide, as one Louisianan said of SREB, "the Good Housekeeping seal." For the larger states, however, the clearinghouse function is less important because they are more often the data points for other states.

Federal Sources

Federal sources of technical information and analysis were not very important across the states visited. Respondents who received information from federal sources often did so through a nonfederal purveyor such as their state's congressional delegation or through a quasi-public organization such as the Kentucky Science and Technology Council. States with a large federal presence like New Mexico found that presence an important source.

Personal Sources

Personal sources of technical information and analysis were important across the range of states and were the most important source in the highly partisan environment of New York. The size of a state and the level of professionalization of its legislature does not seem to have any influence on the importance of such personal sources.

Specialized Sources

A number of states have specialized sources of technical information and analysis—not connected with universities or the executive branch—that are important to the legislators and staff who deal directly with them but relatively unknown to other legislators and staff. Examples include the Kentucky Science and Technology Council, the Kentucky Long-Term Policy Research Center, and Minnesota Technology, Inc. Each of these organizations is a quasi-public institution with a variety of roles, ranging from providing advice to the legislature on a formal and informal basis, to serving as a technology development agency, to helping the state and its businesses take advantage of federal and other development programs.

3. Characteristics of Useful S&T Policy Support

Respondents cited similar characteristics of useful technical information and analysis in all 11 states. Leading the list was trustworthiness of the source, followed by process-related characteristics such as accessible, timely, nontechnical language, convenient format, and content-related characteristics such as accurate, nonpartisan, relevant, current, goal-oriented, and anticipatory.

Trust

The most significant characteristic mentioned was trust. "The comfort level has to be high," said a legislator from Ohio. "You tend to trust those that you know, that you can judge whether you value or don't value their information," in the opinion of a legislator from Wyoming. "The sources most important to me are those that I can trust, that are reliable," declared a member of the New York Assembly. "In a profession in which reliability and trust are the most important variables, known quantities control your ability to succeed." A Florida staffer explained that members of his legislature

> seem to be most persuaded by hearing information of whatever sort, but including science and technology issues, from someone that they consider to be a credible source . . . A member is much more apt to be persuaded by the same piece of information if it is coming from a trusted staff member or a trusted lobbyist from the executive branch or trusted lobbyist from the private sector, a trusted trade association, a trusted constituent, a trusted personal friend whom they believe has expertise and credibility in that area than receiving that same identical piece of information in a written report from some third-party organization, even if that third party may have a national prominence and reputation in that area.

Another Florida legislator found he could trust his personal staff "because they would understand how [the information] would affect me personally at home in my district. They understand the types of individuals that I represent." In terms of committee staff, he could trust "their institutional knowledge and also their ability to ferret out information from the agencies, cut to the quick, and come up with recommendations."

Process Characteristics: Accessible, Timely, Nontechnical Language, Convenient Format

Respondents viewed process issues such as accessibility, timeliness, and format presentation as part of what goes into developing trust.

Accessibility was the key characteristic mentioned in Louisiana. Staff are "readily available on a day-to-day basis," and lobbyists and executive branch agencies are accessible "because it is in their self-interest to reach out to legislators and provide them with information." A legislator from North Carolina said, "I trust my own research staff probably the most because I can keep going back and digging." States with short sessions such as Georgia and Kentucky cited the importance of "immediacy of response and accessibility" as primary factors in getting information. In Wisconsin, with year-round sessions, accessibility is also important. "The legislature is a reactive institution and information has to be readily available. One of the reasons that lobbyists are so effective is because their information is very easily accessible," said a staff member. In Kentucky, lobbyists "know how to convey information . . . They can meet after hours and there's a trust that builds up." A Florida staffer put it more bluntly. "Lobbyists are here all the time. . . . They're in your face . . . and [their] persistence can pay off."

Respondents also considered format important. "Reports, academic work, simply don't compute in members' minds very well . . . The key skills are to be able to reduce everything to three-quarters of a page and be able to brief them on the elevator," said a Florida staffer. A legislator from New Mexico has instructed his technical aide "to go out and talk to people and find out what the problems are. I don't want you sitting in front of a computer. Then come back and talk to me about what you have learned. I don't want it in writing." Legislators need presentation of options rather than just raw data. "What members are looking for is not just being able to go to somebody with expertise. What they are looking for is setting out what the various options are. There are very few issues where it is just a hard, cold fact," said a New York staff director.

Legislators mentioned that it is important to translate technical language into plain English. "Legislators like myself," explained a state representative from Wisconsin, "are not technicians, and some of the things we have to do get into language that scares legislators away. So they ignore the issue rather than have to grapple with DNA or megabytes or whatever, and as a result it is very difficult to get them interested and involved in the issues." New York staff members agreed that a key to useful technical information is to make "it understandable to someone who hasn't much time." It was also very important for staff "to have the ability to translate the jargon, and you can only do that if you understand it yourself."

Content Characteristic: Nonpartisan

Respondents generally agreed that, in the words of a legislator from New Mexico, "partisan information is not credible." In Wisconsin, nonpartisan policy support is considered one of the main reasons for the credibility of their legislative support agencies. A staff director explained:

> Leaders of both houses and both parties have done whatever they can to insure that nonpartisanship or bipartisanship survives. We know that it is in neither of our interests if we move to a partisan bent on any subject, because once we are there we can never get ourselves back. It also means we are able to hire good people who don't feel coerced into a partisan position, don't feel coerced into fund raising, don't feel coerced into campaigns, all of the things that we are not interested in doing, but in fact we are able to hire people who are interested in government and public policy and seeing that issues are handled with professional caring.

Even partisan staff from Ohio and New York concurred that partisan policy support was not useful. Said one Ohio caucus member, "We certainly wouldn't put anything out there that was not factually correct. That is a prescription for losing, maybe not in the short run, but certainly in the long run. [We] wouldn't have lasted as long as we have if we had done that. So I would say that in terms of accuracy, we are very good." A New York partisan staff member observed that "we have an obligation to the people we are working for to lay things out in a straightforward fashion. If you put out things that are factually correct, then legislators are going to know more about the issue, and with better information legislators are going to make better policies and then better politics. Then they win and the institution clearly wins."

Content Characteristic: Current, Relevant

Both legislators and staff considered current and relevant information as critical. "To use old data is reckless, particularly in light of the fact that if your computer systems are up and working, you can have up-to-the-month [information]," said a Minnesota senator. A senator from New York said that for him "technical information has to be very 'goal-oriented' to be useful. It must focus on an existing solvable problem. It's not people going off and doing papers because someone thinks it is a good idea and it just sits there." A legislator from Wisconsin agreed. "It's very difficult for someone to sit down and read a journal on, say, telecommunications, talking about all of the things that you could do, without any real focus on how policy affects that technology and how that policy is going to affect constituents. I think that often times the presentation is too focused on the technical and not enough on the applications or policy." Contrasting staff work with external sources, a Florida staffer said that "Once you look to the academic community for solutions, they seem to have trouble in dealing with them in a relevant sort of a way."

A senator from New York explained that, for him, "technical information has to be very goal-oriented to be useful and must focus on an existing solvable problem. It's not people going off and doing papers because someone thinks it's a good idea and it just sits there." On the other hand, a legislator from Minnesota saw the need to offset the reactive nature of legislative bodies with information that anticipates future technological developments, "not just after they have hit the front page." However, he, too, cautioned that studies that are too far out in front don't get too much attention from busy legislators.

4. Legislative Use of Technology

Given the current dynamism of computer technology, it is no surprise that the states visited were generally in the midst of many changes in the computer technology they use and how they use it. North Carolina illustrates the scope of change: ten years ago, the legislature had six word processors and ten terminals running two programs; by summer 1994, the legislature had seven networked minicomputers, approximately 500 personal computers (PCs), and an internal e-mail system handling 100,000 messages per month during the session. Something of a common model exists among legislatures in which all staff have PCs linked to a local area network (LAN). The variety occurs in areas such as the extension of the network to district offices, the use of computers by legislators themselves, and the degree of public access. Because of the rapidity and novelty of technical change, training has become an important issue as well.

Staff initially used computer technology for bill-drafting and bill-tracking functions. With the proliferation of PCs, uses have expanded to general word processing and some graphics applications. Indeed, some staff who see barriers to communicating technical information and analysis to legislators hold great hopes for computer technology to enhance their ability to present and communicate data in an attractive, entertaining, and informative way. Legislatures on LANs use their internal e-mail systems heavily, and some committees in at least one legislature conduct all their business via e-mail.

Among the important policy areas for computer use are legislative redistricting, demographic projections for social services, and economic forecasting. Ohio and North Carolina used computer resources heavily for their 1990 redistricting, and the latter even made their redistricting program available to the public so interested persons could attempt to draw their own district maps.

Internet, Other Electronic Networks

Despite the recent and rapid advances in legislative use of computer technology, the Internet and other electronic network resources are still not very important sources of technical information and analysis. Although internally networked, staff often do not have modems on their personal computers and must instead perform any kind of electronic search through a "gatekeeper" such as a librarian or senior staffer with access to a modem.

Many staff and legislators are quite optimistic about the potential—and for most, it is still potential—of the Internet as an information resource. Others, however, are more skeptical about how the answers to specific, policy-oriented questions will be available to them. Staff who use electronic sources find commercial providers such as Lexis/Nexis, WestLaw, and Dialog quite useful. Some also used NCSL's LegisNet and other regional networks and bulletin boards such as South-Eastern Regional Vision for Education (SERVE), headquartered at the University of North Carolina, Greensboro. There is some sense that more direct Internet access to policy and technical information may undercut some of the functions of the clearinghouses. Internet use goes both ways, and now many of the legislatures are themselves available to the public through the Internet. For example, Minnesota has a legislative gopher that makes available the text of bills and resolutions, bill tracking, bill summaries, votes, committee schedules and assignments, members' addresses and biographies, and the state statutes. The Internet, however, is not without its symbolic politics. As one senior staffer in North Carolina put it, "Frankly, many people want [an Internet connection] because they want to put forth a high-tech image that's fashionable. So they would like to have Internet. . . . They want to put their Internet e-mail addresses on their business cards."

Issues in Legislative Use of Technology

Procurement and Management

Computers in the legislatures are often the decision of legislative leadership, and thus there are differences between the upper and lower houses of the same legislature in terms of hardware, software, access, etc. For example, in Florida, the House had PCs for staff several years before the Senate did. In Louisiana, where the House and Senate have separate staffs but a single LAN, internal e-mail has created novel linkages. In New York, the Senate has Internet access, but the Assembly is still discussing questions of security, cost, and freedom of information.

Because procurement of computers, both for the legislature and for executive agencies, is an expensive and risky proposition, some legislatures have developed technical capacities to assist in procurement (in some cases developing them only after having been "burned"). As in the case of the Florida Joint Information Technology Resources Committee, such advisors for procurement decisions can then move on to provide technical information and analysis for broader policy decisions.

Generational Change

There is a sense among many of the respondents that a generational change is occurring among legislators in which the older legislators—labeled by one legislator the "legis-auruses"—are resistant to or at least nonparticipatory in technical change, while the younger legislators are at the forefront of it. As staffers in Minnesota suggested, some legislators suffer from "technophobia" and "the old guard, the ones whom I feel I need to offer to make a photocopy for," are still around. One legislator in Georgia who supports the generational hypothesis, however, suggests the driving force is something other than age: "Had not my business dictated me into the computer business . . . I probably wouldn't be in it." One New Mexico legislator insisted that "once legislators find out what power there is in being able to access all this information, they will become more interested in having computers." In North Carolina, however, it was not the power of information processing that led to computer and e-mail, but rather that the Speaker set an example of the use of e-mail as a communications and management tool that sent everyone scrambling to keep up.

Electronic Democracy

There is considerable hope among the respondents that computers and electronic communications will enhance the quality of democratic governance by increasing the accessibility of important information, including technical information and analysis. One legislator from New Mexico declared that with a computerized legislature, "this will finally be a democracy. . . . The inability of government to reach people will change and our constituents will get all the information they want . . . and all the excuses they can stand."

Some respondents see potential short- and long-term downsides, however. One staffer in Minnesota is concerned that e-mail messages will be printed out and then will take on "a reality of its own and you have to live with it forever and ever . . . like a position paper." Others are concerned about freedom of information issues and the security of public networks and databases.

Some even question the suitability of electronic communications to the legislative environment, particularly at the state level. It is not clear, for example, whether laptop computers will allow citizen-legislatures to live longer or kill them more quickly. As one senior staffer from North Carolina equivocated, "I don't know. I would like to say . . . it allows it to live longer. But again, the fact of the matter is, dialing in from home or on the road, it's just more work at home. It makes you a legislator even when you're not in Raleigh." One staffer in New Mexico finds e-mail "helpful to send documents to the typist," but finds the telephone and the fax machine "more effective and more efficient . . . to share information or get information from somebody." Another staffer from North Carolina expresses the same sentiment: "There are a lot of people who seem to think that [computers] are going to be a bright new tomorrow, and I don't think that's going to happen. . . . [In] this arena, I don't think we'll ever get away or should get away from direct personal contact."

5. Technical Information in a Political Environment

Constituents and Representation

Technical information and analysis is obviously only one part of legislative decision making, and respondents across the states indicated that only rarely was it the most significant or definitive part. Most often, it is just part of the mix in the decision-making process. Or, to put it directly, as one Florida staffer did, "Technical information doesn't vote." There did seem to be a subtle difference between staff and legislators, however, with staff slightly more cynical about the role of technical information and analysis and legislators a little more optimistic.

Respondents expressed a not-surprising consensus that the opinions of constituents were usually more important than technical information and analysis, but they also made allowances for types of issues and legislative styles that rendered technical information more or less important. Respondents often distinguished "technical" issues from "emotional" issues. The characteristics of technical issues included their long-term nature, their complicated elements, and their lack of partisan dimension; whereas, emotional issues were those with a serious partisan dimension, where leadership had staked out positions, or those issues appealing to a deep personal commitment on the part of legislators or constituents. On technical issues, respondents said, legislators were more likely to follow the technical information, and on emotional issues, they were more likely to follow their constituents.

Even on some emotional issues, however, some respondents tried to secure technical information and analysis to help forge a consensus. For example, in North Carolina, where one emotional issue was a conflict over foul air from industrial hog farms, "you've got to balance the equities there between two very powerful groups of constituents, and the only way that is going to be done is to have very good and very accurate technical information." Similarly, in Florida during a recent special session on abortion—mentioned in several states as the exemplar of an emotional issue—the legislature heard from a number of experts about fetal development and related subjects.

Respondents also often distinguished between two legislative styles, corresponding to the classic "delegate" versus "trustee" distinction. Delegate legislators represent their constituents by making decisions they believe their constituents would, whereas trustee legislators make decisions based on their own judgment. Trustees would be more likely to make use of technical information, even in opposition to constituent opinion.

Representatives dealing with technical issues also expressed interest in the use of technical information and analysis not only for decision making but also for educating their constituents. As one junior Kentucky legislator said, "I try to use [the technical information] in a process of educating them on why I'm making decisions the way that I am." Or, as a New Mexico legislator said, "On strictly technical issues, technical information is more important than opinions of my constituents. . . . I represent the district I grew up in, and many of the citizens did not go off to college as I did. I will try to educate them on the issues." One legislator from New York even provided a procedure for the representative-as-educator to follow: "The role of the good legislator is to repackage complicated issues involving science and technology and put them into very stark, human terms so that they can be understood by everyone. You look for metaphors and motifs that can be understood by your constituents."

Legislating

With respect to the role of technical information and analysis (from staff) in the legislative process, respondents felt it was most important to legislators when they were drafting legislation. It was also important, but slightly less so, when legislators were deciding how to respond to legislation introduced by other legislators and when they were evaluating previous legislation or administrative actions. Technical information and analysis was only somewhat important for helping legislators decide what issues were important to address in the coming session, and what issues were important to consider beyond the current session. And it was still less important when legislators were deciding how to vote. The responses from staff and legislators were essentially the same with respect to these questions, as were the state-by-state responses.

Some respondents suggested that the relative importance of technical information and analysis provided by staff at various stages in the legislative process may change as a result of legislative term limits, particularly in the agenda-setting stages. Both emphasizing the importance of technical information in bill drafting and distinguishing it from other technical pursuits, one Florida legislator said, "It may not be a dissertation, but writing a piece of legislation that affects the lives of 14 million people is something that can't be taken lightly." Nevertheless, as one staffer in New Mexico observed, "every decision is a political decision in a representative democracy. . . . There's an infinite number of facts in the world on any issue that one could use . . . [and interest groups win] by emphasizing their facts and de-emphasizing or avoiding somebody else's facts." Because of this political flexibility of facts, the timing of the use of technical information and analysis in the legislative process is important: if the information is too early, no one is interested; if it is too late, positions have hardened and are difficult to alter. As one Wisconsin observer said, "I think science applied to an issue before it heats up can do some good. Once some of these other political considerations begin to play up, I think science will get pushed out of the process."

Legislatures, Executive Branch, and Lobbyists

There was nearly unanimous agreement across respondents in all states that the technical information and analysis provided by staff has increased the independence, authority, or power of the legislature vis-à-vis both the executive branch and lobbyists. Respondents found staff vital not necessarily to produce information independent of the executive branch (because the legislatures are not well-enough or technically enough staffed for that), but rather to "look at the expertise that exists in agencies, evaluate their studies and reports, look at the lobbyists' reports . . . and evaluate those . . . and give [legislators] a professional opinion as to which of those reports are more likely to be reliable and reflective of the policy the committee is trying to pursue."

Legislative-executive rivalries are deeply seated, and each state has a unique history. But respondents almost invariably described executive agency staff in the same way they described lobbyists, as interested parties and policy advocates who, while not playing fast and loose with the facts, would still slant them in self-serving ways. As one former legislator from Georgia said, "The reason we needed [a research office was] simply trying to get the best information possible that we could make a decision on, from somebody who did not have an agenda. And when you get stuff from the administration, for example, you've got to assume that there's an agenda there." In Kentucky, increased staff support for the legislature was one of the explicit changes implemented in the mid- and late-1970s to help make the legislature a co-equal branch with the executive, since the executive "no longer had a monopoly" on information and analysis. In the words of one Wyoming legislator who emphasized the importance of staff to a part-time legislature compared to the full-time executive, "We'd just be whipped without them."

Respondents also found technical information and analysis from staff vital in reducing the influence of lobbyists. As one staffer from Florida suggested, staff are "another source for triangulation" for members among the various positions of various lobbyists. Another Florida staffer attributes "more and more members asking harder and harder questions of the lobbyists" to a technically competent staff. Or, as a Georgia legislator described, "Vis-à-vis lobbyists, we understand that they will be telling us their side, and often times if you have one good lobbyist and one poor lobbyist on the opposing side, there's not much balance there. Then we use the . . . research staff to ferret out a balance of information."

Despite this near unanimity, there was also a strong undercurrent of belief among respondents that, for various reasons, legislatures have not yet come far enough in their efforts to achieve co-equal status with the executive branch and sufficient independence from lobbyists. As one staffer in Georgia lamented, "There's simply not enough of us. . . . We cannot specialize enough to be able to get into some of the finer details . . . [and] until that happens, I think the legislature will be at a disadvantage vis-à-vis the executive branch." As a staffer in Louisiana suggested, "Lobbyists are the guys that help them get re-elected. . . . [Legislators] are going to listen to the lobbyist before they listen to me, in real politics." Respondents in Minnesota, New York, and Ohio voiced similar perspectives, especially, for one Ohio observer, because "pro-active mechanisms in the legislature are almost nonexistent."

Barriers

The barriers to the provision and use of technical information and analysis in state legislatures can be usefully grouped into supply-side barriers and demand-side barriers. Supply-side barriers are those encountered in the production of information; demand-side barriers are those encountered in its consumption.

The primary supply-side barrier is time; staff feel that they do not have adequate time to produce information and analysis for legislative use. The time barrier has many dimensions, most of which are structural and political in origin and thus impact differently in different states. The timing of legislative sessions is one such barrier, with a great deal of work loaded into preparing for sessions and drafting and redrafting bills at the beginning of sessions. When legislatures are in session, there is little time or opportunity for members to exchange information with staff;

but when the legislature is not in session, communications over a long distance with members who are not focused on legislative business provides yet another difficulty. One staffer in Florida called this dilemma a "communications nightmare."

Another important supply-side barrier is the ability of staff to gather quality data. Difficulties in data gathering include lack of access to electronic databases, incompatibility of hardware and software among various potential sources of data, uncertainty about the accuracy or credibility of information, lack of cooperation from potential sources of information, and the volume of information that might be relevant but that is inaccessible. The inherent uncertainty of much technical data is also a barrier; as one Kentucky staffer said, "There's a lot of controversy and dispute in the scientific community, and I think that makes it difficult for those of us who are not scientists." A third supply-side barrier is that staff who, although generalists, have more expertise than legislators, need to be able to translate technical information and analysis in order to communicate to legislators.

On the demand side, there is also a time barrier in that legislators feel time pressured and may not be able to spend enough time to formulate the correct questions and to assimilate and use all the information that staff and other sources produce. There is also a set of attitudinal and intellectual barriers to the provision of technical information and analysis. As one Florida staffer said, "sometimes [legislators] don't seem real interested in knowing the facts," or they have "a tendency to either glaze over when the whole subject matter comes up or there's . . . that possibility of disinterest—'Oh, that's too technical. I wouldn't understand it.'" One Georgia staffer said of legislators, "A lot of them are farmers and businessmen—especially from the rural areas—who haven't really dealt with technology much, who don't really understand it themselves, and [who] maybe have never used a computer in their lives. . . . To get them to understand all that is the most difficult part I have."

Competing sources of information also provide a demand-side barrier. One Louisiana staffer maintained that "our members generally have such a good working relationship with the lobbyists that any attempt to give them information that is not accepted by the lobby tends to be dealt with in a jaundiced way." Competing goals provide another demand-side barrier. As one staffer in New York suggested, the reelection goal often supplants the good policy goal: "Members of the Assembly and Senate are always running for office, trying to nudge their way to the front to get media attention. This is not a good match with S&T issues, which require a greater attention span."

Underlying these specific barriers is a more general barrier of the resources devoted to the staff's production of technical information and analysis. More resources could mean lessening the burden of time and increasing the availability of technical expertise through the benefits of specialization and division of labor. Ultimately, however, the question of resources is where the supply-side and the demand-side connect, for it is through their own mechanisms that legislators set the ability of staff to supply them with information.

6. Legislative Satisfaction

The average level of satisfaction of legislators with the technical information and analysis to which they have access, on a 5-point scale where 5 is most satisfied, is 3.86. The modal response (23/53) was 4, and slightly more legislators were more dissatisfied (17 responses) than were more satisfied (13 responses). On average, staff marginally overestimate legislators' satisfaction of technical information and analysis from all sources; and they marginally underestimate legislators' satisfaction with information and analysis from the staff themselves. Levels of satisfaction vary little state to state and seem to bear no direct relation to the level of professionalization in a legislature, suggesting that there is some "equilibrium" in the legislatures between the demand for technical information and analysis and the supply.

Despite the general satisfaction of a majority of legislators, another message comes through strongly from respondents: legislators do not necessarily know enough not to be satisfied. As one staffer from Ohio suggested, "Legislators are satisfied, but they need more technical information and analysis and don't know they need it. They don't know what they don't know." Another staffer from Georgia voiced a similar belief, saying that legislators seem satisfied, "but I don't think they understand why they shouldn't be satisfied. . . . They could be snowed very easily, and they could be impressed really easily, and they perhaps should be a little more critical of technology and information coming from technology and what it all means." And in Louisiana, "Are they satisfied that they got the gaming report? Yeah, it went like hotcakes. . . . They thought this was great information to have. . . . But if they realized that there's the same kind of data out there on environmental issues and education issues that's not being brought to them in this very user-friendly report, then they'd say, 'Well, hell, why aren't I getting that information?'"

Specific sources of residual dissatisfaction include: a desire for "information keyed to their district boundaries in a lot more detail than is typically available from any attainable source at reasonable cost"; the need for "coherent" and "effective synthesis"; less technical information so that "it would make it a little easier" for the citizen-legislator "to make decisions [and] feel good about decisions"; unreasonably increased expectations, especially those wrought by computer technology (e.g., "Well, just give me this out of the computer. That's all I want. Just press that button there."); the lack of availability of particular kinds of technical expertise internally; and information overload. Partisan concerns only seemed a source of dissatisfaction in New York, and North Carolina and Louisiana exhibited some dissatisfaction between the chambers.

An important aspect of legislative satisfaction also seems to be the appreciation of uncertainty in technical information and analysis. As one legislator in Florida said, "It can never be good enough; [in] science . . . there's a certain amount of impreciseness. . . . You can't be absolutely certain about this stuff." Uncertainty drives the search for information, and "the more information they get that causes them to think more long term, the more information they need." One legislator from Florida rationalizes the situation this way: "Do I think that I have an in-depth knowledge of most of the subjects that I vote on or deal with? And the answer is 'no.' But then I think that I'm not supposed to have too technical or too detailed knowledge about many of these issues. I think you're expected to have a broad view, so I think that a lot of the times we're voting with a great degree of ignorance."

When asked to assess the work of the staff in producing technical analysis and information, respondents were almost uniform in their perceptions that staff provide accurate and unbiased information. Respondents were somewhat less impressed with the ability of staff to provide timely information and to present that information in useful formats. The responses suggest that the institutional controls to ensure accuracy and lack of bias among staff members are adequate, but that a more important locus of reform might be enhancing the ability of staff to meet deadlines and produce more readable documents.

7. Recommendations

Respondents in all states recommended improving access to legislative technical information and analysis with one major caveat: change does not come easily to legislative institutions. The complexity of dealing with a large, diverse

membership, short-term political time frames, fiscal constraints, and the reactive nature of legislatures in general all
contribute to preserving the status quo. Three respondents
from New York presented views on the prospect of legislative
change.

An acknowledged legislative expert and former key staff
member of the New York legislature observed, "Changes of
the legislative culture won't happen incrementally. There
would have to be a big blowup for fundamental reform." A
member of the New York Assembly thought that improvement was necessary, but that it would not be easy. "There
is room for improvement, but the big issue is how do you
inform 211 people with widely divergent interests and how
do you give them enough information so that they can make
the right decision?" he asked. A key New York staff member
felt that the transformation of society caused by the information revolution made it a "great time for change. Clearly,
leadership has always been interested in information that
they can use to their advantage, but now there is a need to
think in longer terms. Assembly leadership is putting more
emphasis on longer-term planning, and clearly technology
will be driven through almost everything we do in the future.
Good politics is a long-term endeavor."

Despite the barriers, respondents offered specific recommendations to improve the ability of state legislatures to
acquire and use technical information and analysis.

Internal Sources

Computer Technology

Respondents in all states recommended continued
improvement of computer technology and training for staff
and interested legislators. In such a fast-moving field, some
of these recommendations may have already been adopted,
especially those involving staff access to the Internet. One
computer-literate legislator from Wisconsin suggested that,

at the beginning of each session, every legislator should be offered hands-on computer training. A senator from New Mexico said that he "would give a laptop to every legislator and train them and tell them, 'if you want quick information, this is how you access it.'" He said that he was creating a subject index from reading technical magazines and other publications so that if "I need certain statistics, I can get the index, switch it onto my laptop, and then try to get it and use it in debate." A House colleague agreed: "It's time to move out of the Dark Ages with the stubby pencil and onto the floors of the House and Senate [with laptops] so we stop winding up with five volumes of statutes and amendments." A legislator from New York concurred that computerization of bills would save money and space. "We don't need to store a thousand copies of every bill in a cubby hole. When someone wants a bill, just print it," he explained. A staff member from Minnesota observed that there is a great deal of "technophobia" among legislators, however, and that only "when we can get computer programs that can use voice commands in ordinary English" will legislators not be "frightened off" and not "feel that they don't have the time to learn all that."

In addition to computer training, a staffer from Florida suggested that legislators should have training in using staff resources. "You have to prepare the audience to be able to benefit" from technical information and analysis. A legislator from Wisconsin said that while it might be helpful if more legislators had scientific backgrounds, what was really needed was for legislators to "be comfortable with . . . basic scientific principles," which he thought could come from "basic 101-level undergraduate classes and perhaps even reading what is available at newsstands, so that legislators can separate what is reasonable from what is unreasonable."

There were recommendations for the creation of technical information clearinghouses that would be electronically accessible and would organize information in a way easily retrievable by legislators and staff. An Ohio senator stated that it would be helpful to "have one specific place to call." It was also important that legislative databases be "put in the public domain," said a staffer from Louisiana. At present, 42 states have made some sort of electronic legislative information available to the public.

Recommendations for in-house legislative expertise in making decisions about state purchasing of computer systems was mentioned by several respondents. In New Mexico, where five percent of the state budget is spent on computer technology, a senator explained, "We don't have anybody, so we rely on Los Alamos . . . and Sandia, and they are helping. . . . But they are basically saying, 'It's time you guys recognize you need to start building up this expertise within your own camp.'" A state representative from Ohio said that the House is "just starting to get computers, and we need to be sure that we are coordinating technological equipment. We purchased [one] system this year and found that it was not compatible or transferrable." Minnesota relied on a scientifically trained legislator to guide the legislature in making the appropriate decisions on the purchase of computer technology for the state's higher education system.

A Wisconsin state representative recommended holding discussions on the ethical and constitutional implications of information technology as part of an in-house course on technology use or perhaps at a public policy institute connected with the state university. "You can get a lot of technical expertise and that's fine," he observed, "but you remember that while the Nazis were great technicians, they were a little short on ethics."

Technical Staff Expertise

In all 11 states, respondents felt that because legislators are so busy with their other legislative duties, internal staff must play a key role in providing S&T policy support if the legislature is to fulfill its role as a co-equal branch of government. Methods recommended for increasing expertise included adding full-time, technically trained staff to research offices (such as the staff scientist of the Wisconsin Legislative Council); offering more training and education opportunities to existing generalists on research staffs; hiring part-time experts for specific assignments (as was done in Minnesota to develop health care legislation); hiring technical analysts as personal aides, and hiring technically trained interns from universities or through professional societies such as ASME.

Those who favored bringing in new expertise over in-house training for existing staff questioned whether staff generalists could learn enough science to be able to interpret and translate technical information for legislators and whether they could develop professional networks to keep current on new scientific advances. On the other hand, there was concern that people with scientific backgrounds may be temperamentally unsuited to performing effectively in a legislative environment. One Florida legislator observed that because staff "tend to be too cloistered . . . and not given enough breadth of experience," they should be given more opportunities for field exposure. This might also allow staffers to incorporate more qualitative sources of information into their work in order to balance the quantitative data that now controls the "well-trod path from information to policy."

While respondents expressed little support for the creation of separate S&T research agencies, one Minnesota respondent suggested appointing a joint legislative commission on technology with trained, permanent staff to concentrate on complex issues such as telecommunications during the interim. In New York, where a legislative commission on S&T already exists in the Assembly, respondents made various recommendations to increase its technical service function for individual legislators beyond its general research mission.

Personal Staff

Several legislators in two states (New Mexico, New York) felt that the most effective method of providing them with S&T information and analysis was through personal staff with technical expertise. A member of the New York Assembly, who himself has a technical background, has hired a technically trained person to serve as his one allotted personal staff person and considers him his most important source of S&T policy support. As a legislator deeply interested in technical issues, he ideally could use two or three additional staff with the quality of scientific training of his present staff person.

A senator from New Mexico also hired a technically trained personal aide to assist him during the session in his work as a chair of a committee dealing with many environmental protection issues. Because the New Mexico legislature operates with short sessions and long interim study periods, he recommended that his personal staff be available during the interim as well. In opposition to the hiring of personal aides was the question of cost, the decrease in direct contact of legislators with their constituents, and the potential for creating an independent, entrepreneurial but unelected policymaking arm with a great deal of influence. As a New York senator with 300,000 constituents commented ironically, "When I left my staff position and was elected senator, I lost power."

Standing S&T Committees

In general, there was little support for establishing standing S&T legislative committees and, indeed, several states that once had them have discontinued them or folded them into other committees. The chief reasons cited were the S&T committees' lack of clear focus as well as turf problems with issue-specific committees. In addition, a long-time legislator from North Carolina suggested that extreme specialization can lead to staffers becoming policymakers. One former key New York staffer supported the creation of a science and technology committee whose mission would be to develop state S&T policy and deal with other states, regions, and the federal government on S&T issues. "Having the congressional House Committee on Science and Technology has been very useful in Washington and could be in Albany," he said. A legislator from New Mexico felt that the Interim Committee on Science and Technology, which currently must be reappointed annually, should be turned into a permanent standing committee. "If we created a science and technology standing committee by statute and gave them a statutory charge of what this committee does, that would make it stronger," said a state representative. "It would also bring a lot more focus in the press to those issues. The interim committee gets very little press coverage," he added. A senator agreed, saying that "the interim committee doesn't give enough emphasis given that technology is one of our major assets in this state and should play a more vital role." Turf battles between the new S&T committee and other committees could be "avoided because committees can meet jointly or the Speaker can make the chairs members of overlapping committees."

Although there was no consensus over method, there was broad recognition that improvements in the ability of internal legislative mechanisms to provide technical information and analysis are necessary. Nevertheless, there was also great awareness on the part of legislators and staff that any recommendation that increased legislative costs would be met with opposition.

External Sources

Universities

There was a strong and broad consensus among the respondents about the desirability of better relations between legislatures and state universities, but there was little consensus about how better relations might be achieved, especially since attempts had failed in the past. Almost characteristic of this predicament is Wisconsin, which is seeking to reinvigorate the Wisconsin Idea through its Commission for the Study of Administrative Value and Efficiency and its recommendations to integrate the state's knowledge resources, particularly universities, into its policymaking.

Respondents would like to see the universities be both more active in assuming public service responsibilities (at the institutional and individual level) and more accessible to legislators and staff in their search for technical information and analysis. On the other hand, as one university administrator in Minnesota indicated, legislatures also have to learn to articulate more clearly their specific needs for technical information.

Some legislators and staff recommended that something as simple as a directory of university researchers and research topics be made available. But elsewhere such directories (and Internet sites) had been deemed insufficient because research topics tended to be specified not by legislative interests but by university interests, which were not sensitive to political agendas, timetables, and other specifications. Some respondents suggested that universities designate a single contact person for legislative requests, but in Louisiana this model did not work well because legislators and staff were wary about submitting their questions through an intermediary.

In cases where legislators or staff did find interested and relevant faculty members, money often became an issue. The fact that universities often lobby the legislature for appropriations and that they are, as one Minnesota respondent described it, seen as just another group of special pleaders with their hands out at budget time, only serves to complicate the problem.

Often respondents suggested that their best contacts with university researchers were on a personal or informal level, suggesting that developing some ways of building informal rather than formal contacts could be more rewarding. In some states, such as Florida, law students intern for committees, and it might be possible for science and engineering students to perform similar internships.

One area of successful, formal interaction has been revenue forecasting in states like Louisiana, where an academic economist has a constitutionally specified role to assist in the consensus conference that develops the revenue forecast. The desire for such a role was also expressed by a staffer in New York. Another anticipated formal connection is through the technology centers being created in Ohio, which will necessitate the nurturing of university-legislative relations. Not only will this assist universities in their academic and training roles but also enable them to better enable them to offer technical expertise to the legislature.

In addition to increased responsiveness to legislative requests for technical information and analysis, respondents wanted public universities to be more proactive and to assist staff in anticipating the development of new issues with scientific or technical content. To this end, some respondents suggested that universities might organize briefing sessions, video conferencing, newsletters, or other programs for communicating current and anticipated developments in S&T. These programs could range from regularized, pre-session briefings, which occur in some states without a particular S&T focus, to mini-courses for staff on generic approaches to S&T issues (such as how to evaluate S&T sources), to more intensive presentations designed to educate nonspecialists on particular issues.

Such programs could also create something like the consensus conferences, already in place in Florida and Louisiana on revenue estimating and other technical questions. Gathering together both stakeholders and providers of technical information and analysis and attempting to clarify areas of agreement and disagreement during interims, smooths the way for policymaking during sessions.

Executive Branch and Intersectoral Institutions

In several states, such as New Mexico and Ohio, respondents recommended that the legislature strengthen its ties to preexisting executive branch committees on science and technology (e.g., governors' advisory boards), or, as in New York, that the state create such committees. In states such as Georgia which have advisory boards with ex-officio legislative representation, these committees are important for the particular legislators and staff involved.

Recommendations for increasing the role of quasi-public technology development agencies, such as exist in Ohio, New York, and Minnesota, in providing technical advice to legislators were also suggested. The enabling statute of Minnesota Technology, Inc., for example, includes legislative science and technology advice as part of its mission, but at this early stage in the agency's development, this function has yet to be implemented. But just as with the state universities, there is an inherent conflict of roles for organizations that both perform technology development with state support and provide technical advice to often contending parties within the legislature.

One North Carolina staffer suggested that some state organization should function to inform the legislature about and to help focus state efforts to attract money for science, technology, and economic development. Such an institution could also serve as a nexus for the variety of political interests in the state—the legislature, the executive branch, and the congressional delegation. A respondent in New Mexico recommended improving electronic access of the legislature to outside groups, including the federal government with whom there "should be a better technical relationship." In states with intersectoral institutions, such as

Kentucky with the Kentucky Science and Technology Council, and Georgia with the Georgia Research Alliance, these functions seem well served.

Regional S&T Office

A respondent in Minnesota suggested exploring the possibility of establishing a regional science and technical research office along the lines of a regional OTA. He felt that since neighboring state legislatures deal with many of the same issues that require technical information, such as nuclear waste disposal and use of bovine growth hormones, a jointly funded regional technology office staffed by respected technical experts might be a cost-effective method to reduce duplication of effort. The regional office could also be responsible for anticipating important science and technology issues of mutual concern to participating state legislatures which presently the state research offices do not have the time or expertise to handle. Such a regional office could be patterned after preexisting regional clearinghouses similar to the Southern Regional Education Board, which offers data and policy information to 13 southern states.

Other organizations with a national scope might provide additional technical information and analysis. ASME, for example, currently runs two programs—the State Government Coordinator Program and the State Government Fellow Program—that allow retired or semi-retired ASME members to contribute their technical skills to state legislators and executives. A newly chartered Institute of Technology Assessment, created in the wake of the dismantling of the U.S. Congressional Office of Technology Assessment, also might be able to provide technical information and analysis to state legislative clients.

Despite the barriers, respondents recognized that legislatures need access to technical information and analysis if the public interest is to be served. As a New York legislator explained, "[Staff] should be given the expertise to help legislators do their job and figure out what the public interest is. Too often we define that from competing special interests. That is, if we balance off the special interests and they're all not unreasonably unhappy, we think we have served the public interest. It seems to me that is a pretty minimal definition of the public interest. The other interest out there is the public—the broad interests of 18 million people, and we have to figure out how they fit into the puzzle."

WHAT WORKS:
SCIENCE AND TECHNOLOGY INFORMATION AND ANALYSIS FOR STATE LEGISLATURES

Introduction

Success or failure in the provision of technical information and analysis to state legislatures is significantly a function of the history, institutions, and procedures peculiar to individual states. Nevertheless, we can make some generalizations from our observations in the 11 project states about various arrangements that seem to have established a track record of satisfaction with the legislators and staff involved—in other words, "what works." These arrangements will not be desirable for all state legislatures and, even if desirable, will not necessarily be implementable. But they can certainly suggest examples that legislators and staff in each state might find provocative, and they might then be able to craft these examples into acceptable alternatives to fit their own unique situations. Even the process of contemplating such examples—if only to eventually reject them—may help legislators and staff develop a more nuanced understanding of their needs for technical information and analysis and how those needs are best fulfilled.

In some cases in this description of what works, an arrangement will seem to have fallen short of its goals or still left its customers in the legislature unsatisfied. We have included such examples for several reasons. First, it may be the case that the causes of dissatisfaction were identifiable and particular to the state or the immediate environment. Second, it may be the case that in our judgment, or the judgment of those involved, a less-than-satisfactory arrangement was still necessary but merely insufficient to the greater task at hand. Third, it is certainly the case that a great deal can be learned from bad examples as well as from good.

The standards of what works, and what is necessary and sufficient, also vary from state to state. One cannot treat every state legislature as if it were a "little Congress," and yet the mega-states like New York and Florida are nearly of national scale and complexity. We found certain problems to be consistent among states even of varying size, such as difficulties in retaining specialized experts on staff, relating with state universities, and planning long-term policies. But the acceptability of solutions to these common problems, again, will vary. Given these caveats, we hope the discussion below provides some informed guidance for state legislators and staff wishing to improve their access to technical information and analysis.

Internal Sources

The internal structure of a legislature and its staff organizations is a particularly sensitive topic and a difficult area in which to offer suggestions for improvement. All the legislatures we visited "work." But given our specific interest in what works best with respect to the provision of technical information and analysis, we make some observations and suggestions about legislative organization and the internal sources of information available to legislators.

The availability of research staff support to all legislators regardless of chamber, party, committee, or seniority is a vital aspect of the provision of technical information and analysis. Early in this century, the state of Wisconsin recognized the importance of centralized, nonpartisan research staff, and thus became the model for a number of other states as well as for the Congressional Research Service of the Library of Congress. Given general agreement among the legislators and staff interviewed that there are few—if any—sources of disinterested information external to the legislature, the ability of staff to provide disinterested information, and critical scrutiny of information from interested sources is essential. The need to be responsive to legislators with various points of view is an important and extraordinary discipline of central research staff. Staff who belong to research offices serving just the members of one party or one chamber are not fully subject to this discipline. As Wisconsin recognized, centralized research staff further serve a democratizing role among legislators: it helps level the playing field of information and influence within a legislature, so that legislators with varying educational levels, professional backgrounds, etc., can participate more fully in governing decisions and better represent their constituents.

Staff in the existing research offices tend to be generalists. The nonspecific nature of their expertise creates a number of difficulties, ranging from a lack of confidence and ability among the staff to assess the credibility of external technical information, to problems in communicating the substance of such information to legislators, who are likely to be even less specialized, particularly in technical matters. In most states that we visited, research staff achieve some degree of specialization by serving only a small number of committees, whereas in other states with larger staffs, committees per se had their own staff.

None of the states seemed particularly satisfied with how it resolved the tension between specialization and generalization. Many legislators and staff agreed that some greater specialization among staff was needed, even if it was not likely to be forthcoming for political or financial reasons. Recommendations for improving the specialized knowledge of staff—for example, continuing education, training, and field work—were more forthcoming than examples of concrete attempts to do so. Other recommendations included augmenting the existing generalized staff with a small number of individuals having specialized knowledge. These individuals could range from a staff scientist—one person available to all legislators, such as in Wisconsin, to consultants such as those hired by the Minnesota legislature to help with health care, to interns with technical backgrounds.

Just as law students or public policy students work with legislative staff organizations for academic credit and little or no pay, students or professional scientists and engineers can perform internships as well. The American Society of Mechanical Engineers (ASME), for example, maintains a small but successful internship program for state government, particularly encouraging the participation of its retired or semi-retired members. The New York Legislative Commission on Science and Technology is one organization that has a fellow from ASME. There are other successful models on the national level, for example, the American Association for the Advancement of Science Congressional Fellows Program for professionals, and the Massachusetts Institute of Technology Washington Summer Internship Program for undergraduate students. Legislative internships would be particularly valuable for science and engineering students seeking alternatives to the standard career path of the doctoral degree then an academic or industrial research position. Internships for science and engineering students would also be an excellent way to foster additional informal contacts between the legislature and universities that would be a resource beyond the duration of a particular internship (see below).

For staff as well as legislators, committee work is an excellent means of developing substantive expertise. Unfortunately, for this purpose, the jurisdictions of committees in state legislatures are not very stable, often changing substantially with each biennium or succession in leadership. This unstable political environment is not conducive to the development of substantive expertise, or to the management of some long-term issues that often have important technical content. Some of the legislatures we visited had seen fit in the recent past to create standing committees for science and technology, but dissolved them shortly after creation with very few real accomplishments. One stand-out exception, Georgia's Senate Committee on Science, Technology and Industry, is well integrated with an unusually diverse group of external sources of technical information and, more importantly, it has significant jurisdiction over economic development in the chamber. For standing committees on science and technology to be successful, in most instances they need a broader jurisdiction, including some area of important application such as economic development or environment and natural resources.

The flexibility of state legislatures in dealing with committees, however, turns into an advantage in other ways. Many states take advantage of interim or study committees, which meet between legislative sessions, to explore policy issues. These committees hear testimony from, and in some cases include in their membership, experts from the private sector, academia, etc. State legislatures also create ad hoc committees, often of joint nature, to deal with emerging issues, for example, the Water Policy Committee in Florida. Such temporary committees allow the legislatures to gather talented legislators and staff to address an immediately pressing issue without having to commit resources to maintain the committee over time. Although this problem-solving approach to committee work represents ad hoc-ism at its best, it is still reactive in nature.

To deal with the problem of proactive or prospective analysis, legislatures usually rely on external sources of information (see below), particularly those from the private sector, including lobbyists, but also on quasi-public institutions created for the specific purpose of prospective policy work, like the Kentucky Long-Term Policy Research Center. Using sources inside the legislature to provide prospective analysis is more difficult. Staff are generally too few in number or not expert enough to perform the independent, original analysis required to be proactive, although such staff perform the compilation and assessment of external analyses that are often sufficient for a reactive legislature. Nevertheless, some of the larger states, which are capable of maintaining specialized staff units for research and analysis—such as New York's Legislative Commission on Science and Technology and the Economic Research Office of the Ways and Means Committee, or Florida's Joint Information Technology Resources Committee and its Office of Economic and Demographic Research—get some prospective analysis. The smaller states have to rely on staff initiatives, where they occur, for any proactive information. One example is the Kentucky Legislative Service Commission's "scanning" program, in which designated staff members identify from their normal reading topics of potential interest to the state and contribute the reading selection and a brief analysis to a monthly newsletter.

Committees and legislative research offices house the vast majority of state legislative staff, but in a few of the states we visited, personal staff were important sources of technical information and analysis and, where available, were particularly adept at merging technical and political information in a way that members could both understand and trust. It takes an enormous commitment on the part of a legislator to find and manage a technically trained personal staffer, but for some legislators in New York, Minnesota, and New Mexico, for example, the commitment pays off handsomely. Personal staff is an expensive proposition, although individual legislators could also make use of technically trained interns, as discussed above with respect to committees.

One of the tensions between legislators and staff, who even if not possessing specialized expertise are often more familiar with technical information than legislators, is the frequent lack of ability to communicate technical information easily. In fact, legislators in our study were more satisfied with the accuracy and the objectivity of staff work than they were with its timeliness or its presentation in a clear and useable format. So even if internal staff manage to increase their level of expertise, some still greater increase in their ability to communicate with legislators is warranted.

Again, in this area we found more exploratory suggestions than actual working models. Staff in some states have been experimenting with audio tape reports for legislators to listen to while on the road or videos to view when back in their districts. Videos have often proved unsatisfactory, however, because they usually are just "talking heads" rather than a dynamic presentation of information. As with the gathering of technical information and analysis, staff and legislators hold great hopes for improvements in its communication and presentation capabilities with access to new computer technology and software. But also, as with using computers for research, staff need sufficient training in using them for disseminating information to legislators.

External Sources

Among the variety of external sources, the institution with the greatest resources and a clear obligation to support the informational needs of state government is the state university system. One of the most common perceptions among the staff and legislators we spoke with was that relations between the legislature and the state university were not satisfactory. They attributed this failure to both the university and the legislature, blaming the former for not being concerned and engaged enough with practical policy problems, and acknowledging that the latter do not know the right questions to ask. But just as common was the belief that the state universities are unique repositories of expertise and the hope that they could be tapped effectively to help inform public policymaking.

Staff and legislators in most of the states recounted various, and usually insufficient, attempts to improve relations with the state university. In North Carolina, for example, legislators described their interest in having available something as simple as a directory of researchers. But in Kentucky, the staff had compiled such a compendium, only to find it not particularly useful because it was organized according to the research interests of the faculty rather than the policy interests of the legislature. In Louisiana, the state university charged a vice chancellor with the role of legislative liaison, but staff and legislators were uncomfortable with this arrangement—not wanting to reveal their interests and possible intentions to an intermediary, highly placed in the university administration and, unlike staff, not bound by confidentiality requirements.

One sophisticated example of a good, working relationship between a subunit at a university and the legislature is the Vinson Institute of Government at the University of Georgia. The Vinson Institute has five divisions with 40 faculty, all on salary at the university. In 1977, the state received a grant from the National Science Foundation's (NSF) State Science, Engineering and Technology Program to create a university-based legislative research capacity and to hire a science advisor for the legislature. The legislature hired the science advisor, who remains with the Vinson Institute to this day, and maintained three or four people at the institute's Legislative Research Division. After the initial NSF support expired, the institute had to seek grant funding—a task made more difficult because the work product had to satisfy not only the grant-givers but also the legislature. About ten years ago, the Legislative Services Committee decided to grant the institute approximately $100,000 annually to support a student assistant and other aspects of the policy research.

The Vinson Institute selects its own work agenda and publishes a public policy research series on such topics as environment and natural resources, education, seat belts, and health care. These reports, written by faculty members, are distributed to committee members and leadership, or sometimes to the entire legislature. The institute has also produced more-in-depth books on wetlands, growth management, and recycling, and it presents an orientation conference for legislators that includes substantive sessions for incumbents as well. Other departments or institutes of government and public policy have long-standing service relationships with their state legislatures (the Institute for Public Policy and Social Research at Michigan State University maintains a database of such programs), and in other states, legislatures have created university-based centers for providing technical advice and assistance to state and local government, such as the New Mexico Engineering Research Institute and the Wyoming Science, Technology and Engineering Authority. The Vinson Institute continues to be successful in this role, however, largely because of its reliance on the science advisor, who has become personally well known and trusted within the legislature.

This element of trust is an essential part of providing useful technical information and analysis, and although executive agencies of state governments, for example, are among the most important sources of technical information, staff and legislators do not always trust them. State legislatures have become much more independent and assertive over the last generation and will likely continue in this trend, especially where, as in much of the South, new partisan competition has reformed a century's worth of political patterns. Given the potential for a further erosion of trust by partisan and institutional forces, the role of interbranch and intersectoral organizations in providing neutral fora for the discussion of technical information and analysis becomes even more important.

Some of these organizations are often based in the executive branch but have legislators as ex officio members and often work closely with legislative staff. They also have membership from the private sector, including representatives from industry and academia. Examples include the Governor's Advisory Council for Science and Technology in Georgia and the Governor's Science and Technology Council in Ohio. (In New Mexico, the Governor's Technical Excellence Committee has no legislative membership, a situation that some in the legislature find wanting.) Some states have also created quasi-public organizations which deal directly or indirectly with the legislature to provide technical information and analysis, serve as a focus for technology development and other R&D programs, and perform other tasks. Examples include the Kentucky Science and Technology Council, the Georgia Research Alliance, and Minnesota Technology, Inc. Such organizations can assist in informing and planning policy by bringing together elites in these corporatist environments, and they can also provide a nexus for the increasingly important task of maintaining communications vertically between people in state government and the state's congressional delegation over technical issues. However, these organizations perform less well in making policy in a fashion closer to the people, as is often alleged for policy formation at the state, as opposed to the federal, level.

Another type of institution used in some states to resolve conflict between the legislative and executive branches over technical questions is the consensus conference. Used in Florida and Louisiana, and in other states not in our study, consensus conferences most often take on the challenge of estimating the revenue that state treasuries will receive based on models of the local and national economy. Known as revenue estimating conferences, these mechanisms bring together principals from the legislature and the executive branch (and, in the case of Louisiana, the state university) to agree on technical assumptions that go into the model in order to prevent each branch from playing politics with the revenue estimates. With the consensus conference quite successful in the limited application of revenue estimating, Louisiana and Florida have attempted to apply the conference model to other areas such as demographic projections, but without much success. It seems that in other areas, the stakes are not high enough to warrant the principals' placing themselves in the constrained environment of the conference.

Conclusion

The legislators and staff in our study were nearly unanimous in seeing the importance of and need for technical information and analysis in the state legislative process. Although many legislators and staff are generally satisfied with their current ability to acquire technical information, others are not satisfied and most view the need for information and analysis as increasing over time. They identify particular shortcomings, including the lack of specialized experts on staff, the scarcity of prospective analysis, and poor relations with state universities, as in need of redress.

The discussion above has attempted to describe how some of the legislatures are solving some of these problems in the acquisition of technical information and analysis. What works in one legislature may only be suggestive, however, of what may work in another. Nevertheless, there are a number of alternatives for increasing and improving access to information, such as the use of professional and student interns, that impose few costs on the legislature and complement other goals such as strengthening ties between the legislatures and the universities as well. Similarly, legislative participation in intersectoral institutions creates a conduit for information and informal relationships at relatively low cost.

Sometimes investments may be necessary, and maintaining a competent, sophisticated, and nonpartisan internal staff is an investment that can pay off in terms of maintaining legislative independence vis-à-vis the executive branch and lobbyists. Even without a great deal of specific expertise, internal staff organizations can scrutinize externally generated information in the crucible of the variety of partisan and jurisdictional interests in the legislature. With additional expertise, specialized internal staff can provide the legislature with independent information and analysis for more independent policymaking. Providing state legislatures with better access to technical information and analysis will require changes and, naturally, few if any changes will occur unless both legislative leadership and rank-and-file legislators recognize the need for increased or improved access. But, however difficult and costly changes may be, failure to change is apt to be more difficult and costly still.

STATE PROFILES

AND

STATE REPORTS

FLORIDA
STATE PROFILE

ENTERED UNION:
March 3, 1845 (27th admitted)[1]
LAND AREA:
53,997 sq. mi.—U.S. rank #26
POPULATION:
13.7 m (1993 est.)
U.S. rank #4
Density per sq. mi. 249.8[2]
DEMOGRAPHICS:
White 10.7 m; Black 1.8 m; Hispanic 1.6 m;
Asian .2 m; Native American .04 m
ECONOMY:
GSP: $244.6 b (1990); U.S. rank #6[3]
Agriculture (net farm income): U.S. rank #3
Manufacturing (total income): U.S. rank #14[4]
Mining (total income): U.S. rank #22
Per capita personal income: $20,857 (1993)[5]
Unemployment: 7% (1993)
Number of patents: 1,950 (1991); U.S. rank #10[6]
Number of SBIR awards: 451 (1983-91); U.S. rank #13
State technology development agency:
Enterprise Florida (nonprofit organization receiving
public and private support); budget: FY '94
$12.6 m
EDUCATION:
High school graduation rate: 61.1%; U.S. rank #49[7]
State and local government expenditures for higher
education: $2.6 b (1989-90); U.S. rank #45
(by % of total spending)

Academic R&D expenditures: FY '91 $439 m;
U.S. rank #12[6]

POLITICAL:

U.S. Senators: 1 Democrat, 1 Republican[5]

Congressional Representatives: 23 (8 Democrats, 15 Republicans)

Governor—4-year term

Since statehood: 37 (31 Democrats, 4 Republicans)[8]

Since 1970: 5 (3 Democrats, 2 Republicans)

Current Governor: Lawton Chiles (D), 2nd term[5]

State Legislators: 160[1]

State Senators: 40; 4-year term

1994: 20 Democrats, 20 Republicans

1995: 19 Democrats, 21 Republicans[9]

State Representatives: 120; 2-year term[1]

1994: 71 Democrats, 49 Republicans

1995: 63 Democrats, 57 Republicans[9]

Length of session: 60 calendar days (session may be extended by a vote in both houses)

Annual salary: $22,560; per diem living expenses $75; Senate President and House Speaker each receive an additional $8,772/year

State budget: FY '93 $30.1 b; FY '92 $27.1 b;
FY '91 $25.2 b[10]

Legislative budget: FY '92 $83.4 m[11]

Total staff: 1,774; U.S. rank #5[12]

[1] *CSG Book of the States*, 1994-95.

[2] *World Almanac*, 1995.

[3] *State Rankings*, 1994.

[4] *Gale State Rankings Reporter*, 1994.

[5] *Almanac of the 50 States*, 1995.

[6] *Partnerships: A Compendium*, 1995.

[7] *CQ's State Fact Finder*, 1993.

[8] *Encyclopedia Americana*, 1992.

[9] *State Yellow Book*, Spring 1995.

[10] U.S. Dept. of Commerce World Wide Web census page <www.doc.gov/ CommerceHomePage.html>.

[11] *State Government Finances*, 1992.

[12] NCSL, 1988.

FLORIDA
STATE REPORT

Interview Profile

Legislature: 26 (3 senators, 5 representatives, 18 legislative
           staff)

Findings

1. Need for Science and Technology Policy Support

There is a strong consensus among the respondents in
Florida about the legislature's increasing need for technical
information and analysis. Although a few respondents
believe that, as one staffer said, "the need's always been the
same [and] the meeting of the need is probably as deficient
as it ever was," or that "the need for the information has always remained the same; now the question is more the availability and the access," most respondents recognize that, in
the words of another staffer, "things are much more sophisticated than they used to be."

Some respondents attribute the increasing need for
technical information and analysis to the sophistication and
complexity of contemporary life. "The general incorporation
of technology in our everyday life has meant that it's become
a factor in a lot more decisions," said one staff member.
Policymaking has become more involved, as "the issues that
Florida faces as a legislature are exceedingly complex [and]
traditional structures—committee organization, for example—simply don't adequately address the kinds of complex

problems that we have to find solutions to." Another staffer suggests that there has been "an evolutionary process" from a "highly politicized, nonsubstantive type situation to more involvement with . . . substantive issues, things that require expertise."

Others offer specific policy areas and trends involved in the increase, citing the issues of environmental policy and health care reform most frequently. Environmental policy has been particularly demanding because of the Everglades Forever Act and other resource management questions; and health care reform is important given the state's large population of the elderly and retirees. Prominent among the trends cited are demographics, which will soon render Florida the nation's third most populous state and force the state "to realize in the last decade that there really are some limitations on our natural resources . . . that the future Floridians can enjoy the bounty that this state has offered." Demographic trends have also produced an incredible diversity among the population, both culturally and by age-cohorts (largest number in nation over 80 and under 7 years of age). Still others who see an increase attribute it to the idiosyncrasies of staff directors and legislative leadership, an incremental increase in the sophistication and expertise of staff—in part in response to increasing sophistication of lobbyists—and an increase in sophistication of legislators themselves, who "have careers that also demand that they become more and more skilled in terms of the use of technology, so as a result they are always wanting to know, 'Has this type of analysis been done?' 'Do we have statistical information on this, this and this?'"

Although environmental and health care issues seem to dominate, other important issues requiring technical information and analysis include education reform, telecommunications (including global positioning systems [GPS] for navigation), space science and technology, human services (including welfare reform and child support enforcement), economic development, banking and trade, casino gaming, redistricting, and revenue forecasting. In the words of one legislator, "I can't think of any that don't require" technical information and analysis.

2. Internal and External Sources of S&T Policy Support

Internal Sources

The Florida legislature has a large and extremely differentiated staff structure. Florida legislators have access to personal staff (aides), staff of standing committees, staff of joint standing committees, and staff under the Joint Legislative Management Committee. The standing committee staff are by far the most important source of technical information and analysis. The staff of the joint committees are also important, although, as with other specialized sources, their importance varies widely according to the interests of the user.

All standing committees have their own permanent, professional staff whose primary duties are research and analysis. They are responsible not only to committee members but also to all members in their chamber, and they serve at the pleasure of the chamber's leader. The House and Senate each have their own bill-drafting offices, so committee staff are generally relieved of this task. A typical committee staff might consist of a staff director, a senior analyst, two analysts, an intern, and two support staff.

The Joint Legislative Management Committee, with somewhat more than 200 employees, provides support for more centralized tasks in six divisions: Administrative Services, Economic and Demographic Research, Legislative Information, Legislative Library Services, Statutory Revision, and Systems and Data Processing. Of particular importance in the provision of technical information and analysis is Economic and Demographic Research (EDR). EDR has 14 professionals, most with graduate degrees in economics, statistics, or mathematics. The principal mission of EDR is to provide revenue estimates for the legislature's participation in a revenue estimating conference with the executive branch (Florida's conference served as a model for Louisiana). EDR writes standard reference documents for the legislature and the governor's office on tax options, expenditure forecasting, etc. (which are also used by private sector interests). It also provides statistical and other research support to standing committees.

The revenue estimating conference originated in Florida in the late 1960s as "an informal consensus-building process that has since become quite formalized" and is now being used in areas other than revenue forecasting. The revenue conference began as a simple exercise in estimating how much money the state had to spend, but then expanded into attempting to understand and reach consensus on the assumptions and inputs to that figure, like the nature of the national economy, the state economy, and demographic trends. Now, the revenue estimating conference actually consists of subconferences on each of those topics. The conferences have principals, who have veto power over findings, and participants, who have only power of persuasion. The conference votes only through the application of vetoes. "Everybody has to agree or keep talking, or you go home." The principals are the EDR director, the staff directors of the Finance and Tax Committees from each chamber, and a representative from the governor's Office of Planning and Budgeting. Other agencies provide other participants. In addition to the revenue estimating conference, there are conferences on Medicaid, AFDC, child welfare, criminal justice, juvenile justice, and the state's insurance program. There are rarely nongovernmental participants because "they're not very helpful." Oftentimes "they've been somebody with a political ax to grind." Academics "kind of shy away from" the conferences because they find themselves "doing something that we all learned in graduate school was wrong. We were all—all of us who studied economics and statistics—were taught, if nothing else. Don't use regression techniques to make point estimates. . . . [But] that's basically what we do, and we don't really have much of a choice in the matter because the Appropriations Committee can't appropriate a range." EDR does let contracts to university researchers for some forecasts—for example, long-term population and local area economic forecasts.

The Florida legislature has four joint standing committees, two of which—the Information Technology Resources Committee and the Auditing Committee—have significant roles in providing technical information and analysis. The Information Technology Resources Committee evolved from an ad hoc joint select committee constituted in 1981 in the wake of a "procurement debacle" in the executive branch over a mainframe computer. In 1983, the legislature chartered the Information Technology Resources Committee as a standing committee. The committee began with three staff persons, but in the late 1980s, the Speaker of the House encouraged the committee to take on additional projects and provided additional staff; the committee now has a staff director, three analysts, an attorney, an administrative assistant, and a half-time intern. The committee has been working on assessing a potential state role in developing a GPS system for use by harbor pilots. The committee likes to "nurture" its informational role, trying "to incorporate all sides of an issue and gather all the facts from all the sources."

The Joint Legislative Auditing Committee is charged with conducting financial audits of government programs for the legislature, but over time, much like its federal counterpart, the General Accounting Office, it has become more interested in performance audits. Some audits, particularly financial ones, are done annually, while others are done at the request of the governing committee.

In addition to these extant committees, the Florida House had the Science, Industry and Technology Committee.

Previously called the Science and Technology Committee (which had been chaired by the current Speaker Peter Wallace), the Science, Industry and Technology Committee existed from 1987 to 1991. The committee had a staff director, three analysts, and an attorney, and it handled legislation pertaining to the spaceport, sunset reviews of electric and gas utilities, and telephone regulation, among other issues. With the further addition of the lottery and consumer services to its jurisdiction, regulatory issues began to dominate the committee's agenda, and in 1991 it was reconstituted as the Regulated Industries Committee.

In 1995, the legislature created the Joint Select Committee on Water Policy, with a staff director, two analysts, an intern, and a secretary. The committee will "address issues of water quality and quantity going into the twenty-first century." The committee staff will concentrate on generating information on natural water systems, assessing regional and sectoral needs, and collecting information on technologies of water supply and purification. The committee will deal heavily with scientists and engineers in the state's five water management districts.

Perhaps because of the variety of specialized sources available to them, legislators are not a particularly important source of technical information and analysis in Florida.

External Sources

The Florida legislature appears to use external sources of technical information and analysis in a slightly different way than other states, perhaps because of the size and diversity of its internal sources and the forces which created them.

Executive agencies are the primary external source of technical information and analysis, but they seem much less important than the staff (especially compared to some other states where executive agencies were rated as more important). One legislator complained that the "time span [for] getting information [from agencies] is unbelievable," and he was not sure whether "they're not as responsive, or that it takes them that much time to be able to dispense the information to us, if they're just overworked . . . or what it is."

Lobbyists also ranked highly in importance as sources of technical information and analysis, but although the information is important, staff "understand that the information . . . is strictly to benefit that profession or industry." Or, as another staffer said, "Not that I don't trust their data. It's just that I would have to review their data. . . . My decisions are not made based upon what data they give to me." Nevertheless, as one staffer emphasizes, lobbyists "offer more timely, more practical solutions to problems in kind of a short-term perspective" that the legislative environment encourages.

Public colleges and universities did not rank as very important sources of technical information and analysis for the legislature. As elsewhere, there was a great deal of variance in the responses, as some respondents saw these institutions as very important and others as not at all important. Not surprisingly, respondents attached to education committees found the public colleges and universities more important than those not associated with education committees, and the kind of information and analysis sought by such respondents tended to focus on questions of enrollment, etc. Another staffer steeped in medical issues recalled a number of times that the public universities provided important technical information and analysis, either as the result of appropriations, formally through hearings (including in a special session on abortion), or informally through telephone calls. But one legislator not involved in education issues thinks "that the state universities can be of more help than they are. . . . I just don't think that the research . . . they've done has . . . been applicable to the areas that I've been involved with." Another staffer also believes that the public colleges and universities "are not realizing their potential . . . [because] they tend to deal with the esoteric aspects of research rather than really pragmatic applied research that is needed for decision making by our legislature." Internal expertise allows the legislature to use the universities in a more selective fashion, as described by one staffer: "In most cases we don't go to the university system unless we know that because of time we can't do it in-house or because of a lack of expertise we cannot do it in-house."

Respondents also have a varied perspective on national and regional organizations that support state government—like the National Conference of State Legislatures (NCSL) and Southern Regional Exchange Board (SREB)—as sources of technical information and analysis. While some respondents found them very important, technically reliable, and timely, others have found them less important because "Florida is not only a different state than most states, [but] it's also usually ahead of other states. So when you deal with these national organizations, . . . we've already done that. . . . We do something here and Georgia copies it; so we're not going to go to Georgia to find out how to do it."

The professionalized nature of the staff nevertheless does not seem to have interfered with the use of personal sources of technical information and analysis, which are still rated as fairly important. Federal sources of technical information and analysis were only as important in Florida as elsewhere, although respondents volunteered the names of several federal sources, including the former Office of Technology Assessment, suggesting direct contact with federal sources rather than contact mediated by congressional delegations, quasi-public organizations, or other intermediaries.

3. Characteristics of Useful S&T Policy Support

Despite the existence of a large and professionalized staff in Florida, the top concern for useful science and technology support remains the issue of trust. As explained by one staffer, members of this state legislature . . . seem to be most persuaded by hearing information of whatever sort, but including science and technology issues, from someone that they consider to be a credible source. . . . A member is much more apt to be persuaded by the same piece of information if it is coming from a trusted staff member or a trusted lobbyist from the executive branch or trusted lobbyist from the private sector, a trusted trade association, a trusted constituent, a trusted personal friend whom they believe has expertise and credibility in that area, than receiving that same identical piece of information in a written report from some third-party organization, even if that third party may have a national prominence and reputation in that area.

A good part of what goes into developing that trust is providing information in a timely fashion in a way easily integrated into the legislative process. Legislators "have to some degree to rely on somebody else's pre-screening, as it were." As one legislator described it, "Personal staff I trust because they would understand how [the information] would affect me personally at home in my district; and they understand the types of individuals that I represent. . . . Committee staff, I trust their institutional knowledge and also their ability to ferret out information from the agencies, cut to the quick, and come up with recommendations."

Contrasting staff work with external sources, one staffer said that "the staff know how to communicate to the legislators, understand how to organize it so that members can use it effectively. Reports, academic work, simply don't compute in members' minds very well. . . . The key skills are to be able to reduce everything to three-quarters of a page and be able to brief them on the elevator." Another staffer critiques academic contributions in a similar manner: "Once you look to the academic community for solutions, they seem to have trouble in dealing with it in a relevant sort of a way. They want to define the watch before they tell you what time it is."

Other parts of trust are accessibility, availability, and time. Says one legislator about the importance of lobbyists, "Probably the most important [factor] is their availability and just their presence. They're here. . . . They have a really high degree of credibility to the members." Or, as a staffer put it a little more bluntly about lobbyists, "they're there all the time. That's the bottom line. And they're in your face." And according to yet another staffer, "Lobbying by itself, its persistence can pay off. And there are relationships that develop over time because of that." In many instances, the most trusted lobbyists will be former legislators or staff who have previously "formed some credibility."

The importance of stakeholders in the legislative process also makes the technical information and analysis that they provide important. As one staffer related, "Many times the state agencies and the lobbyists are the . . . major proponents of the legislation that is brought before us. And they are also many times the providers of the technical information that goes along with . . . helping to analyze . . . that decision. So the fact that they are the 'main players' makes them important."

The nature of the market for the technical information and analysis at issue is also important. Unique providers of information, ranging from EDR for state fiscal data to the federal government for census data, are important because of their uniqueness. But unique sources are also pressed into importance because, as with EDR, they "cannot make any mistakes there. So much of what we do is driven by how much money we have, and by the population . . . we are affecting that we cannot make mistakes there."

Behind the demand for information is a legislative prerogative that is only occasionally exercised: firing staff. Says one staffer, "The committee staff [is important] because that's their job, that's what they're paid to do. So they're beholden." Another staffer tells about occasional "'executions' of staff . . . over issues like incomplete information and material, omissions, problems with objectivity. Those are capital crimes here, and those 'executions' have happened more or less annually. . . . So there is quite a bit of policing."

4. Legislative Use of Technology

The Florida legislature has already made many of the technical upgrades that the other legislatures are in the process of making. All of the members' offices in the capitol and in the districts are connected through a local area network (LAN), and the Systems and Data Processing Division of the Joint Legislative Management Committee provides technical support. Because the computerization was led primarily by a former Speaker of the House, there are some differences in the technical capacities of the House and Senate. The House was computerized a few years earlier than the Senate, which just acquired PCs in the last year or two. Each member of the House has a PC-386 on his or her desk whose only application, at this time, is bill and amendment display. A conscious decision was made to go with touch screens out of concern for various barriers to use, from general unfamiliarity with computers to typing skills.

Overall, the Internet and other electronic networks are still not an important source of technical information and analysis for the legislature, although there is hope for the potential of the source. Some of the education staff, however, are involved with the South-Eastern Regional Vision for Education (SERVE), a policy network headquartered at the University of North Carolina, Greensboro, that provides a computer bulletin board, technical assistance, research abstracts, and contacts among education staffers in the region.

Staff attribute to the increased computerization of the legislature an increased ability to perform oversight and "accountability kinds of things," "to examine public policy and examine agency activities and efficiencies and all that."

5. Technical Information in a Political Environment

Technical information and analysis is obviously only one part of legislative decision making, and it is rarely the most significant or definitive part, although in Florida, the technical inputs are as prominent and formalized as anywhere. Despite this prominence and formalization, most respondents in Florida believe that technical information and analysis is less important than the opinions of constituents and legislators. One legislator was blunt about the pragmatic demands of politics: "You can be right, or you can be President, [it's] that sort of thing. . . . If you can't build a consensus, you could be right all day but you're going nowhere. So you try to balance the two." One staffer was even more blunt about the subordinate influence of technical information and analysis: "Technical information doesn't vote."

The respondents have a very sophisticated appreciation of how technical information and political processes interact, however. Beyond the suggestion that the relative importance of technical information and political considerations is issue specific—distinguishing, for example, "emotional" issues or those with serious partisan consequences or strongly staked out leadership positions from "long-term" and "complicated" issues with no serious partisan dimension—respondents talked about the educational and strategic nature of the legislator-constituent relationship.

One legislator explained the educative role this way: "I've always tried to vote what I thought was in the best interests of my constituents. It's getting harder and harder to convince them of that these days. But I suppose if you can say that you've got facts on your side, you can at least go home and defend yourself a little bit more with the ammunition." Similarly, another legislator understands that the way the constituents feel is most important, but "what I get from the committee staff helps me dispense the information to my constituents on what the impact [of their beliefs] would be."

A staffer suggests that "on the technical issues . . . [legislators are] willing to assume that their constituents really don't understand the details and the technology of these things; and then they find themselves in the dilemma of explaining their vote. They're willing to vote the right way. . . . Then their concern becomes more how do they explain this or 'help me explain this.'"

Another legislator explains the strategic element of this role as, "first you make the call on involvement with the issue based on constituents" and then "it's more important to have the information . . . in answer to your position to serve your constituents." But in viewing the use of technical information and analysis strategically rather than academically, legislators are nevertheless not ready to jettison it. As one legislator said, "It may not be a dissertation, but writing a piece of legislation that affects the lives of 14 million people is something that can't be taken lightly."

Florida's robust staff resources do not necessarily make technical information and analysis any more or less important at particular stages of the legislative process. As was the norm, it was most important in drafting legislation and evaluating previously enacted legislation and administrative actions, less important in responding to legislative proposals from other members, and still less important in short- and long-term agenda setting and in voting decisions.

In Florida, as elsewhere, the primary barrier to the provision of technical information and analysis in the legislative environment is time. But the time barrier has many dimensions, and most often these dimensions have structural and political origins. For staff, there are time constraints on data collection and analysis because interims are interrupted by so many special sessions; special sessions are more numerous, in this view, because politics has become more contentious and slower as Republicans have become more competitive in the state. Staff also describe the "communications nightmare" that occurs because time is compressed and scarce during the session, while during the interim, communicating with legislators about complex issues over long distances is also difficult. As one staffer says, "the system is geared toward crisis." Remarking about the demands of the legislative calendar, another staffer said, "You can do a lot of stuff in the interim and anticipate, but when you're in session and you've got to get a quick answer, you've got to go with what you've got. And the politics is such that moving somewhere is considered better than not moving at all; so sometimes you move somewhere to find out the next year that you moved on bad information—but you moved."

Staff are also concerned about the time and availability of legislators "in order to be as thorough and provide as much information and technical analysis" as they feel they should. For their part, legislators feel the time pressure, too, as one indicated that there simply isn't enough time to assimilate and use all the information to which one has access.

Changes in leadership every biennium in Florida make for changes in the agenda and in priorities, so staff have trouble planning longer-term projects. The ever-changing and nonlinear political process renders the planning and use of technical information difficult. As one staffer says, "most of the information sources that our committee is responsible for, at least in my own view, can really be used only if one is approaching this in some kind of fairly rational, organized manner." Some committee staff find the - aspect of time a barrier, given the challenges facing generalists on committee staff. Producing timely data from the most current information is a particular barrier. One staff member even complained of a lack of "anticipatory data."

In addition to timeliness, another set of barriers surround data gathering. Staff have very practical concerns about the quality of data from their sources and their own ability to integrate data from various sources and from incompatible hardware and software. As everywhere, staff find their "being unsure of the accuracy or the credibility of the information" a barrier. Staffers were also frustrated by knowing that data existed but that they had no easy access through the Internet: "There's a whole world of information out there that we're not connected with, and I think it's a shame that they're not utilizing just tons of research out there."

There is also a set of attitudinal and intellectual barriers to the provision and use of technical information and analysis, because "sometimes [legislators] don't seem real interested in knowing the facts." As one senior staffer suggested, both staff and legislators "have to think too hard to understand a lot of it." Another staffer also spread the blame for difficulties on both legislators and staff, saying "most people who are legislators are not here because they're rocket scientists—a few, but for the most part, they're not. And the inadequacy of our [staff's] understanding of the technology and the science information is just enough to provide one more barrier, because unless you really understand it adequately, you can't translate it. . . . That's difficult at our level of expertise." Some legislators may present a barrier by not even giving staff an opportunity to translate: "There's a tendency to either glaze over when the whole subject matter comes up or there's . . . that possibility of disinterest—'Oh, that's too technical. I wouldn't understand it.'"

But translating is a problem because, even with staff's generalist approach, they are still more specialized than legislators, who "don't speak the same language we [staff] do . . . because we get into our little technobabble and it requires spelling things out in much greater length rather than using little short-cuts." In recognizing that "the more technical you get, the less likely you're going to have an audience," staff face the challenge of finding innovative ways to present technical information. They have found computerization somewhat helpful but hope for still more. Some staff have also taken to providing technical information and analysis on audio tapes for their members who commute.

Respondents were nearly unanimous in their belief that the technical information and analysis provided by staff has made the legislature more powerful, authoritative, or independent vis-à-vis the executive branch and lobbyists. A few respondents disagreed with respect to the executive, because they felt the legislature dominated the weak executive branch—fragmented by an elected cabinet—anyway. "Frequently, we've slaughtered the governor's proposals because they're half-baked, they haven't been researched, and they fall apart when you start looking at them. And we're set up to do that. It never ceases to surprise me that the new governors are surprised."

One staffer summarizes the role of staff in checking the executive branch this way: In Florida, the executive agencies "have their own expertise," but they "lobby the legislature" along with other groups and the staff are expert enough to

> look at the expertise that exists in agencies, evaluate their studies and reports, look at the lobbyists' reports . . . and evaluate those; and oftentimes you may find some contradictory conclusions or contradictory use of data. . . . [T]he legislature relies on committee staff with our own set of technical backgrounds to evaluate that and give them a professional opinion as to which of those reports are more likely to be reliable and reflective of the policy that the committee is trying to pursue. So we play that kind of evaluative role in looking at different technical reports and sorting it out for recommending to our legislators.

Legislators are more likely to trust staff over executive agency personnel because, as one legislator explained, "if an agency person gives biased data, data that's not objective, there's not really any consequence from the legislature usually; but if a staff person plays those games, that staff person doesn't last long."

With respect to lobbyists, staff are "another source for triangulation." One senior staffer has heard "more and more members asking harder and harder questions of the lobbyists. So I think members are getting more sophisticated in terms of how they analyze the issues, and the objectivity and the quality of facts and the information that's being presented to them." Just as with executive agencies, it is staff who are responsible to legislators when something goes wrong: "When the information directly conflicts, sometimes it's the staff's ass that's chewed out, not the lobbyist's. I've actually had lobbyists come in, in one of my previous committee assignments, and chew me out for having quoted the CEO of his company in my staff analysis, because he didn't like the quote. The staff analysis was still published with the quote in it."

But for all its sophistication, and perhaps even to some extent because of it, Florida politics is no less contentious. As one legislator recounted,

> I hate to keep going back to the Everglades, but it was one [case] that really was very enlightening for me. But I see more and more the science being colored by the politics . . . and that's just long-term death for everybody. To me the scientific community has got to give the policymakers the straight scoop and not play politics with their data. I saw both sides manipulate that on the Everglades issue . . . so you had to take whatever they were saying with a grain of salt. It had the practical effect of sending us back with the executive agencies or the Water Management District . . . because you kind of felt like the industry scientists and the environmental scientists were not being quite as straight with you as they should have been.

Another staffer was even more disillusioned with the situation because

> what it really gets down to ultimately is my scientist up in the courtroom—my scientist can beat up your scientist. Rarely does science come forward with unassailable conclusions. So you fall back to politics. You can't escape it. Just like in the courtroom. . . . So I have seen some eminent

scientists . . . reduced practically to tears in front of the committee, tucking their tails between their legs and shuffling to the back of the room. . . . Their skills, their knowledge, may be more appreciated in another environment. They probably go away thinking it's just like they said, you shouldn't "cast pearls before swine."

6. Legislative Satisfaction

Despite the high level of professionalization and size of staff, respondents in Florida are no more satisfied with the technical information and analysis provided by all sources, or that provided by staff, than respondents in other states. Legislators "always need more and better data and more up-to-date data and more complete [data]." One legislator agrees, saying that "it can never be good enough; [in] science . . . there's a certain amount of impreciseness. . . . You can't be absolutely certain about this stuff." According to one staffer, what dissatisfaction exists among legislators comes from their desire for "information keyed to their district boundaries in a lot more detail than is typically available from any attainable source at reasonable cost."

One legislator declared flatly, "Do I think that I have an in-depth knowledge of most of the subjects that I vote on or deal with? And the answer is 'no.' But then I think that I'm not supposed to have too technical or too detailed knowledge about many of these issues. I think you're expected to have a broad view, so I think that a lot of times we're voting with a great degree of ignorance."

7. Recommendations

Because of the large size and well-differentiated nature of the legislative staff in Florida, there were almost no recommendations for the addition of new structures or expertise. Some committee staff, however, felt overworked and understaffed, in part because of the high expectations generated in such an environment. "We get these projects that are just so immense that we just don't have the manpower to do an adequate job on the reviews that we're asked to do," says one staffer. A staff director agrees and would like to see some system by which qualified analysts could be hired to work on projects for a short period of time. Preferably, such part-time analysts would have specific expertise to complement the general expertise in the committee staff. This staff director would also like access to an editor or another kind of resource to help staff produce readable, usable documents—"translating the jargon into English."

Respondents also suggested that legislative staff should have more exposure to the work in the executive agency under their jurisdiction "and learn more about it first hand, be out there in the trenches sometimes, to learn really what's going on." One staffer agrees that, particularly with Tallahassee somewhat isolated from the rest of the state, the legislature "could spend more time training us, getting us out there in the real world and seeing some of the problems first hand." A legislator believes that staff "tend to be too cloistered and . . . they're not given enough breadth of experience," so they should attend "conferences, visitations, seminars with various universities, meetings with school boards, maybe go meet some parents' groups, that type of thing." Such field exposure might also allow staffers to incorporate more qualitative sources of information into their work, which one staffer thinks is necessary to balance the "well-trod path from information to policy" of quantitative information.

To combat the primary barrier of time pressure, one staffer suggested altering the legislative calendar not by extending the duration of the session but rather by introducing a mid-session hiatus to allow legislators and staff to "just catch up with all the things that are going on." But the staffer recognizes that "there are political reasons why that can't be done." This staffer would also like to see continued improvement of the computer systems and "more capability of doing original research or influencing the research that's done in the academic centers."

An important area one senior staffer has identified for improvement is to develop more "effective ways of presenting analytical information to members, so that it is in fact used more by them and understood better by them." This staffer also noted that there is no training for members in how to use staff resources. "You have to be able to prepare the audience to be able to benefit" from the technical information and analysis provided.

One legislator believes that the staff have sufficient expertise and should be "more tough" and "brutally frank . . . in dealing with the legislators but also in dealing with the executive people."

GEORGIA
STATE PROFILE

ENTERED UNION:
January 2, 1788 (4th admitted)[1]
LAND AREA:
57,919 sq. mi.—U.S. rank #21
POPULATION:
6.9 m (1993 est.)
U.S. rank #11
Density per sq. mi. 119.4
DEMOGRAPHICS:
White 4.6 m; Black 1.7 m; Hispanic 1 m;
Asian .08 m; Native American .01 m
ECONOMY:
GSP: $136.9 b (1990); U.S. rank #13[2]
Agriculture (net farm income); U.S. rank #9
Manufacturing (total income): U.S. rank #20[3]
Mining (total income): U.S. rank #24
Per capita personal income: $19,278 (1993)[2]
Unemployment: 5.8% (1993)
Number of patents: 757 (1991); U.S. rank #22[4]
Number of SBIR awards: 147 (1983-91); U.S. rank #25
State technology development agency:
Governor's Advisory Council on Science and Tech-
nology Development (operates in a decentralized
manner; many programs are operated by inde-
pendent institutions); budget: FY '94 $29.9 m
EDUCATION:
High school graduation rate: 62.7%; U.S. rank #47[5]
State and local government expenditure for higher
education: $1.5 b (1989-90); U.S. rank #39
(by % of total expenditures)

Academic R&D expenditures: FY '91 $484 m;
    U.S. rank #11[4]

POLITICAL:

U.S. Senators: 1 Democrat, 1 Republican[6]

Congressional Representatives: 11 (4 Democrats,
    7 Republicans)

Governor—4-year term
    Since statehood: 63 (37 Democrats, 2 Republicans)
    Since 1970: 5 (all Democrats)[7]
    Current Governor: Zell Miller (D), 2nd term

State Legislators: 236[8]
    State Senators: 56; 2-year term
        1994: 39 Democrats, 17 Republicans
        1995: 35 Democrats, 21 Republicans[9]
    State Representatives: 180; 2-year term
        1994: 128 Democrats, 52 Republicans[8]
        1995: 114 Democrats, 66 Republicans[9]
    Length of Session: 40 legislative days[8]
    Annual Salary: $10,641; per diem living expenses
        $59 (committee and session days) plus $4,800/
        year expense allowance. Senate president pro tem
        receives an additional $4,800/year. House Speak-
        er receives an additional $63,582/year. House
        Speaker pro tem receives an additional $4,800/
        year.[8]

State budget: FY '96 $10.7 b; FY '95 $10.3 b;
    FY '94 $9.2 b; FY '93 $8.3 b[9]

Legislative budget: FY '92 $18.2 m[10]

Total staff: 679; U.S. rank #15[11]

[1] *World Almanac*, 1995.
[2] *State Rankings*, 1994.
[3] *Gale State Rankings Reporter*, 1994.
[4] *Partnerships: A Compendium*, 1995.
[5] *CQ's State Fact Finder*, 1993.
[6] *Almanac of the 50 States*, 1995.

[7] *Encyclopedia Americana*, 1992.
[8] *CSG Book of the States*, 1994-1995.
[9] *State Yellow Book*, Spring 1995.
[10] Georgia Legislative Budget Office.
[11] NCSL, 1988.

GEORGIA
STATE REPORT

Interview Profile

Legislature: 14 (3 senators, 3 representatives, 8 legislative staff)

External: 3

Findings

1. Need for Science and Technology Policy Support

There was nearly unanimous agreement that legislators need access to technical information and analysis and that this need has been increasing. Among the most important roots of this increase are the general complexity of policy issues, the importance of technology development in the state's economy, competition from other states and countries, the need to improve the quality of education, and the increasing willingness to deal with environmental concerns. Most bills in the legislature do not actually have technical components because most are local bills with little substantive content. But, a number of contentious and pressing issues, such as conforming to the Clean Air Act and managing solid waste as well as recurring uses of economic and demographic data in reapportionment and education financing, demand technical sophistication and capacity. Although Georgia has a large defense establishment, it has not been hit particularly hard by base closings and other common consequences of the end of the Cold War.

Other issues demanding technical information and analysis mentioned include: the costs and benefits of transportation alternatives (including air and ground water pollution, economic and residential development consequences of highway and airport construction and of mass transit); purchasing computer systems for the state and legislature; water and coastal management; emergency defense and management; distributionary effects of tax reform; health care reform; attracting biotechnology firms; agriculture and support for research at experiment stations; gambling; telecommunications (including digital communications for state agencies and local telephone service); and university research and technology transfer.

In response to this demand, Georgia has created a number of new mechanisms over the last few years, including a Senate Committee on Science, Technology and Industry, the Governor's Advisory Council on Science and Technology, and the Georgia Research Alliance. Despite these innovations, some staff feel that staff expertise has not been used to its fullest.

There is some sense in Georgia that the move to greater technical sophistication is in part driven by a generational change among legislators, the younger of whom are more technically oriented than their predecessors (although some dispute this perspective). One long-serving committee chairperson believes that with seniority comes a greater need for technical information and analysis and some greater capacity to get it.

2. Internal and External Sources of S&T Policy Support

Internal Sources

The principal internal resource providing technical information and analysis to members of the Georgia legislature is the staff of the House and Senate research offices. Legislators do not have personal staff and as many as six to eight legislators may share one secretary. The first phone call a legislator usually makes to track down some information is to the House or Senate research staff. Although there are separate House and Senate research offices, there is a joint bill-drafting organization, the Office of Legislative Counsel.

The House Research Office (HRO) has a director, six analysts, an administrative assistant, and a secretary. Analysts usually serve three or four committees that correspond roughly to their areas of specialization or training. Several of the 33 standing committees in the House—including Judiciary, Appropriations, State Planning and Community Affairs, and Ways and Means—have their own committee staff. These staff remained with the committees after the current system was established in part by removing staff from committees and aggregating them. HRO has its origins in the Georgia Educational Improvement Council, an executive organization that mediated educational issues between the State Department of Education and the Board of Regents. The legislature then took over this organization, renaming it the Legislative Education Research Council. Over time, its role expanded to examine other issues in addition to education, and it began to service both chambers. However, because of a conflict between the House and Senate, the latter of which is more executively oriented, the group was reconstituted as the House Research Office. HRO staff serve at the pleasure of the Speaker: the director interviews candidates and makes the recommendations to the Speaker, who makes hiring decisions.

The Senate Research Office (SRO) has nine analysts who serve 24 committees, so there is some specialization of expertise and some generalization. SRO is governed by the five-person Senate Administrative Affairs Committee, chaired by the lieutenant governor, who is the active presiding officer of the Senate. SRO was created by then-Lieutenant Governor Zell Miller, whose request for a joint office had been rebuffed by the House. With its slightly larger staff-to-member ratio, there is perhaps some sense that SRO is a little more pro-active than HRO.

In 1992, the lieutenant governor, believing that the Senate needed more expertise in the area of technical information and analysis, created the Senate Committee on Science, Technology and Industry. The need for expertise had several sources: the distributed nature of Senate jurisdiction in important related areas such as economic development and higher education; the vision of Georgia as the Empire State of the South and the regional headquarters for a large number of high-technology businesses; and the need to establish a legislative capacity to evaluate and oversee initiatives taken by the governor, including the Governor's Science and Technology Advisory Council and the Georgia Research Alliance. The Committee—formed as an alternative to increasing the capacity and expertise of Senate staff—supported the lieutenant governor's political strategy to decentralize the power that comes with access to information. This strategy was also expressed in the appointment of Senator James Tysinger, a Republican, to chair the Committee. (There is little sense, however, that the appointment of a Republican was a conscious strategy to head off partisan questions about technology or industrial policy in which the Committee might engage.) Tysinger is a long-serving state senator and an engineering graduate of Georgia Tech. Since its creation, the Committee has mostly tried to learn about issues and establish an agenda. The Committee has made site visits to the Medical College of Georgia to view a demonstration of telemedicine, and to Georgia Tech and the University of Georgia.

Legislators themselves are only a modest source, at best, for the provision of technical information and analysis in Georgia.

External Sources

Georgia has a well-developed variety of external sources of technical information and analysis, particularly the Governor's Science and Technology Advisory Council, the Georgia Research Alliance, and the Vinson Institute of Government.

The Governor's Advisory Council on Science and Technology was sworn in in March 1992 with a charge from Governor Zell Miller to work on a strategy and mission for the state in science and technology development and to serve as a hub linking the various public and private actors involved in harnessing science and technology. The original council reported to the governor in 1992 and 1993 and developed a list of six strategic initiatives. A new council was sworn in in 1994 with a more specific charge to focus on aerospace and aviation. The council has direct input to the Georgia Research Alliance and the Georgia Partnership for Excellence in Education. Members of the council serve pro bono, and staff support is provided by individual members when available. The council was begun with an appropriation of approximately $250,000 from the legislature, but the funding has been decreased from that level. Its influence in the legislature is narrow but seemingly important through liaisons with legislative staff and through the experience of legislators who, as ex officio members, come in contact with a broad cross-section of private sector individuals represented on the council.

The Georgia Research Alliance (GRA) is one aspect of the relatively special relationship between the legislature and the university system in the state. Created in 1990 by an initiative of the presidents of the six major research universities in the state (University of Georgia, Georgia Tech, Emory, Clark-Atlanta, Georgia State, and the Medical College of Georgia), together with the CEOs of the largest corporations, GRA is a nonprofit organization seeking to improve the research infrastructure in Georgia. Funding for

GRA's office of four staff members comes from the partici-pant universities, foundations, and corporations in roughly equal proportions. Like the Governor's Advisory Council (and other types of commissions), the influence of GRA in the legislature is at times important but narrow, limited by the simple fact that it chooses its own agenda and has direct contact with only a small number of legislators. From 1991–1994, the state invested $58 million in 91 specific projects recommended by GRA on the basis of their potential for economic development through science and technology (with another $146 million in federal, corporate, and philanthropic contributions). As part of their "value-added" function, GRA has also been involved in the federal Tech-nology Reinvestment Program (TRP) to facilitate the transi-tion of defense facilities into the civilian economy. In this role, GRA links the needs of state legislators through the universities to a federal program. In another federative role, GRA campaigned among the 1993 Georgia congressional delegation to get three members—the very first from Geor-gia—on the U.S. House Science, Space and Technology Committee (now the House Science Committee).

The Vinson Institute of Government is the second aspect of the relatively special relationship between the legislature and the university system in Georgia. Although the lineage of the institute goes back to 1927 when it was attached to the law school, its relationship with the legislature on substantive science and technological issues did not blos-som until 1977 when the state received a grant from the National Science Foundation (NSF) to create a university-based legislative research capacity and to hire a science advisor for the legislature. Jim Kundell was hired to provide scientific and technological research and technical assis-tance support for the legislature and was one of three or four people in the Legislative Research Division at the institute.

The institute publishes a public policy research series on such topics as environment and natural resources, education, transportation, and health care. These reports, written by faculty members, are distributed to committee members and leadership, or sometimes the entire legislature. The institute produces in-depth books on wetlands, growth management, ground water, and recycling, and presents an orientation conference for legislators that includes substantive sessions for incumbents. It also publishes a handbook for legislators. In addition to policy research, Kundell provides technical support to key legislative committees and individual legislators dealing with specific scientific and technological matters. After the initial NSF funding expired, Kundell had to "hustle" grants like other researchers, but this task was made more difficult because the work product had to satisfy not only the grant-givers but also the legislature. Finally, about ten years ago, the Legislative Services Committee, comprised of the leadership of the House and Senate, decided on an annual grant of approximately $100,000 to support student assistants, travel, and other aspects of the policy research and technical support functions of the Institute. Today, the Vinson Institute has five divisions with a total of 40 faculty, all on salary at the University of Georgia.

In addition to the connection between the legislature and university provided by the Vinson Institute and GRA, there are a number of less formal contacts, including a legislative liaison for the Board of Regents, and a number of personal relationships between House and Senate staff and legislators—many of whom came through the Georgia state university system or Georgia Tech—and faculty members. In these relationships, though, the responsiveness of the universities is generally due to the desire for good will. In some respects, the resources of the universities are complementary to those of the legislature. For example, a legislative study committee was unable to resolve an issue of defining a turbidity standard in water, so it requested the Board of Regents to appoint a scientific panel comprised of 15 university system people and chaired by Jim Kundell of the

Vinson Institute. Nevertheless, there is still a nagging suspicion in the legislature that more is available within the universities than legislators have access to, and that the universities could be more helpful if only the legislators were more capable of calling on them.

The standard array of executive agencies, in addition to the specialized groups mentioned above, are important sources of technical information to legislators, often because the agencies are involved more in policy development and bring issues to the attention of the legislature. In 1993, the governor created by executive order the Office of Technology Policy (OTP) and, to the extent that the legislature looks to executive agencies for technical information and analysis, it is expected that OTP will be a dispenser of technical information. But, as one legislator said, "Some legislators, including myself, maybe don't trust some of them [because] the information that you get from them might be given to you in such a way as to sway your decision one way or the other."

Lobbyists are important sources of technical information and analysis because, even more than staff and sometimes in contrast with them, lobbyists will provide information without the legislator having to request it or hunt for it. Or, if legislators have to request information, lobbyists are notably quick in providing it. Legislators usually believe that lobbyists don't lie because the lobbyists' only currency is credibility. Nevertheless, they view their connections with lobbyists as "unfortunate."

3. Characteristics of Useful S&T Policy Support

A key to useful technical information and analysis is the ability to trust the source, which is often derived from a feeling of propriety over it. For example, one legislator admitted a "bias" toward one of the regional policy support groups because of his long-time membership on its board and advisory council. Another legislator described the House

Research Office staff possessively as being an extension or "arm" of the legislature to do its bidding. This legislator also described how relationships developed with persons in the executive branch: "Once you develop those relationships, you aren't dependent on them, but it's also the thing where you've got your staff that you feel would be your think tank and you kind of say maybe there's a little slant from the executive, but I think you build up confidence in folks after dealing with them if they've been straight shooters." In other words, staff resources enable legislators to build confidence in other sources of information and analysis, such as the executive branch, by being available to counter any bias until a personal, trusting relationship develops.

The proximity of staff to the demands on legislators make the information and analysis they provide very useful. According to one staff member, "I think it's a combination of accessibility and, I hate to say, trust, but just the fact that the staff is here and it's immediate support for [the legislators]. We have a very short session—it's a 40-day session—so the immediacy of response or accessibility is a primary factor in getting the information."

To be most useful, external sources of technical information and analysis must be somewhat representational or sensitive to the demand-side of policy. The legislature must be attuned to the demands of constituents as expressed through the executive agencies and lobbyists, and because of the representative nature of these sources, their information and analysis has great utility to legislators.

One provider of technical information and expertise suggested that the role of "translator" was an important one to make the information that is available, for example, in the state university system, useful to the legislature. Such information must be scientifically defensible, legally supportable, and understandable. Although there were many pragmatic aspects to evaluating the utility of technical information and its sources—for example, a unique source of information is seen as a useful source—something like technical virtuosity was barely mentioned as a characteristic of useful information.

4. Legislative Use of Technology

In summer 1994, the Georgia legislature was in the midst of a significant upgrading of its computer systems, including a local area network and a personal computer for every secretary and legislator. Because the computer systems were not yet available, the ability of staff and legislators to use electronic networks was negligible. Some were very optimistic about the potential of the Internet as an information tool, but others were more sanguine because they were unable to understand how the answers to specific, policy-relevant technical questions could be available to them. As indicated above, some believe that there is a generational influence to the use of computer-related technology in the legislature. But one legislator who generally supports this hypothesis believes that the primary impetus comes from the occupations of legislators outside the legislature—"Had not my business dictated me into the computer business . . . I probably wouldn't be in it."

5. Technical Information in a Political Environment

Technical information and analysis is obviously only one part of legislative decision making and it is rarely the most significant or definitive part. With respect to the relative influence of technical information versus constituent opinion, two different types of explanations are offered: legislative style (i.e., trustee vs. delegate) and issue content (emotional/salient vs. nonemotional/nonsalient). In these schemes, legislators who consider themselves delegates are less likely to use technical information in opposition to constituent opinion; similarly, on issues with a high salience or a high emotional content, legislators are less likely to use technical information in opposition to constituents. However, legislators describe themselves as being more concerned with technical information and analysis vis-à-vis constituents, fellow legislators, leadership, and lobbyists than staff describe them (that is, legislators describe themselves more as trustees while staff describe them as delegates).

One of the important roles played by staff in providing technical information and analysis in this regard is with respect to the relationship between legislators and constituents. Staff help legislators respond to constituent concerns in a substantive way and help legislators educate constituents on technical issues. As one legislator recognizes, "A good legislator must take into consideration the facts rather than constituents [who] many times are not as well informed as they should be on a given subject and are off base." The legislator's role in these cases becomes an educative one.

The stage of the legislative decision-making process in which the information and analysis from staff appears to be most important is in bill drafting, followed by evaluation of previous legislation. Information and analysis is still marginally important in helping to determine what issues are currently important, in helping legislators decide how to respond to other legislation, and in planning for the long term. As might be expected, it is relatively unimportant in helping legislators decide how to vote.

Respondents discuss several barriers to the provision of technical information and analysis in the legislature. Principal among the barriers seems to be the interest of legislators and the understanding they have of the information and analysis provided to them. One staffer admits that "their understanding of what they're given [is a barrier]. A lot of them are farmers and businessmen—and especially from the rural areas—who haven't really dealt with technology much, who don't really understand it themselves, and [who] maybe have never used a computer in their lives. . . . To get them to understand all that is the most difficult part I have." Staff face the impediment of having "to put [information] in terms [legislators] understand while maintaining accuracy."

Oftentimes, staff suggest, "the legislators who have a specific knowledge-base are not put in a political position to use that knowledge-base. . . . For instance, the group of legislators that made the decision about computerizing the legislature has very little computer knowledge; the group of legislators that has computer knowledge were not asked to be part of that group."

The resources devoted to staff are also a barrier in the provision of technical information and analysis. The relatively small number of staff available and their time commitments reduce their ability to specialize "enough to be able to convey some of the more detailed, more scientific-dependent information that [legislators] may want to know about." According to one staffer, many negative "decisions are made relative to travel or purchasing of equipment and other kinds of things. . . . [And] I think it provides a barrier to sufficient access to the kind of information and technical services that both the staff as well as the membership require." One senior staffer notices a gap in information management technology between the public and private sector: "State government hasn't kept pace with the private sector in terms of information management or management of information services. So it's very decentralized."

Respondents were nearly unanimous in their belief that the technical information provided by staff has given the legislature more power or authority vis-à-vis the executive branch and lobbyists, and that this is a good thing. As one former legislator recalled, "The reason we saw we needed [a research office was] simply trying to get the best information possible that we could make a decision on, from somebody who did not have an agenda. And when you get stuff from the administration, for example, you've got to assume that there's an agenda there. . . . And with somebody over in the research office, they can then go gather this information from all the sources, and hopefully, then we can get it in a straightforward way that's not slanted trying to promote something." Or, as one legislator said with respect to staff and lobbyists, "This is our captive source of objective, independent information. Vis-à-vis lobbyists, we understand that they will be telling us their side, and oftentimes if you have one good lobbyist and one poor lobbyist on the opposing side, there's not much balance there. Then we use the . . . research staff to ferret out a balance of information."

One staff member who disagreed simply felt that what staff was able to do was not enough to counteract the executive dominance in technical information: "There's simply not enough of us. . . . We cannot specialize enough to be able to get into some of the finer details . . . [and] until that happens I think the legislature will be at a disadvantage vis-à-vis the executive branch."

6. Legislative Satisfaction

There is a generally high level of satisfaction in the legislature with the availability of technical information and analysis from the variety of sources in Georgia. The variety is important to this satisfaction because, as one legislator described, "I expect to get a certain flavor on the idea" from one source and a different flavor from another, "but I expect that . . . you sort of mix them up and you usually end up in the right spot." But this is a demanding method. As one senior staff person said, "I would think that the people who know how to ask the questions are probably satisfied." And another staffer suggested that the legislators might be very satisfied, "but I don't think they understand why they shouldn't probably be satisfied. . . . They could be snowed very easily, and they could be impressed really easily, and they perhaps should be a little more critical of technology and information coming from technology and what it all means." What seems to be missing from available information and analysis is "knowing what's available" and "coherent" and "effective synthesis."

7. Recommendations

More than other states, there seems to be great sympathy for increasing the number and expertise of the research staff in the House and Senate research offices, although there is also more sympathy for spending money on computer systems than on personnel. Staff clearly recognize that new information technology also requires new training. One concrete proposal was to have one staff person and one secretary for every four legislators. Another proposal was to have one policy analyst for each committee. One legislator even volunteered a proposal to maintain adequate compensation for research staff. Both legislators and staff feel that one benefit they could receive from adding personnel is a modestly more pro-active relationship and significantly greater specialization. The overall political climate, however, makes spending money on the legislature very difficult. Furthermore, as the Georgia legislature becomes a more partisan institution with greater numbers of Republicans, questions of staffing may begin to reflect partisanship as well.

KENTUCKY
STATE PROFILE

ENTERED UNION:
June 1, 1792 (15th admitted)[1]
LAND AREA:
39,732 sq. mi.; U.S. rank #36
POPULATION:
3.8 m (1993 est.)
U.S. rank #24
Density per sq. mi. 94.5[2]
DEMOGRAPHICS:
White 3.4 m; Black .3 m; Hispanic .02 m;
Asian .02 m; Native American .01 m
ECONOMY:
GSP: $67.5 m (1990); U.S. rank #25[3]
Agriculture (net farm income); U.S. rank #14
Manufacturing (total income): U.S. rank #24[4]
Mining (total income): U.S. rank #6
Per capita personal income: $17,173 (1993)[5]
Unemployment: 6.2% (1993)
Number of patents: 371 (1991); U.S. rank #31[6]
Number of SBIR awards: 23 (1983-91); U.S. rank #42
State technology development agencies:
The Business and Technology Branch (BTB) of the
Kentucky Cabinet for Economic Development
(state run); budget: FY '94 $1.1 m
Kentucky Science and Technology Council, Inc.
(KSTC) (independent)
EDUCATION:
High school graduation rate: 69.1%; U.S. rank #36[7]

State and local government expenditure for higher
   education: $1.06 b (1989-90); U.S. rank #19
   (by % of total expenditures)
Academic R&D expenditures: FY '91 $98 m;
   U.S. rank #34[6]

POLITICAL:

U.S. Senators: 1 Democrat, 1 Republican[5]
Congressional Representatives: 6 (4 Democrats,
   2 Republicans)
Governor—4-year term
   Since statehood: 56 (30 Democrats, 7 Republicans)
   Since 1970: 7 (6 Democrats, 1 Republicans)[8]
   Current Governor: Brereton C. Jones (D), 1st term
State Legislators: 138[1]
   State Senators: 38; 4-year term
      1994: 24 Democrats, 14 Republicans
      1995: 21 Democrats, 16 Republicans[9]
   State Representatives: 100; 2-year term
      1994: 71 Democrats, 29 Republicans[1]
      1995: 63 Democrats, 37 Republicans[9]
   Length of session: biennial, even years; 60 legisla-
      tive days; may not extend beyond April 15[1]
   Annual salary: $100 per diem; $74.80/calendar day
      per diem living expenses. Senate president $25/
      day, Senate president pro tem $15/day, House
      Speaker $25/day, Speaker pro tem $15/day
State budget: FY '93 $10.5 b; FY '92 $10.2 b;
   FY '91 $9 b[10]
Legislative budget: FY '92 $23.7 m[11]
Total staff: 462; U.S.rank #24[12]

---

[1] *CSG Book of the States*, 1994-1995.
[2] *World Almanac*, 1995.
[3] *State Rankings*, 1994.
[4] *Gale State Rankings Reporter*, 1994.
[5] *Almanac of the 50 States*.
[6] *Partnerships: A Compendium*, 1995.
[7] *CQ's State Fact Finder*, 1993.

[8] *Encyclopedia Americana*, 1992.
[9] *State Yellow Book*, Spring 1995.
[10] U.S. Dept. of Commerce World Wide Web
   census page <www.doc.gov/
   CommerceHomePage.html>.
[11] *State Government Finances*, 1992.
[12] NCSL, 1988.

KENTUCKY STATE REPORT

Interview Profile

Legislature: 12 (1 senator, 5 representatives,
             6 legislative staff)
External: 3

Findings

1. Need for Science and Technology Policy Support

There was virtually unanimous agreement that legislators need access to technical information and analysis and that this need has been increasing. Among the most important roots of this increase are the general complexity of policy issues, the role of technology in education policy, the importance of technology development in the state's economy, and the implementation of federal mandates, particularly in environmental policy. Education has been particularly demanding on two fronts: (1) demographic data and analysis is important for projecting educational budgets; and (2) educational reform, passed in 1990, has raised many vexing questions about providing technology in the classroom.

Other issues demanding technical information and analysis include: agricultural issues such as the future of tobacco farming; health care, telemedicine, and the availability of physicians; telecommunications and utilities; higher education and the research and development infrastructure; technology transfer; energy and environmental issues, especially those surrounding the combustion of coal,

groundwater, and the comparative assessment of risk; and scientific and mathematical education and literacy.

In response to this demand, Kentucky has created several new mechanisms over the last few years, including the Kentucky Long-Term Policy Research Center (KLTPRC), the Kentucky Science and Technology Council (KSTC), and the Partnership for Reform Initiatives in Science and Mathematics (PRISM). Despite these innovations, there is some sense that the Kentucky legislature, in the words of one senior senator, "often has to make decisions with inadequate information."

2. Internal and External Sources of S&T Policy Support

Internal Sources

The principal internal resource providing technical information and analysis to members of the Kentucky legislature is the staff of the Legislative Research Commission (LRC). Legislators do not have personal staff. Committees have assigned staff from the central LRC who serve both during the session and in the interim between sessions. Only legislative leadership possess partisan staff members. LRC staff serve members of both parties, all committees, and both chambers of the legislature. LRC staff serve both bill-drafting and research functions, and they are usually receive the first phone call a legislator makes to find a piece of information.

Staff are governed by the LRC itself, a board composed of 16 members from the bipartisan leadership of each chamber. The commission hires the director, and the director in turn hires the staff. The approximately 90-person research staff (of 250 total staff) are organized roughly into committee areas in order to develop expertise. There are also special areas, including budget review, program evaluation, administrative regulations, personal service contracts, and capital construction and bond oversight. An office of economic analysis with a team of six economists provides economic and financial analysis for the legislators and also acts as a resource for other staffers on questions of economics and research design and methodology.

The Legislative Research Commission was created in 1948, but it was not an effective organization until about 1968, when the legislature established the interim committee system to provide some continuity between Kentucky's 60-day, biennial sessions. In the mid-1970s, a movement for greater legislative independence began, and the lieutenant governor, who had been the chair of the commission, lost that position. In 1974, the Speaker and president pro tem of the Senate became the commission co-chairs. After a constitutional amendment in 1992 removed the lieutenant governor as the presiding officer of the Senate, the Senate elected its own president, who co-chaired the commission. LRC has an annual budget of approximately $25–28 million.

Legislators themselves are only a modest source, at best, of technical information and analysis for the legislature in Kentucky.

External Sources

Kentucky has a wide variety of external sources of technical information and analysis for the legislature, but they are still developing and the sources are in many ways still unsatisfactory.

Despite the legislative independence movement of the 1970s, the Kentucky legislature still relies heavily on executive agencies for information and analysis. In some policy areas, the executive agencies do not have a great deal of credibility with the legislature. One senior legislator gave an example of a special legislative session on health care, during which even basic data from an agency had to be cleared through political channels before it could be sent to the legislature. At one point, the legislature created an executive branch commission on science and technology, and legislators sat on the commission. But a court ruling held that legislative membership on an executive branch commission violated the separation of powers.

Lobbyists occupy an important but peculiar position in providing technical information and analysis to the Kentucky legislature. Because the state was for so long dominated by the executive branch, there was little tradition of lobbying the legislature. After the mid-1970s, when the legislature began to assert its role in governing, lobbyists turned more attention to legislators. Personal relationships between legislators and lobbyists have been important. But recently, Kentucky suffered a very difficult legislative ethics scandal known as BOPTROT (named after the Business Organizations and Professions [BOP] committee and the trotters at the race track). New ethics legislation enacted in 1993 has fairly well eliminated the purchasing of meals by lobbyists for individual legislators, since this activity is now reportable. The role of lobbyists as providers of information, however, is still very important.

Just as the personal aspect is important to lobbyists' role, individual, personal contacts are also important sources of technical information and analysis in the part-time and relatively informal legislative environment in Kentucky.

National and regional organizations to support state legislatures, such as the National Conference of State Legislatures (NCSL), are also very important in Kentucky, particularly in their ability to provide information about the activities and experiences of other states. Staff members use NCSL resources frequently to help them get "pointed in the right direction." Legislators also participate actively in NCSL functions, like the study mission to Europe to study models of technology and development institutes which led to Technologies Infrastructure legislation to be implemented by the Kentucky Science and Technology Council.

The Kentucky Science and Technology Council (KSTC) is one organization that deals specifically with science and technology policy issues. As one might expect from an organization with a specific mission, it is very important to people in the legislature familiar with it and not very important to those unfamiliar with it. KSTC was created by statute in 1986 and incorporated as a quasi-public, not-for-profit corporation in late 1987, out of "a perceived need [among university and private sector leaders] to have an organization that was independent, free-standing, [and] entrepreneurial, to pursue science and technology issues and activities in the state." KSTC has limited contact with legislators and staff, although it does testify before committees "not infrequently." On occasion, it has provided informal services, such as linking legislature with consultants, sharing survey results, and sponsoring meetings attended by staff and legislators, among others.

KSTC has also become involved in developing and implementing science and technology policies within the state and in a federative role. The organization works with the state to establish a state-wide R&D infrastructure, including a network of applied research centers, to implement Senate Bill 277, the technology infrastructures legislation. KSTC prepared the state's application to the National Science Foundation's Systemic Science Initiative (SSI), and it manages the subsequent SSI-funded activity called Partnership in Reform Initiatives in Science and Mathematics (PRISM). KSTC also wrote a successful proposal for the Technology Reinvestment Program (TRP) to create a state-wide technology deployment system called the Kentucky Technology Service, and it manages Kentucky's Experimental Program to Stimulate Competitive Research (EPSCoR)—a NSF set-aside for states program as well. In these roles, KSTC sees itself as "an interface not only between the federal and state [governments] but also between the state and firms [in the private sector]." KSTC has a full-time professional staff of nine persons (including two with doctorates) and three administrative assistants. It operates on a direct budget of approximately $1.6 million and coordinates a budget of an additional $5–6 million. The vast majority of the operating budget comes from grants and contracts, with the remainder roughly split between corporate memberships and fees for service.

In 1992, the legislature created by statute the Kentucky Long-Term Policy Research Center (KLTPRC). The center's substantive policy work began only after its first executive director was hired in August 1993. In contrast to the LRC staff, who "have a difficult time finding adequate time to look over the horizon," KLTPRC's "responsibility is to attempt to look over the horizon to identify emerging issues and trends that could have important policy implications in the future." This certainly requires the center "to consult with people who have . . . the scientific expertise" on many questions, but "some of the biggest ones for policymakers are not scientific."

Another reason for KLTPRC's creation was a "feeling" "by the principal architects that we needed a center or institution that was not wholly located within the legislative branch or wholly located within the executive branch." Thus, the 21-member board of KLTPRC is composed of six legislators, four persons from the executive branch, and 11 at-large members from the business and university communities, citizens' groups, and local governments. In the summer of 1994, the center had an executive director, one senior analyst and one research assistant, but it was looking to expand to a total of four or five professional staff. The center is financed by a $1 million endowment created by the legislature, as well as by direct appropriations, which totaled about $500,000 for the first biennium and $635,000 for the second. The center is also authorized to accept gifts, grants, and contracts. One such grant—shared with the Cabinet for Natural Resources and Environmental Protection—is from the U.S. Environmental Protection Agency (EPA) for a comparative risk assessment project called Kentucky

Outlook 2000. A second major project is a study of the future of tobacco production in the state. Legislators and staff who are familiar with KLTPRC have high hopes for its importance in providing technical information and analysis to the legislature and for it to fulfill its mission of looking beyond the next election.

Although respondents recognize the contributions of the public colleges and universities, there is some dissatisfaction lurking in the legislature with their role in providing technical information and analysis. The question of attributing blame, however, seems to be open. According to one senior legislator, "The universities have been quite helpful, but could be more helpful. They give us everything we ask for. We're probably not sophisticated in what we can ask for." Staff see it rather as a question of university researchers being "detached from the General Assembly. . . . They seem to be doing their research, and they don't want to share it with the General Assembly." Or, they are not capable of framing the issues in a fashion usable by legislators.

One senior staffer described one LRC project to "improve the functioning and the expertise of the agency by seeking outside resources, especially through the state universities." The project compiled "a compendium of names and research projects that we felt . . . could give some improvement to the functioning of the role" of LRC staff. Although the compendium was completed, the staff found "a lot of times that research they were doing was not really relevant to stuff we were interested in, quite frankly." Or, staff found the university researchers interested but in need of money to carry out the research. One short-lived relationship with the University of Louisville did develop, but it was "not creating a bridge there of what they were doing on an ongoing basis to what we were doing." Although the responsiveness of the universities was praised, both staff and legislators seem dissatisfied with the piecemeal relations and untapped potential.

3. Characteristics of Useful S&T Policy Support

Familiar, accessible, nonpartisan, and expert are the important characteristics of useful science and technology support in Kentucky, and the staff of LRC generally fit the profile on all counts. LRC staff are the "primary source of information," and legislators will "go to an individual" that they "think is knowledgeable in an area. . . . Their mission is to take care of whatever needs that we [legislators] have . . . [and] if we're not happy, they may be out of a job."

The part-time nature of the Kentucky legislature makes reliance on staff inevitable, especially with the increasing complexity of public policy. Reliance on staff is also inevitable because staff tenure is generally more stable than that of the legislature, where turnover averages about one-third per biennium. LRC staff also combine the functions of research and bill-drafting, so their knowledge of legislative affairs is detailed. Staff are aware, however, that they work for all legislators, and that, to be effective, they must approach this charge without bias or partisanship. More than one legislator indicated a tendency to discount the work of individual staffers who were known not to be good on both sides of an issue.

But lobbyists and people from the executive branch are also familiar, accessible, and expert, and therefore can be very useful even if they are not nonpartisan. As one staff member indicated, the legislators "know the lobbyists, the lobbyists know them. The lobbyists know how to convey the information to them. . . . They can meet them after hours, and they develop a relationship with them. . . . there's a trust that builds up and they believe for the most part what the lobbyists will tell them." According to another long-time staff person, "State agencies are always over here testifying. They're the people that are called in for what's going on and why." Together, the staff, lobbyists, and agency personnel are "the three groups I think that are really an integral part of the process."

4. Legislative Use of Technology

As of summer 1994, the Kentucky legislature was making only scant use of electronic information systems. It is only since late 1992 that research staff have had PCs on their desks. As one staffer said, "I feel like we're kind of in the Dark Ages in that." Electronic networks like Lexis were generally available to research staff only through a "gate-keeper," the librarian, although a few staff persons had their own individual links to the Internet and relied on it greatly ("a 5 or 6 if you have one" on a scale of 5). LRC was in the midst of discussing how to become more connected and hoped to be more significantly on-line by the end of the year. Staff were also looking to their computers to help them present information and analysis in a more useful format. KSTC and KLTPRC seemed a little further along in their use of information technologies than the legislature.

Since the interviews were completed, a great deal of progress in legislative use of technology has been made. All research staff and legislators who have requested them now (fall 1995) have PCs and access to the Internet. LRC also has facilities for video conferencing, and a downlink satellite is in operation. An interactive video conference examining current and future trends in technology, work, demographics, education, and society was offered to research staff.

5. Technical Information in a Political Environment

Technical information and analysis is obviously only one part of legislative decision making, and it is rarely the most significant or definitive part. There seems to be a clear distinction between the perspectives of staff and legislators with respect to the relative importance of technical information and analysis in legislative decision making. Staff seem more likely to view technical information and analysis as generally subordinate to political factors such as the opinions of constituents, other legislators and legislative or party leadership, and lobbyists. Legislators seem more likely to frame the relative importance of technical information and analysis in a specific context: "It depends on the issue." One legislator described the attempt to balance information and constituent demands this way: "My theory is to vote how I think the constituents would want me to vote if they had the information." This perspective also highlights the necessity of orienting technical information to constituents as well as legislators. As another, more junior, legislator says, "I try to use it in a process of educating them on why I'm making decisions the way that I am."

The stage of the legislative decision-making process in which information and analysis provided by LRC staff appears to be most important is the bill-drafting stage. It is relatively less important—but still somewhat important—in helping to determine what issues are currently important, in helping legislators respond to legislation introduced by others, in helping them evaluate the impact of legislation, and in planning for the long term. It is least important, as one would suspect, in helping legislators determine how to vote.

There are a number of barriers to the provision of technical information and analysis in the legislative environment in Kentucky. As elsewhere, a principal barrier is time, particularly staff having the necessary time to develop the information, and to develop the necessary expertise. "It's hard to get legislators to focus and to give staff an adequate amount of time to cover an issue adequately." Staff—mostly generalists and spread among a number of committees—also see "our own lack of knowledge or expertise" in a particular area as a barrier.

The irresolvable nature of uncertainty in technical areas like environmental impacts and economic forecasting is another barrier. As one staffer said, "There's a lot of controversy and dispute in the scientific community, and I think that makes it difficult for those of us who are not scientists." Respondents also recognize that a result that is technically sufficient may not be politically sufficient. As one staffer relates, there are different types of legislators, some of whom rely more on political than technical information for decision making: "If your research is somehow critical of that industry, [the legislators] may discount it and tend to rely on what the lobbyist or their friend has told them. . . . So, I think your biggest obstacles to the research you do are the friendships legislators develop" with interested parties. Another staffer interpreted this situation differently and suggested that differing educational levels among legislators and constituents—rather than friendships with lobbyists—accounted for the differing types of legislators.

In the summer of 1994, barriers existed because of minimal access to electronic sources and limited technical capabilities to gather information electronically and manipulate it for clear presentation on the available software. Some of these difficulties were expected to be resolved with additional hardware, software, and training in the near future. The necessity of maintaining confidentiality in staff responses to legislative requests is widely recognized and rarely a problem.

Respondents were nearly unanimous in their belief that the technical information and analysis provided by staff has given the legislature more power and authority vis-à-vis the executive branch and lobbyists, and that this is a good thing. There is a history of significant legislative-executive conflict in Kentucky, which until the mid- or late-1970s was entirely dominated by the governor. Increasing staff support and changing the timing of legislative sessions in order to reduce gubernatorial influence over the selection of leadership were two of several reforms that increased the legislature's independence. This independence has generated a greater work load for LRC staff, but it is considered worth the cost because the executive branch "no longer has a monopoly" on information and analysis. Staff resources are perceived to have been somewhat less successful, but still important, in balancing the influence of lobbyists, who have become more important in the legislature as the legislature itself has become more important.

It is largely this legislative-executive rivalry that makes KSTC and KLTPRC, which hang between the executive and legislative branches, important: "This is the only forum in which you don't necessarily have that adversarial relationship playing out. It provides an opportunity for . . . high-level representatives of both branches to be part of the same group . . . [and to] present policy options that represent a melding of interests."

6. Legislative Satisfaction

There is only a modest level of satisfaction in the legislature with the availability of technical information and analysis from the variety of sources in Kentucky. One senior legislator concluded simply that "it could be a lot better" because the legislature did not have access to the technical expertise it needed, although it was moving in that direction. Another legislator is generally satisfied, but still worried that "the executive branch has more resources available to get technical information . . . and they will try to manipulate us." One senior staff member suggests that it is younger legislators who are less satisfied with their access to information and analysis because, in their inexperience, they have not yet learned how to use resources. Indeed, one junior legislator wishes that the information provided was a little less technical so that "it would make it a little easier" for the citizen-legislator "to make decisions, feel good about decisions." The problem staff face in providing such understandable information, however, is the dual nature of their audience: "We've got two audiences. We have 'Legislator Z' who ain't no dummy. 'Legislator Z' is a sharp guy, but he doesn't have much training in research methodology. . . . We also write for 'Professor X' . . . in another university who's hired by a lobbyist to knock down our analysis."

7. Recommendations

There has been talk in the Kentucky General Assembly of changing the organization of staffing from one unified staff serving both chambers to separate staffs for House and Senate. But changes in staff organization are largely a question of financing, which is almost universally perceived as quite limited. One possible alternative is increasing the use of consultants. The committee system in the legislature is generally stable and few perceive a great need for a separate science and technology committee, which probably would not have many bills to deal with anyway. Staff would like to see themselves working more productively, without necessarily adding to their numbers. More and better computer facilities, computer training (especially in producing information in more useful formats), and better time management were all mentioned as possible changes. Staff and legislators would also like to see better relations with the university community but can offer few concrete suggestions for achieving new connections. Some legislators recognize the high stakes involved, however, in acquiring technical information; in the words of one, "There's a realization in the General Assembly among enlightened members that nothing is really more important than having good technical information. If you have good technical information, you can control policymaking."

LOUISIANA
STATE PROFILE

ENTERED UNION:
April 30, 1812 (18th admitted)[1]
LAND AREA:
43,566 sq. mi.; U.S. rank #33
POPULATION:
4.3 m (1993 est.)
U.S. rank #21[2]
Density per sq. mi. 98.4
DEMOGRAPHICS:
White 2.8 m; Black 1.3 m; Hispanic .09 m;
Asian .04 m; Native American .02 m
ECONOMY:
GSP: $90.8 b (1990); U.S. rank #22
Agriculture (net farm income): U.S. rank #33[3]
Manufacturing (total income): U.S. rank #33[4]
Mining (total income): U.S. rank #2
Per capita personal income: $16,667 (1993)[5]
Unemployment: 7.4% (1993)
Number of patents: 503 (1991); U.S. rank #27[6]
Number of SBIR awards: 72 (1983-91); U.S. rank #31
State technology development agency:
Office of Technology, Innovation, and Modernization;
budget: FY '94 $2.7 m
EDUCATION:
High school graduation rate: 56.7%; U.S. rank #51[7]
State and local government expenditures for higher
education: $1 b (1989-90); U.S. rank #38
(by % of total expenditures)

Academic R&D expenditures: FY '91 $240 m;
   U.S. rank #25[6]

POLITICAL:

U.S. Senators: 2 Democrats[5]

Congressional Representatives: 7 (4 Democrats,
   3 Republicans)

Governor—4-year term
   Since statehood: 45 (1 Democrat, 44 Republicans)
   Since 1970: 4 (1 Democrat, 3 Republicans)[8]
   Current Governor: Edwin Edwards (D), 2nd term[5]

State Legislators: 144[1]
   State Senators: 39; 4-year term
      1994: 33 Democrats, 6 Republicans
      1995: 33 Democrats, 6 Republicans[9]
   State Representatives: 105; 4-year term
      1994: 88 Democrats, 16 Republicans,
         1 Independent[1]
      1995: 86 Democrats, 17 Republicans,
         1 Independent[9]
   Length of session: odd years—60 legislative days in
      85 calendar days; even years—30 legislative days
      in 45 calendar days[1]
   Annual salary: $16,800; per diem living expenses
      $75 for session and committee work; Senate pres-
      ident receives an additional $32,000/year; House
      Speaker receives an additional $32,000/year

State budget: FY '93 $12.9 b; FY '92 $11.75 b;
   FY '91 $10.5 b[10]

Legislative budget: FY '92 $24.5 m[11]

Total staff: 531; U.S. rank #20[12]

[1] *CSG Book of the States*, 1994-1995.
[2] *World Almanac*, 1995.
[3] *State Rankings*, 1994.
[4] *Gale State Rankings Reporter*, 1994.
[5] *Almanac of the 50 States*, 1995.
[6] *Partnerships: A Compendium*, 1995.
[7] *CQ's State Fact Finder*, 1993.

[8] *Encyclopedia Americana*, 1992.
[9] *State Yellow Book*, Spring 1995.
[10] U.S. Dept. of Commerce World Wide
   Web census page <www.doc.gov/
   CommerceHomePage.html>.
[11] *State Government Finances*, 1992.
[12] NCSL, 1988.

LOUISIANA
STATE REPORT

Interview Profile

Legislature: 15 (2 senators, 2 representatives, 11 legislative
     staff)

Findings

1. Need for Science and Technology Policy Support

There is a general consensus among Louisiana respondents that it is important for legislators to have access to
technical information and analysis and that the demand for
it has increased over time. In addition to the general
response that policy is becoming more complex, the primary
reason cited for this increase is the need to respond to
environmental concerns. This is especially important in a
state with a large oil and gas industry (one of the world's
largest oil refineries is easily visible from the capitol building) as well as a large tourist industry. Federal environmental mandates play an important part in creating this
demand.

Some respondents also believe that a more stringent
fiscal environment has created a higher demand for technical information in an attempt to prevent costly mistakes:
"We can't afford to make bad decisions any more." Some
also attribute the change to a more educated type of
legislator who is more apt to pursue "preventative maintenance legislation" than to react in a "seat-of-the-pants, off-

the-cuff type of approach." A few respondents believe, however, not that the demand for technical information and analysis has increased, but that the ability to supply it has increased. They cite the creation of nonpartisan staff and the beginnings of computerization as indications of this increasing capacity.

Among the most important issues in Louisiana requiring use of technical information and analysis are: environmental issues such as air pollution, wildlife and fisheries, and oil field cleanup; economic development and strategic planning; data gathering and transfer for social programs; education reform; and health care reform.

2. Internal and External Sources of S&T Policy Support

Internal Sources

Staff are an important source of technical information and analysis for the Louisiana legislature, and they are usually the first point of contact for legislators seeking information. Staff are also long-serving and provide a measure of institutional memory despite turnover in legislators, leadership, and committee chairs.

The House and Senate have separate staff. The House Legislative Service (HLS) is organized similar to the structure of the previous Legislative Council. The Legislative Council administered a unified staff from its creation in the 1950s until 1981, when the Senate acquired its own research service, the Senate Research Service (SRS). HLS has about 75 staff members, about half of whom are research analysts, attorneys, or senior administrators. It is divided into four divisions, roughly corresponding to the jurisdiction of the four or five committees assigned to each division (e.g., insurance, industry, commerce, agriculture, and natural resources committees). HLS is supervised by the Legislative Council, composed of 12 representatives including the Speaker, the Speaker pro tem, the clerk of the House, a representative from each of the seven congressional districts, and two members at large. Membership in the council is appointed by the Speaker, who is not required to maintain a partisan balance but nevertheless attempts to do so. The council sets policy and hires a director, who serves at the pleasure of the council.

The Senate Research Service has about 70 members, about 30 of whom are researchers, 30 are clerical and support staff, and 10 are administrators. Roughly two-thirds of the researchers are attorneys. These staffers serve 16 of the Senate's 17 committees. The Office of Fiscal Affairs and Policy Development, with seven professionals, staffs the Finance Committee and the Revenue Estimating Conference (see below). Each committee has one research analyst, one secretary, and one senior attorney (who oversee about two committees each). Most of the staff have mixed assignments of committee work, bill drafting, and research, regardless of their primary assignment. On an annual basis, staff are assigned at least one major subject area and perhaps a secondary area. (This organizational structure is an artifact of the formation of SRS from the Legislative Council, which left the Senate with an awkward mix of very senior central staffers and more junior committee staffers.) Senate staff tend to be more closely associated with particular committees and particular chairs, and a new chair will often bring in new staff for that particular committee.

Senior staff concede that there is some duplication of effort, for example, in bill drafting and in staffing two libraries, but that the roles are really quite different. There is some question about the possible overstaffing of the Senate, especially when the legislature is not in session. Higher Senate staff pay scales also cause some tension.

Legislators are not particularly important sources of technical information and analysis in the Louisiana legislature.

External Sources

Executive agencies are the most important source of technical information and analysis for the legislature in Louisiana, a state with a very strong tradition of executive leadership. The agencies are seen as important sources because of their experience in the day-to-day workings of programs (and not, for example, because of a particular in-house analytical capacity). But executive agencies, like lobbyists, are also viewed with some skepticism because they are advocates (and opponents) as well as sources of information.

Lobbyists rank very highly in importance in providing technical information and analysis to the legislature, largely because they are proactive in bringing information to the legislators and the staff. Similarly important are the regional and national organizations that support state government, such as the National Conference of State Legislatures (NCSL) and the Southern Regional Education Board (SREB). Members and staff find the clearinghouse function of these sources particularly useful, and SREB is bestowed "the Good Housekeeping seal" by education policy people because of its efforts to provide comparable data among its 15 southern state members. SREB data are both widely accepted and used as policy benchmarks; as one staffer said, "We need to be within so much of the SREB average."

Less important than executive agencies, lobbyists, and clearinghouse organizations, but still somewhat important, are public colleges and universities. The relationship between the legislature and the state universities seems to be, like everything else in Louisiana, highly politicized. There is a great deal of politicking over state funding for research centers among the state's universities in different regions (e.g., rivalry between Louisiana State University [LSU] and University of Southwestern Louisiana). Staff explain the lack of specific centers geared toward assisting the legislature by referencing the political culture of the state, which "goes back to the Huey Long days, where because of the political influence and the reaction you got if you were on the wrong side . . . they want to stay in the foxhole and let the wind blow over, and if you stand up and get involved and are seen, first of all, your motives are questioned." Nevertheless, universities promote their expertise when they come to the legislature seeking funds. According to another senior person, "When a university is out here looking for funding, they'll bring along these experts and basically offer them—'Say, by the way, if you ever have a question about the redfish population in the Gulf of Mexico, we've got Dr. So-and-So here who spent the last five years doing nothing but counting redfish roe.'"

But even though universities are forthcoming out of financial self-interest, they seemingly fail to view the provision of information to the legislature as a primary duty, and the legislature could get more information, "an unlimited amount, if we were more active at soliciting it." At one time, LSU created a position for a vice chancellor to serve as a coordinator for handling legislative requests. This innovation did not work well because "[m]embers [of the legislature] are never happy with having that kind of stuff screened." Instead, legislators prefer having "people who have a ready-made reputation on standby that we know to call" directly.

One more formal role for academic input to the legislative process, one not conditioned by the implicit exchange suggested above, is the Revenue Estimating Conference (REC), in which an economist from LSU joins representatives of the governor and the legislature to project state receipts for the coming years. The idea of the conference is to "have a single set of reliable numbers that can be used by all parties in the policymaking and management process of Louisiana." REC, in operation since 1987 and enshrined in the state constitution, worked so well that Louisiana attempted to institute estimating conferences in other policy areas (demographics, economics, education, transportation, social services, and criminal justice). These have not, to date, been successful, in large part because of an apparent lack of interest from the executive branch.

3. Useful Characteristics of Science and Technology Policy Support

Accessibility seems to be the key characteristic in Louisiana for the utility of technical information and analysis. Staff are important because they are "readily available on a day-to-day basis" and in constant contact with legislators. The nonpartisan nature of the staff is also important to their utility. Other sources of information, such as lobbyists and public universities, are accessible because it is in their self-interest to reach out to legislators and provide them with information. The most useful sources are the ones that "bring the information," because staff is not sufficiently numerous or structured to do much independent research. In many ways, the legislature "simply [has] to rely on what the agencies tell us and what the lobbyists and private industry say."

There is also a sense that useful information has an element of experience to it. Executive agencies are important because they "deal with [information] on a day-to-day basis," according to one staffer, and "are actually in the field" and so are a good source of information, according to another.

Comparative information from clearinghouses such as NCSL and SREB is also very useful.

4. Legislative Use of Technology

The use of national electronic networks is currently not very important in the Louisiana legislature, although there are hopes for improvement. Such networks are only available through the library, and one staffer reported that access to such systems as Westlaw or Lexis was restricted to senior staffers. Only one fax machine services several floors' worth of House staff, and it is only recently that staff changed from dumb terminals to PCs. An internal e-mail system was established just in 1994, creating some novel links between the separate House and Senate Research Offices. As one staffer said, the legislature is taking only "little baby steps in technology" right now.

5. Technical Information in a Political Environment

Technical information and analysis is obviously only one part of legislative decision making, and in Louisiana the more political parts are notably robust. There is no apparent consensus among legislators and staff about whether technical information is more or less important than the opinions of constituents, leadership, fellow legislators, or lobbyists. The respondents tended to make a distinction between the two types of information. As one staffer said, the legislative process "has an objective information side and a political side. . . . The amalgam of the information and the politics is with the legislator."

Paralleling this distinction and the classical one between the delegate and the trustee, one legislator made a distinction between the "politician" and the "statesman" and does not "apologize for being a politician." This legislator chides "the guy who comes up here and says . . . 'We are elected to lead our people; if they don't understand, we have to explain it to them.' That might have sounded good 200 years ago, but it's foolish today. . . . I happen to be one of those who always puts my constituents' philosophies first. I hope and pray that enough technical information will substantiate their reasoning."

One senior staffer attributes the ability of legislators to use (and therefore the influence of) the staff to an increase in the length of the legislators' service: "It's funny, but you can almost see it in a first-year legislator. The first-year, 'My people back home tell me, 'Blah, blah.' And the second year, it's, 'Do you think they might be right?' And the third year, it's, 'They're always screwed up on this funding issue; are they still screwed up?' Yes sir, they're still screwed up; 'that's what I thought. I just wanted to check and make sure.'"

As one might expect, the stage of the legislative process in which House and Senate staff have the most influence was drafting legislation. Staff were also rated more important in helping legislators respond to legislation introduced by others and in evaluating previously enacted legislation or administrative actions. They were less important in short-term and long-term agenda setting and least important in helping legislators make voting decisions.

There was some agreement that "the biggest barrier is time" in attempting to provide technical information and analysis in the legislative context. According to one staffer, "You have to scramble around and try to find something. And sometimes you're left with the feeling that you're just not sure that what you've done is right." Time management is also a problem because the workload changes radically between session and interim, and during session there can be conflicts between committee work and research work.

Other barriers identified include: difficulties in computer compatibility and data collection, and in hardware and software familiarity among staff (especially for purposes of clear visual presentation of information); the lack of ability of staff to understand information and jargon (in order to fulfill the role of "interpreter" for the member); the lack of specific expertise, exacerbated by the large volume of work ("They have too many balls in the air to be able to be experts in every part of the issue," says one legislator of staff); the lack of staff resources "to follow through" on projects; a reluctance of those with information to give it up; and the questionable applicability of data that are available.

On the demand-side, there are barriers such as the educational level of legislators and their knowledge of what the legislature has versus what it could have. Another barrier is the influence of lobbyists, because, as one senior staff person asserted, "Our members generally have such a good working relationship with the lobbyists that any attempt to give them information that is not accepted by the lobby tends to be dealt with in a jaundiced way."

There is a strong consensus that the technical information and analysis provided by House and Senate staff has helped make the legislature somewhat more powerful or authoritative vis-à-vis the executive branch, which is very strong historically and constitutionally in Louisiana. This increased legislative authority is particularly noticeable on economic issues. Although one staffer lamented that "I wish I could say 'yes'" to the question of increased legislative authority, a legislator expressed the general consensus that staff

> has brought some balance and perspective. Louisiana traditionally has had a very strong executive branch. And we had to rely very heavily on what the executive branch said as being gospel. The fact that with the . . . technology, which continues to be upgraded on an almost quarter-by-quarter basis, we feel that we're on level playing ground now and that a lot of the information sometimes that the executive branch may give, we refute or we can challenge or we can question because of the fact that we have that same capability and in some cases even more than the executive branch.

Again there is a consensus that technical information and analysis from staff has helped make the legislature more powerful or authoritative vis-à-vis lobbyists, but "in a limited way." As one staffer suggested, "Lobbyists are the guys that help them get reelected, that support them when they need it. They're going to listen to the lobbyists before they listen to me, in real politics." Another staffer allowed that most of the progress with respect to limiting the influence of lobbyists was attributable to registration and disclosure laws. Legislators equivocate on the relative importance of staff and lobbyists. The "politician" above values staff information over information from lobbyists "because it's unbiased."

Other legislators view lobbyists the same way: "Generally, I look for the lobbyists' input and I discount as much as I know I have to discount." The limits of staff's ability to compete with executive agencies and lobbyists is illustrated by the fact that respondents in Louisiana ranked both agencies and lobbyists higher as sources of technical information and analysis than respondents in any other state.

One senior person neatly summarized the political position of the technical information and analysis provided by staff: "We don't provide a lot of particular expertise, but they all know that if they want to test the objectivity [of a] lobbyist or the executive branch [or even] the local universities, . . . they can look to us."

6. Legislative Satisfaction

The level of satisfaction with the provision of technical information and analysis is generally high among respondents in Louisiana. According to one senior staffer, the residual dissatisfaction has to do in part with "the perception, if not the actuality, that there's information out there that for some reason we can't get a hold of." Legislators' expectations have increased with computerization, sometimes without reason or knowledge: "'Well, just give me this out of the computer. That's all I want. Just press that button there.'"

Other staffers also suggest about legislators that "you can give them information . . . and they still don't know what they want" because "they don't understand what they have." Another staffer described it this way: "Are they satisfied that they got the gaming report? Yeah, it went like hotcakes. . . . They thought this was great information to have at this stage of the debate on that public policy issue. But if they realized that there's the same kind of data out there on environmental issues and education issues that's not being brought to them in this same very user-friendly report, then they'd say, 'Well, hell, why aren't I getting that information?'"

But staff also acknowledge that legislators "seem overwhelmed and frustrated. They ask a simple question; in their mind they expect a simple answer. And it's the old joke: they'll sit there and ask what time it is, and me or the college president or the chief financial officer is going to tell them how to build a clock."

7. Recommendations

Recommendations for solving the primary problem of limited time availability for assembling technical information and analysis range from constitutional amendments to additional staff to more formal time management solutions (e.g., pre-filing of bills, which has been implemented). Some among the staff express a desire for greater scientific or technical assistance in their role as interpreters of data. But enlarging the staff risks stirring public ire, and there is little sympathy for differentiating the functions of bill drafting, research, and committee work that adding more staff might imply.

One staffer suggested "a more rigorous system of interim training, development of additional skills by staff in their subject matter areas . . . in continuing education, . . . participation in national conferences," etc. Universities could be more active in this regard, and more responsive to legislative (as opposed to administrative) needs in technical areas.

Staff members propose two additional reforms to improve the use of technology in the legislature. First, decreasing wasted time by adding to the technology available to staff; for example, equipping them with fax/modems would help eliminate the time and effort required to print and fax at the few available dedicated faxes. One staffer also discussed the goal of using technology to make staff-generated information available not just to legislators but to the public as well:

"Make it a database that people can connect with and not just staff; I'd like to put it in the public domain."

Again, a major impediment to implementing any of these recommendations is the strength of the executive branch in Louisiana and the relationship between the governor and the legislative leadership, which "is so tied to the executive administration that there's not that impetus to go out and create the independence."

MINNESOTA
STATE PROFILE

ENTERED UNION:
May 11, 1858 (32th admitted)[1]
LAND AREA:
80,000 sq. mi.; U.S. rank #14[2]
POPULATION:
4.5 m (1992)
U.S. rank #20[2]
Density per sq. mi. 55.2
DEMOGRAPHICS:
White 4.1 m; Black .09 m; Asian .08 m;
Hispanic .05 m; Native American .05 m
ECONOMY:
GSP: $100 b (1990);[3] U.S. rank #6
Agriculture (net farm income): U.S. rank #6
Manufacturing (total income): U.S. rank #18
Mining (total): U.S. rank #13
Per capita personal income: $18,829 (1990)
Unemployment: 4.8% (1990)[4]
Number of patents: 1,533 (1991); U.S. rank #12[3]
Number of SBIR awards: 302 (1983-91); U.S. rank #19
State technology development agency:
Minnesota Technology, Inc.[3]; budget: FY '94 state
$5.48 m; federal $2.75 m; total $8.23 m
EDUCATION:
High school graduation rate: 90.9%; U.S. rank #13
Proposed University of Minnesota budget 1996-97:
$1.37 b
Academic R&D expenditures: FY '93 $332 m;
U.S. rank #17

POLITICAL:

   U.S. Senators: 1 Democratic Farm Labor [DFL],
      1 Independent Republican [IR][2]
   Congressional Representatives: 8 (6 DFL, 2 IR)
   Governor—4-year term
      Since statehood: 60 (13 Democrat [9 DFL],
         47 Republican [2 IR])[5]
      Since 1970: 6 (4 DFL, 2 IR)
      Current Governor: Arne Carlson (R), 2nd term
   State Legislators: 201[6]
      State Senators: 67; 4-year term
         1994: 45 DFL, 22 IR
         1995: 42 DFL, 25 IR
      State Representatives: 134; 2-year term
         1994: 85 DFL, 49 IR
         1995: 71 DFL, 63 IR
      Length of session: 120 legislative days in biennium;
         since 1973 meet annually[2]
      Annual salary: $27,979; House: $48 per diem, up to
         $600 housing during session; Senate: $50 per
         diem, up to $500 housing during session; House
         and Senate majority and minority leadership
         additional $11,192[2]
   State budget: FY '94-95 $19.5 b; FY '91 $17.8 b;
      FY '89-91 $16.2 b[7]
   Legislative budget: FY '95 $48.9 m; FY '94 $46.9 m;
      FY '93 $48.2 m; FY '92 $48.9 m[7]
   Total staff: 804; U.S. rank #10[8]

[1] *Information Please Almanac*, 1994.
[2] *CSG Book of the States*, 1994-1995.
[3] *Partnerships: A Compendium*, 1995.
[4] Hanson, *Tribune of the People*, p. 38.
[5] *Journal of the State Government*, 1988.
[6] Minnesota House of Representatives Information Office.
[7] Minnesota Legislative library staff.
[8] NCSL, 1988.

MINNESOTA
STATE REPORT

Interview Profile

Legislature: 9 (1 senator, 3 representatives, 5 legislative
         staff)
External: 5

Findings

1. Need for Science and Technology Policy Support

There was general agreement among those interviewed that technology is playing an increasingly important role in issues that come before the legislature, particularly in the areas of economic development, environmental protection, agriculture, telecommunications, energy, and governmental science and technology policy. One legislator felt that "virtually everything can trace its roots to some sort of technology." Another legislator said that it was "difficult to give an overall percentage because in almost every committee there's something that has some kind of science component that ought to be looked at."

Examples of some issues coming before the legislature that required some technical information or analysis include: creation of a new government information council, building codes based on new technologies, implementation of the 1993 science and technology policy statute, Minnesota Public Outreach funding, technology transfer, developing the region as the gateway for North American free trade, dry cask storage of radioactive wastes, telecommunications and information systems, energy policy and alternative energy sources, light rail transportation, leakage of underground storage tanks, electromagnetic field side effects, synthetic bovine growth hormone labelling, genetic engineering, food irradiation, DNA evidence in judicial proceedings, computerized state lottery, computer-based modelling systems for evaluating gambling proposals, distance learning, and university engineering facilities construction.

Respondents agreed that the need for science and technology (S&T) information and analysis had increased over the past decade. They cited as primary reasons the "complexity of the world that we deal in today," the importance of technology to the state economy, and education reform. Considered somewhat less important were competition from other states and countries (reflecting Minnesota's relative geographical isolation and self-sufficiency), and executive S&T activities requiring legislative response. Least important were the impact of the end of Cold War because of the few federal facilities located in the state, and the need to respond to federal mandates since Minnesota is often "out in front" of Washington, for example, in such areas as special education, open enrollment, charter schools, site--based management, health care, and information infrastructure. The only area where legislators and staff differed was the impact of lobbyists: legislators felt it was not a particularly important reason for increase in need and staff found it a significant issue.

Respondents also cited the growing interest in technical issues by a younger generation of legislators. As a staff member explained, "Legislators are wanting to know more detail about what they are deciding about. The baby boom generation is generally better educated, and as a result, they ask more questions." A senator, keenly aware of the importance of new information technologies to the legislative process, expressed "the frustration that policymakers experience when the most recent data that they are dealing with is four years old. To use old data is reckless, particularly in light of the fact that if your computer systems are up and working, you can have up-to-the-month data."

2. Internal and External Sources of S&T Policy Support

The Minnesota legislature reflects a state that has traditionally taken public service seriously and has made information about its government open and accessible. Minnesota generally sees itself as a leader, not a follower, on emerging public policy issues such as health care and telecommunications. It is in transition to a high-tech economy both in manufacturing and agriculture and is headquarters to 29 major corporations. Minnesota has a long history of commitment to quality education and ranks number one in the country for high school graduation rates. There are plans to wire the entire state in a telecommunications network to permit distance learning and eventually create the Minnesota Electronic University.

Internal Sources

The Minnesota legislature has established an extensive two-tier system of institutional mechanisms for access to information: one actively partisan and the other rigorously nonpartisan. In the first category are the House and Senate majority and minority caucuses whose main function is to provide information to legislators for political purposes. In the second category are the House and Senate Research Offices, and the Legislative Library, which serves both branches. The ethic of nonpartisanship is so strict that in the House Research Office, there is even a requirement that staff may not have participated in any political campaign "in any way."

Respondents considered the House Research Office and the Senate Research Office the major institutional mechanisms available to legislators for technical information. Both have staffs of approximately 25 professionals, most of whom have advanced degrees. As expected in a legislative agency, many are attorneys. The Legislative Reference Library is staffed by approximately ten professionals. Staff compensation ranges from the low-$30,000s to mid-$60,000s. Except in computer technology, these organizations do not have in-house S&T expertise, and respondents generally agreed that this deficiency should be remedied.

The research offices and library were created in 1969 for the principal purpose of "providing professional staff to the members so they did not have to rely so much on lobbyists from the growing number of organizations that were essentially providing the staffing on a loaned basis," explained a research staff member. Previously, a county "essentially loaned [its staff] to the legislature, and it became very difficult, of course, under those circumstances, to have a high level of confidence in those staff positions." At the end of the 1970s, the research offices and library became separate organizations, each with its own director, charter, and mission statement.

The research offices operate on a two-track system for technical information. First, they respond to requests from individual legislators or committees. As an example, in 1992, the Committee on Health Care instructed the House and Senate research offices each to hire an additional employee with health care expertise to develop legislation to create Minnesota Care, the state's health care policy. Staff also identify areas where questions are likely to arise and conduct primary research, if necessary. For example, on a "driving while intoxicated" (DWI) issue, staff went out with the state highway patrol when they were making traffic stops. "Each person who was stopped was given a questionnaire and a dollar bill to answer it," reported a staff member.

The most important recent issue for House Research dealt with nuclear waste storage. "What we did was pivotal to the deliberations, maybe not the outcome because, at the last hour, the legislature just caved in to the utility and said, 'You got it,'" said a staff member.

> What we did was to review a combination of legal and technical issues. They had to go hand in hand. A third piece was economic information. We reviewed the history of the entire event, which included administrative law judges, decisions, public utilities commission decisions, [and] some old state law that came into play. So we reviewed the history of the issue from an administrative perspective. We reviewed from a technical perspective what it was that the local utility was asking for: What are dry casks? What is the arrangement of nuclear fuel in the cooling pool of a power plant? What happens to the radioactivity of the old fuel assemblies that were pulled out of the core of the reactor 11, 12, 13 years ago, and have been sitting in this fuel storage pool for those last 12 years? What is their condition now, and what will happen when we move them into the dry casks? What is the difference between a transportable cask, a fixed storage cask, and a dual purpose cask? In the way of price, availability, what they can be used for? These are all things that we provided information on for them.

Senate Research is similarly staffed with generalists. "We look for people who can do the work, and we look for people with the right kind of personalities," said a staff official. "They have 67 bosses who don't necessarily call about technical questions. They quickly get into other issues, so you have to have people who are very sensitive to the realities of working in a legislature. We have a person in charge of the computer systems who has a degree in computer science, but a pure science degree is not a high priority in our office," she said.

Other comments, however, reflect the general need for more technical expertise either through hiring of new personnel with technical backgrounds or additional technical training for the present staff. Said one legislator with a strong technical background, "On science and technology issues, I think you have staff that have picked it up on an ad hoc basis, but I don't think there is anyone there who really understands fundamental science." Another ranked the research offices' technical performance as "uneven" and said that "by and large, I am better off doing my research through my personal staff."

A committee chair who is recognized by his fellow legislators as one of the most technically competent members in the House ranked his personal staff member as the most important internal mechanism. Entitled to hire a committee administrator who doubles as his personal staff, he hired a person who had the ability to provide him with technical information and analysis even though she has had no formal technical training except one college course in statistics. She admitted that she needs some more technical background and that she requires assistance "if the issue is very technical." The fact that she, as committee administrator, also has to respond to approximately 50 committee members' requests on a wide variety of issues during a session underscores the complex nature of her duties—and all for $32,000 a year.

Another important resource available to legislators is the Legislative Reference Library, which received very high marks from two technically trained legislators. "They actually are spectacular at getting information and chasing down references," said one. Library staff conduct literature and data searches and sometimes primary research in response to direct questions. They provide requested information in a useable format but perform only limited analysis for legislators. They are heavily used, averaging 75 requests for information a day: 60 percent from legislators and 40 percent from the public. The staff has no in-house technical expertise except in computer technology.

A recent example of a request made to the library was by a senator who wanted to know if a missile could pierce the dry cask being proposed for off-site nuclear waste storage. The librarians found the answer from an ordnance professor at George Washington University whom one of the staff knew. He responded with a four-page memo about the kinds of tanks and missiles that could break through 16-inch thick concrete cask. The senator was one of the few Republican senators who voted against the proposal. When asked why Georgetown was contacted instead of the University of Minnesota, the librarians answered that they did not know whom to call there, a situation not unique to Minnesota.

Respondents also mentioned legislators known for their technical knowledge as a good source of policy support. "There is no question that in this process you rely a lot on other legislators," observed one legislator. As an example, a legislator with a doctorate in biophysics has been instrumental in the drafting and passage of legislation dealing with DNA fingerprinting, computer systems, and natural resource protection, among others. In addition, her influence on science and technology issues in the public arena has gone beyond the confines of her state through her articles published in national scholarly journals.

Drawbacks to relying on legislators as mentors were also mentioned. "There are just not that many people who have technical backgrounds," stated a legislator. A University of Minnesota faculty member felt that

> there are key legislators who are a source of knowledge about technology, but the willingness of other legislators to accept that is the barrier. In today's climate, with everyone talking information superhighway and so on, what you have are legislators jockeying for position to be able to say, "See, I sponsored a bill on the information superhighway, and I want to bring it home to the state, to the citizens of my great state, my great county, my great whatever." So, you have multiple bills on the same subject. And you have confusion and oftentimes ill-informed and ill-formed legislation because of it.

External Sources

Respondents cited the state university, the executive branch, and lobbyists as the most frequently used external resources for technical policy support. These resources are generally accessed through personal contacts that legislators and staff have developed either through their full-time occupations or after long-time legislative experience.

The legislature has many ties to the University of Minnesota. It appoints the Regent Selection Board and controls the annual $500 million university budget. Many legislators are graduates, and legislative spouses number among the faculty. The Legislative Library and House and Senate Research Office staff have full access to the University Library, its reference librarians, and the Internet, for which there is no charge. The university is "convenient, large, and there is a lot of talent there," said a Senate staff member. "Members who live in university districts develop strong relationships with certain departments, such as agriculture." Recently a new service within the university relations office was established to provide public access to networks of experts. A faculty respondent mentioned that this could be made available to the legislature "along with everyone else."

Respondents observed, however, that at present there is no systematic, organized method for legislative access to university expertise. "It's who you know and are you going to take the time to track it down. It is very, very cumbersome, time-consuming work, knowing that you are making the first of probably five to seven phone calls before you get the person who knows about a particular issue. If you had to go through that process to find an answer about whether a missile could penetrate a dry cask, I mean you feel that 'I wouldn't want to do this again,'" explained a legislative staffer. From the university perspective, there was concern that if the university provides a resource for legislators, they might not be prepared to use it. "If there's a way to do it," a faculty member said, "I suspect it would come through a more systematic, better-organized effort that would focus around their legislative staff."

Respondents cited the executive branch as another source of science and technology policy support. Because of the imbalance of resources between the full-time executive branch and the part-time legislature, legislators and legislative staff often look to state agencies for technical information. As a key Senate staff member explained, "The Minnesota legislative branch has gotten stronger and better at legislating over the last two decades, just like other states have. But you are still at a huge disadvantage with the executive branch and their resources, so we continue to rely on information from governors from Minnesota. We react to their budgets, and even when you have a governor who comes from a different political party and we seem to be disagreeing a lot publicly, in the final analysis what we end up passing is 90 percent of what he proposed in the first place."

The fact that the current governor holds the highest record for vetoing legislation of any governor in recent Minnesota history indicates that the two branches frequently do not share common agendas and, therefore, information from state agencies may not be reliable for legislators to use. One long-term house staffer said bluntly, "I don't trust any of them, especially not the political appointees." Others said it depended on the issue and the quality of agency leadership and expertise. "It really depends on the issue and the level of trust on a particular issue, the particular agency that they are dealing with, who the governor is, and the politics involved."

From the agency perspective, one administrator said that her agency was available to provide information to legislators to help them develop public policy, but "few are interested. They have too many issues competing for their attention. For legislators to be able to take the time and get involved to the point where they understand the implications of technology is very difficult."

Respondents cited lobbyists as another important source of technical policy support. Lobbyists are strictly regulated in Minnesota. As one legislator explained, "I have talked to lobbyists who have worked in multiple states who say that in Minnesota, Wisconsin, and Iowa, the type of lobbying is a lot less expensive. It is more of an information provider. We've always had strict laws on disclosure. Everything is prohibited. You can't even get a cup of coffee from them." A state representative said she found that "lobbyists can be very helpful and I don't trash them, but sometimes the public and private sector can get too intertwined." Another legislator explained that "on the whole, I have gotten accurate information from lobbyists, but it is necessary to get an additional point of view about the information they provide."

An outside observer of the legislative process critiqued the indirect influence of lobbyists:

> Lobbyists make a big effort to put the technical information in front of the committees. But with virtually any scientific endeavor, there are lots of different ways of looking at the information and different approaches to studies and different conclusions to be drawn. . . . Where the system is weak is that the lobbyists . . . are the sources of the technical information that is received and played in the media, in public perception, and in how the legislature is informed. For example, dry cask storage is apparently deemed to be exceedingly safe. But that's just because [this company] is a great big company and they buy lots of statisticians and they can buy lots of reports that make it look okay. They are going to launch this great big technical argument. I guess what I'm saying is people receive this information without the perception that it is coming from an inherently biased source. And it is.

Minnesota has established Minnesota Technology, Inc. (MTI), a quasi-public technology development agency whose enabling statute identifies it as the S&T advisor to the state legislature. This identity is not widely known, partly because the agency is still in the early stages of its development and does not have the technical staff to provide this service. "Maybe later when we are stronger, an advisory role to the legislature would not be inappropriate," said a staff official. However, MTI manages Minnesota Project Outreach, whose main purpose is to supply technical information to small and mid-sized businesses. They have contracted out this service to TelTech, a national technical knowledge company headquartered in Minneapolis, providing access to 3,000 databases. TelTech has been provided to the legislature through a state subsidy. At the time of the interviews, it had not had wide legislative use but was seen as having potential as a source of technical information.

3. Characteristics of Useful S&T Policy Support

Legislators put special emphasis on: accurate and up-to-date information, now more readily available through computer technology; the importance of getting information on time, an issue often not appreciated by academic sources; and the need to offset the reactive nature of legislative bodies with information that anticipates future technological developments, "not just after they have hit the front page." Legislative staff, on the other hand, stressed the importance of having enough background to translate technical information into language accessible to the layperson since legislators rarely have scientific backgrounds. "Most legislators are not real good at anything technical. That is not the kind of people they are," said a research staff member. "These are political people, so you really have to be careful and lower the level of sophistication. You have to be accurate and be able to convey information in nontechnical language, which means you have to have a lot of background to do this." Another staff member mentioned the problem of having enough time to respond. "The time frames around here can be very tight, and sometimes we don't have enough time to verify everything," she said.

Both legislators and legislative staff stressed the importance of a high level of comfort with an information source either through positive personal experience or through its reputation.

4. Legislative Use of Technology

House, Senate, and Library research offices are computerized and networked. Within the last two years, the *House Journal* was put in word-processed format on the computer network to speed up access to information. "We are more useful now to the members than we have ever been before because we have access to tools that we didn't have before. And I think that will continue," said a staff member. Library staff was offering training sessions for legislative staff about the library's electronic resources. "It would be pretty difficult to set up training sessions for legislators, because they are not here when they are not in session. But I am not discounting it for the future," said a library official. One of the plans for summer is to offer one-on-one training on using the Internet for anybody who is interested within the legislative community, including legislators. "Not the technical part—how you get into it—but rather what you find when you get there."

In 1995, information about the Minnesota House and Senate became fully accessible on-line through the Minnesota Legislature Gopher. The available information includes: daily bills and resolution introductions and text; bill tracking; House Research Office bill summaries; final house votes; weekly and daily committee schedules for House and Senate; biographies of representatives and senators and their committee assignments, office numbers, and e-mail addresses; and Minnesota statutes.

Legislative computer operations and Internet access is under the supervision of the Select Committee on Technology. The House publication *Session Weekly* reported that "the goal of the Internet access is to provide as much information as possible in a user-friendly format to increase citizen participation in the legislative process and give the public equal footing with lobbyists when it comes to following legislation."[1] However, a staff member saw problems with "electronic democracy" and raised the question of elected officials being on-line and open to messages from their constituents. "A legislative response can be put in hard copy and then it takes on a reality of its own, and you have to live with it forever and ever. It's like printing a position paper or something. And so politicians are nervous about that and with good reason."

Among some legislators, interest in technology is high. Legislators who wish to use their own computers are now hooked up to the research office network and can be reached by e-mail. A senator explained that his approach to technology was very parochial. "I come from 270 miles from here, and the only negative to where I live is distance. To have access to economic growth, medical services, educational services, entertainment through telecommunications, it is very important to my district. For instance, I live in a little town [of] . . . about 400 or so people. I go into town and I can teleconference from the headquarters of the phone company there." Other legislators have a problem with "technophobia." "If we provided computers to all of our members, half of them would never get turned on. It would be a stupid waste," said a research staff member. Another commented, "We still have a lot of the old guard, the ones whom I feel I need to offer to make a photocopy for," she said.

There seems to be a generational divide over technology with the older members resisting change. They consider themselves "people persons." One legislator calls them "legisauruses." However, change seems inevitable, not only because of the influx of younger, computer-literate members but also "ironically through the partisan, political end and not the policy end," said a legislative aide. "In order to facilitate their campaigns, get them better organized, free up more of their time to do the essential meeting people and trying to persuade voters and so forth, candidates will have to use computers no matter what their age. There is an old saying around here, 'You can't be a good senator unless you are a senator first.'"

5. Technical Information in a Political Environment

Technical information in a political environment can be the overriding issue, part of the mix, or irrelevant. As an example of the latter, a legislator who represents a farming district supported his constituents' opposition to synthetic bovine growth hormone and voted for a labeling law that allows dairy farmers to identify their milk as hormone-free, even though he had no real evidence that hormone-enhanced milk poses a health risk. In a similar example in which information was irrelevant, one legislator wanted more technical information in and an adequate health and ecological risk analysis prior to the placement of a large, potentially damaging metal-shredding machine near her Minneapolis district. She was able to eliminate a veto threat from the governor not by making the technological arguments, but by pointing out that the owners had gone to jail once before for cheating the city on a scrap metal deal.

On the other hand, several legislative issues in Minnesota have been decided almost entirely on the basis of technical information. A specific example concerned the purchase of a new state computer system. A computer scientist from the University of Minnesota notified his legislator that the new state computer system about to be purchased and installed by the state education system was unworkable. Consulting with legislative staff and outside experts, the legislator was able to raise enough questions so that a special subcommittee of the House Appropriations Committee was established to review the issue. After much research and testing, the subcommittee did indeed find the computer system to be inadequate and the purchase was withdrawn. The subcommittee was then continued to establish a data processing control board to oversee all state computer operations and to review the future course of state computer development.

More frequently, legislation involves a combination of both technical and political issues such as the recent debate over a utility's request to permit off-site dry cask storage of nuclear wastes. The proponents and opponents provided conflicting technical arguments concerning the safety of the storage method to legislators and the media. On this issue, as in many others, technical information played an important role in the debate even though, in the end, political and economic considerations were credited with the final legislative decision to permit the storage. Respondents agreed that for technical information to have the greatest impact, it had to be introduced early in the debate, not after positions had hardened.

In terms of constituent opinions versus technical information, a legislator observed that "it depends on the issue. I live in a dairy area and my constituents want artificial growth hormones labeled, and so we are going to label it. But on the ground current/stray voltage question, you see yourself as an educator as well as a legislator." Another legislator found the role of educator minimal in comparison to the advertising that proponents and opponents of controversial technical issues, such a nuclear waste storage, can generate. The opinions of leadership and other legislators was not cited as a major factor in decision making, although one legislator reported that when he disagreed with a committee chair, "he didn't win, and what happened was that my bill didn't go anywhere."

In response to questions about the importance of technical information at specific stages in the decision-making process, answers indicated that it was most important in bill-drafting, followed by responding to legislation filed by others, and evaluating enacted legislation and administrative action. Somewhat less important was the use of technical information influencing voting decisions and determining issues for the current and future sessions. At these stages, other influences are more important. In terms of technical information giving more power to the legislature in relation to the executive branch and lobbyists, one legislator felt that the policy support services needed more resources before they could match those from outside the legislature.

Fundamentally, the interviews revealed that the main barrier to the use of technical information in a political environment is what one respondent called the "mismatch" between legislators and science and technology. Legislators are not elected because of their technical expertise and represent people who are, in general, also not technically literate. Scientists, on the other hand, generally do not have either the interest or skills to deal with the political process.

6. Legislative Satisfaction

In 1989, the Senate president asked the associate dean of the Hubert Humphrey Institute to conduct a study of the Minnesota legislature because he felt that while the legislature, in "Lake Wobegon" terms, was "above average, it could do better."[2] Interview responses reflected that this was still the prevailing opinion. Generally, those interviewed expressed satisfaction with policy support but had a few suggestions for improvement. A senator thought there was not enough anticipation of issues. "By nature, legislatures are reactive. We try to institute different kinds of staff and processes to get us into a more vision-oriented approach, but it is a tough thing to do." He also recognized that little in-house technical expertise is available and that this is "probably an area where they are going to have to concentrate on finding somebody who comes out of that background."

A state representative said that she did not have enough access to information, "but it is not as bad as those states where there is no recognition of technical issues. The understanding here is much higher, but the major problem is that neither the legislature nor the executive branch regard scientific and technological information as a priority." A staff member also thought there was room for improvement. "I think legislators think they have enough, but I think they are wrong. If legislators call here for technical information, they only have a certain budget of time and energy available. And if they spend minutes or hours trying to get information out of us, that's time that they could have spent getting it from a truly qualified technical source, if they only knew it was there. That's why I said the problem is not the number of sources, it's the quality and accessibility. I don't consider us to be a quality technical source because often we have to give disclaimers. We have to say, 'Look, we aren't experts in this.' So, we give a reference many times."

A caucus staff member explained that legislators' level of satisfaction depends on the issues. "On the nuclear waste storage issue, I don't think that any legislators, particularly ones opposed to nuclear storage, thought they had enough information—and they might never have enough information. On the other hand, I think, generally speaking, legislators are satisfied with the amount of information that is provided," he said. A research staff member explained that legislators "each have their own individual personal demands and levels of satisfaction, but if I were to lump them together and shoot for the average, I guess I think they probably would like more information in some areas than we are able to provide."

In terms of outside resources, there was some feeling that available sources are sufficient, but legislators "don't know how to access it or know whose data is reliable." Information overload is also a problem. A legislator commented that "for in-depth analysis, unfortunately, the university gives you so much detail, and it takes so long to get back to you, that it isn't all that useful."

7. Recommendations

Research Offices, Library, Personal Staff

Strengthening in-house expertise was the most frequently mentioned recommendation as well as the most feasible. Because legislators are so busy with their other legislative duties, respondents felt that internal staff must play a key role in providing S&T policy support. This internal staff must be in place first in order to know how most effectively to profit from external sources of information. Even more importantly, respondents felt that legislatures should keep control over their policy support mechanisms by developing their own in-house expertise if they are to fulfill their role as an equal branch of government.

In general, legislators favored the hiring of additional staff with science backgrounds, and staff supported additional education and training for current personnel. The concern raised by the staff was that people with scientific backgrounds are incapable of performing effectively in a legislative environment. Some legislators disagreed and referred to the Science, Technology and Public Policy program at Harvard University's Kennedy School of Government as an example of the training for the dual-career path. They also questioned whether generalists can ever learn enough science to be able to interpret technical information and develop the professional networks to keep current on new scientific advances.

There was no support for the creation of a separate S&T research office. It had been tried once before in the 1970s as part of the National Science Foundation State Science Engineering and Technology program and had been found not cost effective, an opinion that still holds.

Joint Interim Legislative Commission on Technology

In Minnesota, the legislative leadership appoints legislative commissions and often serves on them as well. The commissions operate during the interim, have permanent staff, and are able to concentrate on complex issues when more time is available for thorough study. Also, their recommendations reflect the opinions of both chambers. Rather than coming to the conference committee stage with drastically different solutions that may or may not be resolved, their concurrence of opinion often results in major legislation. Telecommunications was singled out as an area needing the concentrated and coordinated attention that an interim commission on technology could provide.

A standing legislative S&T committee, as distinct from a commission, was not recommended. The legislature has experimented with various S&T committees since the 1970s, but they either have not survived or have been folded into issue committees. A key legislative aide observed, however, that "one could make a strong case that it deserves more attention than we give it."

Legislative Use of Computer Technology

A member of the University of Minnesota faculty suggested that every legislative office should be on a local area network (LAN) that is connected to the Internet and that computer training should be made available to legislators and their staffs. In his opinion, legislators need to understand the capabilities of computer technology, and the only way to do this is for them to learn how to use it. Others disagreed and said that to provide computers to all members "would be a stupid waste of time because half of them would never turn them on." Respondents looked forward to more user friendly computer programs. "When we can get computer programs that can use voice commands in ordinary English and understand what we are trying to tell them, it will reduce technophobia tremendously. The hoops you have to jump through now frighten off a lot of legislators. They don't feel they have the time to learn all of that," said a key legislative aide.

Legislative Access to University S&T Expertise

A university administrator recommended three steps to improve legislative access to university expertise. First, the legislature would have to clearly state its needs for technical information; second, the university would have to acknowledge its obligation as a public institution to make its resources available on an organized, systematic basis, probably "focused on legislative staff, not legislators"; and third, the state would have to make a serious commitment to the development of an information infrastructure that would put Minnesota on-line and make effective legislative-university interaction feasible.

Respondents clearly stated that the development of a legislative-university S&T network needs leadership from both sides. Whether such leadership exists remains to be seen. The creation of an organized legislative-university S&T support will not be easy considering the realities of the cultural divide between academic and political worlds. From the academic side, providing technical policy support to state legislators is not highly regarded. Universities do not recognize or reward such service as being important for faculty in their pursuit of tenure, and on a personal level, colleagues are often disdainful of spending time with those they perceive as being both indifferent and ignorant. These attitudes are communicated to the legislative branch, further reducing rapport between the two groups. Another barrier is that the university, with its lobbyists actively at work in the corridors of the state house, is often seen as just another special pleader with its hand out at budget time.

Minnesota Technology, Inc. Legislative Advisory Role

There was a recommendation that the Minnesota Technology, Inc. develop its legislative advisory capabilities in such a way as to carry out this part of its statutory mission, but at the same time not jeopardize legislative support for its primary responsibility of economic development. One respondent suggested that MTI educate the legislature about the Minnesota Public Outreach program and request increased public funding for this service.

Midwest Regional S&T Research Office

Understanding that the digital revolution may, in time, make geographical boundaries obsolete, a legislator nevertheless suggested that since individual state legislatures generally have not invested in separate S&T research offices, it might be useful to explore the possibility of creating a regional S&T research office. Participating states would subsidize an office with a small number of technical experts trained to respond to science and technology information and analysis needs similar to the former congressional Office of Technology Assessment.

S&T Constituent Education

A legislator recommended increasing efforts to bring science and technology issues to the public. Knowledgeable legislators can play an important role in educating their constituents. In addition, he suggested that private sector groups, such as the Minnesota High Tech Council, make a concentrated effort to inform the media on science and technology issues and to reinforce linkages with the university, technical colleges, and elementary and secondary schools. He recognized that organizing science literacy programs in schools and communities across the state is a long, slow process, but he felt that from these efforts a greater understanding of basic science and technology concepts on the part of the public and their legislative representatives could emerge.

NOTES

1. February 10, 1995, p. 15.

2. Hanson, *Tribune of the People* (Minneapolis, Minn.: University of Minnesota Press, 1989), p. xi.

NEW MEXICO
STATE PROFILE

ENTERED UNION:
  January 6, 1912 (47th admitted)[1]
LAND AREA:
  121,365 sq. miles; U.S. rank #5
POPULATION:
  1.6 m (1993 est.)
  U.S. rank #36[2]
  Density per sq. mi. 13.0
DEMOGRAPHICS:
  White 1.1 m; Hispanic .6 m; Native American .1 m;
  Black .03 m; Asian .01 m
ECONOMY:
  GSP: $26.7 b (1990); U.S. rank #39[3]
  Agriculture (net farm income): U.S. rank #32
  Manufacturing (total income): U.S. rank #42[4]
  Mining (total income): U.S. rank #14
  Per capita personal income: $16,297 (1993)[5]
  Unemployment: 7.5% (1993)
  Number of patents: 246 (1991); U.S. rank #35[6]
  Number of SBIR awards: 431 (1983-91); U.S. rank #14
  State technology development agency:
    New Mexico Economic Development Department,
      Technology Enterprise Division, and the New
      Mexico Industrial Network Corporation (a non-
      profit corporation); budget: FY '94 $1.26 m
EDUCATION:
  High school graduation rate: 68.2%; U.S. rank #39[7]

State and local government expenditure for higher
education: $666.4 m (1989-90); U.S. rank #4
(by % of total expenditures)
Academic R&D expenditures: FY '91 $163 m;
U.S. rank #29[6]

POLITICAL:
U.S. Senators: 1 Democrat, 1 Republican[5]
Congressional Representatives: 3 (1 Democrat,
2 Republicans)
Governor—4-year term
Since statehood: 25 (17 Democrats, 8 Republicans)
Since 1970: 6 (3 Democrats, 3 Republicans)[8]
Current Governor: Gary Johnson (R), 1st term[5]
State Legislators: 112[1]
State Senators: 42; 4-year term
1994: 27 Democrats, 15 Republicans
1995: 27 Democrats, 15 Republicans[9]
State Representatives: 70; 2-year term[1]
1994: 52 Democrats, 18 Republicans
1995: 46 Democrats, 24 Republicans[9]
Length of session: odd years, 60 calendar days; even
years, 30 calendar days[1]
Annual salary: none; per diem living expenses $75
(limit of 60 legislative days in odd years). No addi-
tional compensation for leaders in both houses.
State budget: FY '93 $5.6 b; FY '92 $5.2 b;
FY '91 $4.5 b[10]
Legislative budget: FY '92 $10.2 m[11]
Total staff: 369; U.S. rank #32[12]

[1] *CSG Book of the States*, 1994-1995.
[2] *World Almanac*, 1995.
[3] *State Rankings*, 1994.
[4] *Gale State Rankings Reporter*, 1994.
[5] *Almanac of the 50 States*, 1995.
[6] *Partnerships: A Compendium*, 1995.
[7] *CQ's State Fact Finder*, 1993.

[8] *Encyclopedia Americana*, 1992.
[9] *State Yellow Book*, Spring 1995.
[10] U.S. Dept. of Commerce World Wide
Web census page <www.doc.gov/
CommerceHomePage.html>.
[11] *State Government Finances*, 1992.
[12] NCSL, 1988.

NEW MEXICO
STATE REPORT

Interview profile

Legislature: 12 (6 representatives, 4 senators, 2 staff)
External: 7

Findings

1. Need for Science and Technology Policy Support

Respondents agreed that legislators have a need for science and technology policy support. As a senator explained, "I need technical information all the time. I need it to be able to formulate legislation and state policy." A leader of the House of Representatives explained, "Almost every area may be affected by some sort of technology. I cannot think of an area where technical components would not be required involving major public policy issues in New Mexico."

Examples of technical issues before the legislature include: environmental protection, such as water quality and quantity; ambient air quality; the Apache Mescalaro Reservation monitored retrievable storage project for high-level nuclear waste; the Waste Isolation Pilot Project (WIPP) for military nuclear waste; handling and transporting hazardous waste materials; landfill regulation; integrated solid waste management; waste tire recycling; economic issues such as defense conversion and technology transfer; space port and single stage orbit rocket technology; creation of a telescope complex ("cosmic explorer"); biotechnology;

energy research; retail wheeling of electricity, mining laws, and coal technology; state technology development policy, technology and international trade, and economic forecasting; telecommunications issues including the information highway, computer technology and computer literacy; equitable technology distribution in K–12 schools; access to technology for Native Americans; social issues such as health care technology; the human genome project; computerization of the court system; security technology; and DWI computer tracking.

Respondents felt that the need for technical policy support had increased over the past decade, paralleling the dynamic growth of the state. Population is estimated to have nearly doubled since the early 1980s, making it one of the fastest growing states in the union. One legislator asked, "How are these people going to support themselves? Are they going to take the water that all of us use? Are health services available? Schools? Everything?"

The fact that New Mexico is seen as having lots of open land for dumping of wastes from other states has also increased the need for legislative action. In 1989, a construction company from Baltimore bought 25,000 acres in southern New Mexico to create "the world's largest landfill," said a staff member. "Again, we were being treated like some poor third-world colony, and the public was justifiably outraged." The legislature is attempting to deal with these issues with more emphasis on strategic planning, which in itself requires technical analytic capability.

Respondents said that the most important reason for the increased need for technical information and analysis was the importance of technology to the state economy, followed closely by the end of the Cold War, which affects the state's large concentration of federal weapons research facilities. Next in importance were the increased complexity of issues, the use of technology in educational reform, and federal mandates requiring state implementation. Of less significance were competition from other states and foreign countries, and executive branch initiatives requiring legislative response. Commented one legislator, "Ten years ago, we were still seeing ourselves as involved with an extractive and service industry, and it never dawned on us that the service industry was going to be led by technological advances. New Mexico is now being seen by the outside world as a place to come to, and companies are looking to move here, for example, Intel, Synetics, and Phillips. It used to be that they wanted to know if you needed a visa to get here and 'what language do you speak?'"

The influx of high-tech companies is requiring the legislature to focus on education and training issues, especially the use of computer technology. Explained one legislator, "We've got kids that travel 75–80 miles one away in a school bus. Costs $4,800. We could educate them through telecommunications at half the cost. We've got to start using our imagination. Then there is the matter of access, particularly as it affects Native Americans living on reservations where often the basic infrastructure of water and electricity is lacking."

In 1994, the legislature passed the $8 million Education Technology Act, which established the Education Technology Bureau in the State Department of Education to develop criteria for bringing computer equipment, maintenance, and training for every student in New Mexico on an equitable basis. "We have the capability of programming any language that is documented, including Navaho, and the university is now working with the Pueblos to document their language. We have the capability and technology to be able to retain the culture and heritage of our multicultures, which is really important to New Mexico," said one of the bill's sponsors.

Referring to the complex new issue of telecommunications, a legislator stated that "we now need to know such things as different bandwidths, what they can carry, the difference between copper wire and fiber optics." There is considerable competition between software companies to provide the technology, and the legislature "needs the expertise to decide which is the best technology and not the one with the most political clout."

Another indication of the need for more information is the political pressure on government to be more responsive. As a staff member explained, "There is a great deal of pressure on state legislatures now to perform better. That inherently places a burden on the legislators, especially the citizen-legislators, to become more informed and more current on technical knowledge than they were required to be in the past." Keeping up with technological change is, however, not an easy task. "We have created a democracy to govern our society, and the democratic process is slow to respond to change," said a staff member. "And yet, the need to upgrade the technical information and comprehension of that information is critical. I have a hard enough time keeping up with the information in my field."

2. Internal and External Sources of S&T Policy Support

New Mexico's citizen legislature reflects the multicultural heritage of its 1.6 million Native American, Hispanic, and Anglo residents. Although geographically large, its population is still relatively small, ranking 36th in the U.S. As one legislator remarked, "New Mexico is a small state, in some ways a conservative state, and ideas have to take root and float through the constituencies. I'll tell you how small we are. I can meet my constituency in the supermarket. I can go to the grocery store and find that my ice cream has melted before I get out of the store." One representative has one precinct with 28 voters in it. "We have little towns all over this state where for people to get a tooth taken care of, they've got to travel 100 miles one way. When I leave my little town to come to Santa Fe, I drive 190 miles without a single stop sign."

Internal Sources

Legislative leadership considers the most important internal sources of technical policy support to be the three central legislative agencies: the Legislative Council Service, the Legislative Finance Committee, and the Legislative Education Study Committee, whose full-time staffs frequently work together. Said one representative, "On budget issues, I would go to the Finance Committee. On technical legal bills, I go to the Legislative Council Service. On education, I would go to the Education Study Committee. I have often gotten a member from each of those staffs together with one as a head. I can call staff and ask them to contact university presidents or federal laboratory directors for information. I don't have to call them myself." These central staffs are particularly important since representatives do not have personal staff and senators have no more than two, and even then, only during session.

Of the three committee staffs, the Legislative Council Service was the most frequently mentioned resource for S&T policy support. It was created in 1951 to provide the legislature with a professional cadre of experts in both bill drafting and policy research. Similar to many other states, it was based on the Wisconsin model, which a staffer described as "the best council with the best staff, for whom I have a lot of respect."

The Legislative Council Service serves as the management committee for the legislature. It is co-chaired by the speaker of the House and the president of the Senate, who appoint a director to hire staff to carry out the day-to-day business of the legislature. There are 15–20 full-time professionals, most of whom are attorneys, with several having some science background. Salaries are in the $30,000–55,000 range, which are considered "good" for New Mexico. During the interim, the council service has also, from time to time, contracted for some additional assistance for specific committee assignments. The council service is responsible

for drafting all bills, staffing standing and interim committees, preparing committee agendas and committee reports,
preparing *The New Mexico Legislative Handbook*, and
managing the building. At the request of legislators, it also
produces memos and speeches and serves as the mechanism for contacting the National Conference of State
Legislatures (NCSL) and other organizations. It is available
to all 112 legislators on a nonpartisan basis and responds
to approximately 10,000 requests a year. "We work for both
Republicans and Democrats, and we work under a confidentiality law. When a legislator makes a request, we cannot
divulge that information to another legislator or anyone else,
no matter what the subject," explained a staff member.

Although the council service received high praise from
most of the legislators interviewed, its technical expertise
was called "fairly limited." Explained a representative, "The
Legislative Council staff are skilled in legislative matters and
as a conduit of information, but that doesn't give me access
to what is going on in cybernetics, or the information
highway. If I want to ask technical questions, I go to a
technical person." Another respondent thought that "the
problem of a legal mind trying to translate technical information into a scientifically sound piece of legislation was
very difficult." A legislator with a strong technical background did not use the council service staff for technical
information "because they are not technically trained."
Another legislator, however, found that the council service
"would work real hard to find the right person or at least
some written information, so I think that would be a good
entrée into the system. They will know who to talk to, what
the trends are, because they are bright and will learn. Over
time, they can be a very good resource."

The Legislative Council staffs the interim committees,
which play an important legislative role given that the short
sessions leave little time for the study of complex technical
issues. Interim committees also give legislators "the opportunity to meet with witnesses and hear them on a more

informal basis." Members are appointed jointly by the Speaker and Senate president, and there is a good deal of interest in serving, since important legislation is frequently developed from the work of interim committees for the coming session. The two interim committees most concerned with technology issues are the Radioactive and Hazardous Materials Interim Committee, which was established by statute in the early 1980s, and the Science, Technology, Energy and Defense Conversion Interim Committee, which must be reappointed every year. The impermanence of the S&T interim committee concerns some members, but the importance of the issues under its review has encouraged its continuation. There is no standing committee on science and technology.

As mentioned above, only senators may hire personal staff, and generally staff are not hired for technical skills. However, the chair of the Senate Conservation Committee, which handles many technical issues, took the unusual step of contracting with the university for a technically trained analyst to staff his committee and serve as his personal aide during the session. The analyst, selected from over 50 applicants, holds B.S. and M.S. degrees in civil and environmental engineering from the University of New Mexico and is a New Mexico-registered professional engineer. He began his involvement with the legislative process in 1989, when he was asked to advise in the drafting of the New Mexico Solid Waste Act of 1990. A lobbyist later cited this act as "the closest [he] had ever seen the New Mexico legislature [come to surpassing] Congress on legislation."

The chair considers his technical analyst as his most valuable source of science and technology policy support and entrusts him with a great deal of responsibility. He calls the advisor his "trusted evaluator." In addition to reading and reporting on all bills before the committee, the analyst will negotiate between contending parties when necessary. Through this process, "an historic compromise agreement on amendments to the state Endangered Species Act was negotiated." Although the aide works formally for the senator only during the session, he remains available during the interim period as a friend and advisor, and "through him and his network, we can anticipate what issues are going to be important."

Legislators themselves can also be good sources of technical information. As a staff member explained, "In any legislative body, it is just a traditional way of doing business for an individual member to give great credibility to another legislator whom he knows is interested in a particular subject area." "We have 112 legislators," said a legislator, "and you find at least one or two [who] are experts in any field you are interested in. I deeply respect legislators. They do their homework. The beauty of talking to your fellow or lady legislators is that they are expert in a particular field, and they also understand the legislative process." Another legislator mentioned that "we are getting more people in the legislature that have technical expertise, so that resource is increasing."

External Sources

Universities, colleges, and federal laboratories were most frequently mentioned as important technical resources for the legislature. The academic institutions include the University of New Mexico (UNM), the New Mexico Institute of Mining and Technology School, and New Mexico State University, whose expertise on agricultural questions and border development between Mexico and New Mexico one representative identified as "very helpful."

Legislative-university communication generally occurs through personal contacts. In addition, the UNM has an institutional mechanism for working with state and local governments on technical issues such as waste management, Superfund cleanup, and alternative wastewater collection and treatment systems. The New Mexico Engineering Research Institute (NMERI) is a stand-alone facility affiliated with UNM's College of Engineering. It employs about 150 people and is self-supporting through its government and private sector contracts. It was from this program that the staff analyst for the chair of the conservation commission was selected. A senator confirmed that the universities "have accommodated us," but added that "it would be nice if they would appreciate more what the role of the legislature is."

Some legislators cited the federal laboratories at Los Alamos, Sandia, and Phillips as useful sources of technical information. "It wouldn't be unusual for me to call the heads of the labs or someone that works for them when I need information. They are a very good source of technical information, and the tours they offer legislators are also particularly useful," said a technically trained state representative. He thought the labs "go out of their way to help state legislators with information, although the information may not be presented in a useful format for most legislators." Another legislator spoke highly of the assistance that Los Alamos and Sandia gave the legislature on the use of computer technology for managing state government. "They came up with a really fine piece of legislation," he said. Laboratory personnel see their relationship to state government as "very important" and work in partnership with both the legislature and the executive branch on a pro bono basis. Employees are encouraged to "give advice, facilitate meetings, and run for public office on the county and legislative level." With the end of the Cold War, "we are no longer an island and are becoming involved with competitiveness and start-up businesses," explained a laboratory executive.

Not all respondents expressed confidence in the federal labs as a source of policy support. A leading environmental legislator commented, "I have a horrible prejudice against these people because of the way they have treated us in the past. They have some real PR problems because they have been dumping toxins in the water system for 45 years." He also said that any hope of the labs' changing their military mission to domestic use was unlikely. "The same laboratory management people are trying to do something completely different in the same old way. You are not going to get very many new ideas with the same old group."

The fact that Los Alamos pays no state taxes because of its nonprofit status was a source of friction for some state legislators. Also causing resentment is the fact that the Los Alamos K–12 school system is exempt from the state funding formula and receives additional support from the federal government in order to attract and keep scientific staff. Recently, the Los Alamos senatorial district was divided into four districts, a move which one respondent described as an effort to broaden legislative oversight of the laboratory and reduce its influence in the legislature.

In addition to the federal labs, legislators also cited federal agencies, such as the Department of Defense and the Department of Energy, as sources of technical information. They mentioned that the close relationship with the New Mexico congressional delegation and their staffs permits exchange of information which was "very helpful. We are a small enough state so that type of thing is possible."

Respondents identified the executive branch as another important source of technical information. "I find them most responsive," commented a legislator. "After all, we control the purse strings, and they aren't going to bite the hand that feeds them." Another legislator found them less reliable because "they represent the governor and are not an independent voice but come from a certain perspective." A legislator cited the 1992 Strategic Plan, which the Governor's Technical Excellence Committee (GTEC) developed for the utilization of the state's technological resources for economic development as a helpful source of information.

Respondents considered lobbyists as useful sources of information, but not without additional verification. "They get me accurate, dependable information faster than any other way. But we need more than one source on complex issues. We need the council staff, or we could become victims," explained a legislator. Another said that she uses them "only so they can introduce me to someone that I can talk to, not themselves." Echoing this was the comment of a council staff member, who said, "I tend to try to find the person who is the technical research person as opposed to the front man or person paid to lobby the legislature. Specific companies can be good sources of information on pollutants from manufacturing plants, [but] then I double check with EPA or an environmental group."

Some legislators cited the Energy Council as a good source of technical information. The council is composed of legislators from nine energy-producing states who meet four times a year to develop regional and national energy policy recommendations and to exchange state legislation. According to a member from the New Mexico legislature, "The Energy Council does long-range thinking and leaps beyond the normal objectives of greed and desire for immediate satisfaction. We look at the long-term interest of our states and the country." Another important source of technical information mentioned by respondents was the national media, such as *Newsweek* and *Business Week* magazines. "Technical depth is immaterial," commented a legislator. "The point is they are reporting on these topics, and there is nothing out of date in what they say. They are bringing people along and their information is reported back through my constituents." Some respondents also mentioned NCSL as useful for finding out what other states are doing.

3. Characteristics of Useful S&T Policy Support

Respondents considered credibility the most important criteria for useful technical policy support, followed by accessibility, timeliness, and manageable format. Legislators stated that for information to be credible, it has to come from a trusted source and be accurate. As one legislator explained, "I am accustomed to my sources and they are accustomed to me, so that they provide me with information I can understand. They have learned what I consider to be useful and important. Partisan information is not credible." Respondents stated that the source also had to be easily accessible and provide the information on a legislator's timetable. Said one staff member, "I know where to go within the university system or I can get a name real quick and get a quick answer. Somebody who doesn't return phone calls just isn't going to get used." Quick responses are particularly essential in New Mexico because of the short legislative sessions.

Respondents also mentioned that nontechnical language and a format that legislators—with too much to read and too little time—can use easily were important criteria for useful technical information and analysis. Several respondents identified the detailing of pros and cons and a discussion of options rather than just raw data as essential. In terms of useful format, one senator asks for only verbal briefings only from his technical advisor. He has instructed him to "go out and talk to people and find out what the problems are. I don't want you sitting in front of a computer. Then come back and talk to me about what you have learned. I don't want it in writing." His advisor explained, "Once I have the technical information, I put it in a form that a layperson can make sound decisions on. I can take highly technical stuff and sit and talk to the senator, and afterward he'll go into a committee room and have just the right nuances of the issue." Another legislator finds it possible to reduce the paper glut by listening to tapes prepared by various groups on the long trip from his home district to Santa Fe.

4. Legislative Use of Technology

The New Mexico Legislature operates a centralized legislative computer system under the direction of the Legislative Council. In 1994, the council subscribed to Dialog and Lexis/Nexis, and the council librarian had access to the Internet and, through the state library, to other databases. All computers are compatible and use the same word processing software. Explained a staff member, "We are not on the cutting edge, but we are not really far behind."

Computer-literate legislators were strong proponents of greater utilization of computer technology by their colleagues. "We are trying to computerize the legislature, but unfortunately most of legislators are not too interested now," explained a representative. "But once legislators find out what power there is in being able to access all this information, they will become more interested in having computers." "It is important to understand the ability of computers to revolutionize education, health care, [and the] management of state government," said another legislator. "I got through a memorial to bring the legislative side of state government into the electronic age. We should put fiber optics in the capitol and have computers on every legislative desk, on the floor of the House, and in committee. I am trying to push them to get some laptops so we can just carry them around and plug them in." With a computerized legislature, "this will finally be a democracy," declared a representative. "The inability of government to reach people will change, and our constituents will get all the information they want—and all the excuses they can stand," she added.

One legislator complained that he was not allowed to plug in his own computer in the capitol. "They have a policy of not letting you plug it in, so I plugged in my computer anyway and dared them to pull it out. Some ridiculous policy of not tapping into the main system. That is not my intent. They are paranoid and think that if you tap into the system, you will wreck it. I don't think we have a technical person taking care of these things, so they just say 'No, we don't allow it.'" Other legislators were not interested in using computers themselves. A Legislative Council Service staff member explained, "I don't think there will be a computer on every legislator's desk. We will eventually make them available to all, but I doubt that they all are going to use them. A lot of legislative business just doesn't need it, and it is inappropriate to try to force a technology to a problem where access is really not necessary. I think software still has a few generations of improvement to go for it to be truly accessible. I find e-mail is helpful to send documents to the typist to get the bill or memo out faster. But the telephone and fax machine are still more effective and efficient for me when I am trying to share information or get the information from somebody."

5. Technical Information in a Political Environment

How and when a legislator uses technical information to make political decisions depends a great deal on his or her background, experience, and operating style. In general, respondents found technical information to be most useful in bill drafting, followed in importance by responding to legislation filed by others and evaluating administrative action. It is less important for determining issues for current or future sessions, and least important for influencing voting.

There is general agreement that access to technical information from reliable sources had given the legislature more power in dealing with the executive branch and lobbyists, although some respondents felt that the balance still favored the governor and his staff. In regard to lobbyists, a legislator felt that "technical information gives me a lot more power re lobbyists. They don't wag me, and I don't fit into their patterns. I'm now out ahead. But then they also don't give me contributions." Technical information was also seen to play an important part in relation to the opinions of political actors. A long-term senator stated that the information he received from his trusted technical advisor was "more important than the opinions of anyone except the legislative leadership." Regarding the opinions of constituents, a state representative explained that "on strictly technical issues, technical information is more important than opinions of my constituents. They are not apt to have a technical background, and they know I do. I represent the district I grew up in, and many of the citizens did not go off to college as I did. I will try to educate them on the issues. I also try to do that with other legislators if the issue is strictly technical." Legislators thus attempt to serve a dual role as both representative and educator.

Technical issues, however, are often intertwined with the political process. "Basically, every decision is a political decision in a representative democracy," said a staff member. "Hence, a lot of scientists get very annoyed and impatient or disappointed in the political process because it doesn't necessarily place the right answer in the scientific sense first. Some of them literally have instructions from their directors that they cannot get involved in the political process, and it takes a lot of red tape just to get them even to be allowed to come testify in a completely non-self-interest kind of way." It is also true, he continued, that

> different interest groups are very skillful at selecting their facts and that there's an infinite number of facts in the world on any issue that one could use. The democratic process gets manipulated, or the media get manipulated, depending upon who they go to for their information. And the sources of information are going to try to maximize their benefits to them from the political system and from government by emphasizing their facts and de-emphasizing or avoiding somebody else's facts. But that is the democratic process, and there is going to be pressure for the legislatures to weigh the advantages and disadvantages, and ultimately their decision will be based on the perceptions of the voters.

The complexity of dealing with technology is compounded in a citizen legislature because of lack of time. "People don't understand how much time it takes to do the public's business and at the same time take care of jobs [and] family," explained a legislative leader. "Yet, it is the legislature that has to deal with very complex issues, including the impact of technology on our citizens." In an effort to deal with these complex issues, the legislature has recently created the Horizons Task Force to develop ideas for the future. A legislative leader explained that:

> The Task Force has free rein and has been asked, "If you could redo the world, what would you want the state to look like in 2020?" We are trying to bring everybody together to say, "Okay, you're doing something over there. How's that going to affect me over here?" I'm talking about the guy that owns the local garage down there, saying, "Hey, I'm working on these cars, and are you doing something over here that's either going to make my job more expensive, or am I going to be without a job, or going to need to expand my business? Whatever it is, I'm going have to bring somebody else in if I am going to survive." The Technical Vocational Institute is training young men and women to develop microchips. Well, that's nice, and that's fine, but are we going to train everybody to make microchips and forget that we need young men and women trained to be bakers, butchers and candlestick makers?. . . . Or are you going to sit behind this machine and have images pop up and it is going to be an image rather than a word? I don't know. That's not bad. I'm not saying that it is wrong. I'm just saying is, is that what we want?

6. Legislative Satisfaction

Legislators were generally very satisfied with the internal policy support services provided by the central legislative staff. One legislator commented that "the staff have done a pretty remarkable job and have kept us pretty much up to par. The salaries are competitive, but even more important is the relationship and respect they get for assuming that position." Another legislator stated that "the Legislative Council ranks with the best, and they have been ranked. They are paid well for New Mexico. People like to work there.

We give them a lot of latitude. They are protected. They have the right to think."

Although many legislators shared this opinion, several also recognized that the technical capability of the council is "pretty limited." Explained one legislator, "I don't really have the internal support people I would like on technical topics. They are very good when they know where they are, but in terms of technical support staff, they are not my source of information." Another commented that "the council doesn't have the technical expertise. I have enough outside resources because I know where to look for them. I would guess your average legislator would not."

Another general problem mentioned by some legislators was the lack of personal staff who could provide technical research assistance. "We are always getting all of this paper, and most of us have little time to read it," said a representative. The one legislator who had hired a technical expert as his personal staff member was very satisfied with the arrangement and wished he could have his staff for the entire year, not just during the session. "It is more important to me to have my own staff year-round than have science and technical staff added to the Legislative Council," he said. On the other hand, other legislators thought that it was preferable to increase the technical expertise of the council which would be available to all legislators.

Some respondents cited short sessions as a problem in making informed decisions on complex technical issues. "During the session, we deal with 2,000 bills. Sometimes, we deal with 20–30 bills in one committee hearing," said a staff member. "We're trying to deal with too much business in too short a time. A member who doesn't sit on the interim committee may hear 20 minutes of the discussion and then vote. Literally, the last five weeks in the 60-day session, we have met at four o'clock in the morning. I may have 20–30 bills in a two-day period that I have to read, review, try and find out the issues."

In terms of outside resources, satisfaction with university support was high, and respondents reported good relationships between legislators and faculty. Satisfaction with federal laboratories as a source of technical support was mixed. For some legislators, the labs are seen as the best source of technical information. Others said that "if the labs were available to us and at all interested, it could make a big difference, but they just don't get it. And I think there isn't a good feeling for how important the legislature's role is, and everybody else gets a lot of mileage out of diminishing that role."

The executive branch was also reported as helpful to some and not to others.

7. Recommendations

Legislative Council Service Technical Expertise

Some respondents recommended increasing the technical capability of the Legislative Council Service. However, they also raised questions about what kind of person(s) could best fill the technical role. As one legislator stated, "Unless you have a person with an extremely broad background, you won't do a very good job of getting the whole picture." A staff member also stated that "in a citizen-legislature, it's just not a full-time job to have a science and technology specialist."

Personal Staff

Several legislators recommended that policy analysts be available as personal staff for legislators, not only during the regular session but also during the interim period. One senator explained that "personal staff are not available after the session. There are Legislative Council Service staff, but I guess the whole problem with interim committees is that while that is going on, we as individual legislators aren't as able to make the best use of it. I don't have somebody who gets me ready for those meetings, who sits with me at them, who follows up on what I want to do from those meetings." Another senator said,

> I think we should have a technically trained staff person. The system that we have in New Mexico is that our votes are equal, but how we vote and how we make that decision is unequal for new legislators. The more experienced legislators tend to have staff, and sure, they say "use my staff," but there isn't the time or the convenience as there would be for instructing your own staff and spending more time on certain issues. I think I'll start talking with other legislators and see if we can become serious about changing the system.

A representative who has no personal staff explained, "It would be nicer if I had a regular office and office staffing and was able to keep up on a more regularized basis. Here in New Mexico, you are just sort of out alone once the legislature ends. We will connect again when the interim committees begin during the summer, but it's still not the same as a more regularized system."

S&T Standing Committee

The majority of respondents did not support the creation of a standing science and technology committee. They felt that science and technology issues are adequately addressed by the existing committees, that there are already good "interlocking relationships" among them, and that turf battles over jurisdiction would result. On the other hand, proponents claimed that such a committee could focus on the importance of technology and provide a permanence that the present interim S&T committee does not have. "If we created a science and technology standing committee by statute and gave them a statutory charge of what this committee does, that would make it stronger. It would also bring a lot more focus in the press to those issues. The interim committee gets very little press coverage," said a representative. A senator agreed that "the interim committee doesn't [get] enough emphasis given that technology is one of our major assets in this state and should play a more vital role." Turf battles between a new S&T committee and other committees could be "avoided because committees can meet jointly or the Speaker can make the chairs members of overlapping committees."

Legislative Use of Computer Technology

Computer-literate legislators recommended providing computers, preferably laptops, to all legislators who wanted them. "It is time to move out of the Dark Ages of the stubby pencil on the floor of the House and in the Senate, too. And with laptops, we can stop winding up with five volumes of statutes and amendments," said a representative. A senator recommended that there should be "some form of computerized indexing system of state publications and state information available to every legislator, as well as access to outside information, including a better technical relationship with the Feds." He also said that he is trying to create a subject index for himself by reading technical magazines and other publications, so that if "I need certain statistics, I could get the subject index, switch it into my laptop, and then try to get and use it in debate."

A senator recommended acquiring in-house expertise on the purchasing of computer equipment. Almost five percent of the annual state budget is spent on computers, and "most of us are scratching our heads, and 'wondering where does all this money go?'" he said. "We don't have anybody, so we rely on Los Alamos and Sandia computer scientists, and it is helping us a little bit. But they are basically saying, 'It is time you guys recognize you need to start building up this expertise on your own.' We just spent $150 million last year, and where is it? We have had some systems that have never been implemented. So, we need to develop that expertise."

Technology Policy Education for Legislators

In addition to computer training, a senator declared that the legislature needs somebody to educate them about how information technology can create jobs:

> Now, that is something that would help. If the Kennedy School or the Carnegie Corporation wants to do something, then train us as policymakers to understand how to take advantage of a resource like Sandia to create jobs using communications technology. I need to know what kind of jobs are going to be available in the next ten years because of communications . . . This is a perfect place for a data transmission link to Mexico. You run those wires here, turn left, and you go down to Mexico . . . If we knew what kind of jobs were going to be created by this information superhighway, we could bring some home. We could figure out ways to supplement that here. But first you've got to know what is out there, and then you've got to know how to craft the policies and the legislation that will help implement it. And then you have to have an executive branch or bureaucracy that is willing to cooperate.

Strategic Planning

A legislator recommended changing the Governor's Technical Excellence Committee to the New Mexico Technical Excellence Committee (NMTEC) and giving it a statutory charge and some funding to provide information directly to the legislature. He further suggested that legislative involvement could be established by including legislators on the committee and by assigning someone from the Legislative Council Service to attend GTEC/NMTEC meetings.

Lengthen Sessions/Pay Legislators

Although attempts to lengthen the session and provide salaries for legislators have consistently been defeated by ballot, many of those interviewed felt that short sessions made it difficult to deal with complex technical issues and that the interim committee meetings lasting a day or so over the summer and fall months were not really an adequate substitute. One legislator suggested that the legislature meet for 20 weeks with sessions on Mondays, Thursdays and Fridays and committee work on Tuesday and Wednesday. Legislators would be full time, salaried, and expected to be at the capitol during that time. "Then we could get something done," declared a legislator. "But I don't think it will ever happen. It will never change, and it is a horrible shame. And the people don't understand that we are their representatives up there. Special interest is all full time and salaried, and we're not and it's too bad. We are not empowered to identify problems and find solutions."

One legislator said that he "suspected that our legislature would get more technical people involved if the pay was better. Now, it is difficult for anybody who doesn't work for themselves or isn't retired to be in our legislature." Technically trained himself, he knows firsthand how often he is called on by his colleagues for technical advice and thinks more people with his background should be encouraged to run for the legislature.

NEW YORK
STATE PROFILE

ENTERED UNION:
July 26, 1788 (11th admitted)[1]
LAND AREA:
47,224 sq. mi.; U.S. rank #30
POPULATION: 18 m (1990);
U.S. rank #2
Density per sq. mi. 381[2]
DEMOGRAPHICS:
White 13.4 m; Black 2.9 m; Hispanic 2.2 m;
Asian .7 m; Native American .06 m
ECONOMY:
GSP: $466 b (1990); U.S. rank #2[3]
Agriculture (net farm income): U.S. rank #28
Manufacturing (total income): U.S. rank #4[4]
Mining (total income): U.S. rank #25
Per capita personal income: $24,623[5]
Unemployment: 7.7% (1993)
Number of patents: 4,965 (1991); U.S. rank #2[4]
Number of SBIR awards: 973 (1983-91); U.S. rank #5[6]
State technology development agency:
New York State Science and Technology Foundation;
budget: FY '94 $22.9 m
EDUCATION:
High school graduation rate: 65.1%; U.S. rank #43[7]
State and local government expenditure for higher
education: $4.4 b (1989-90); U.S. rank #48
(by % of total expenditure)
Academic R&D expenditures: FY '91 $1.4 b;
U.S. rank #2[6]

POLITICAL:
   U.S. Senators: 1 Democrat, 1 Republican
   Congressional Representatives: 31 (17 Democrats,
      14 Republicans)
   Governor—4-year term
      Since statehood: 53 (22 Democrats, 17 Republicans)
      Since 1970: 5 (2 Democrats, 3 Republicans)[9]
      Current Governor: George Pataki (R), 1st term
   State Legislators: 211[1]
      State Senators: 61; 2-year term
         1994: 26 Democrats, 35 Republicans
         1995: 26 Democrats, 35 Republicans[10]
      State Assemblymen: 150; 2-year term[1]
         1994: 100 Democrats, 50 Republicans
         1995: 94 Democrats, 56 Republicans[9]
      Length of session: no limitation
      Annual salary: $57,500; per diem living expenses
         $89 ($130 in NYC metro area and out-of-state
         travel; $45/partial legislative day; Senate presi-
         dent pro tem receives an additional $30,000/
         year; Senate minority leader, an additional
         $25,000/year; House Speaker, an additional
         $30,000/year; majority and minority leaders, an
         additional $25,000/year[1]
   State budget: FY '96 $32.4 b (proposed); FY '95
      $33.4 b; FY '94 $32 b; FY '93 $31 b[11]
   Legislative budget: FY '95-6 $177.2 m; FY '94-5
      $167.5 m; FY '93-4 $167.8 m[10]
   Total staff: 4,157; U.S. rank 1[12]

---

[1] *CSG Book of the States*, 1994-1995.
[2] *World Almanac*, 1994.
[3] *State Rankings*, 1994.
[4] *Gale State Rankings Reporter*, 1994.
[5] *Almanac of the 50 States*, 1995.
[6] *Partnerships: A Compendium*, 1995.
[7] *CQ's State Fact Finder*, 1993.
[8] *CQ's Who's Who in Congress*, 1995.
[9] *Encyclopedia Americana*, 1993.
[10] New York State Government
    Information Gopher.
[11] *New York Times*.
[12] NCSL, 1988.

NEW YORK
STATE REPORT

Interview Profile

Legislature: 15 (2 senators, 3 Assembly members,
              10 legislative staff)
External: 2

Findings

1. Need for Science and Technology Policy Support

Respondents agreed unanimously that a great many issues before the legislature need technical information and analysis. As one legislator said, "Everything [needs S&T support]. I feel the need for technical information all the time." Examples include:

Environment and Health: state implementation of Federal Clean Air Act; Environmental Trust Fund; feasibility of wetland mitigation bank; low-level nuclear waste; PCB water contamination; dredging New York City harbor; salt mine collapses; water purification technology; lead toxicity; asbestos removal; environmental technology incubator; food irradiation; breast and prostate cancer prevention and treatment; social and ethical impacts of DNA-based genetic testing; licensing of genetic counselors; surrogate motherhood; bovine growth hormone; AIDS; prison health; carcinogenic effect of low-level radiation; disabilities research and medical technology development; Lyme disease; Medicaid funding;

Economic Development: funding for Brookhaven and Rome National Laboratories; industrial technology extension service; defense conversion; development of biotechnology industry; economic and revenue forecasting; computer analysis of income/tax cuts distribution; high-speed rail;

Education: University Centers of Advanced Technology (CATs); K–12 science/math education; junior and senior S&T high schools in depressed urban areas; technology training for disadvantaged students;

Information Technology Policy: building the information highway; public electronic access to legislative information through the Internet; publicly funded, computer-generated, targeted, constituent information mailings; storage durability of computerized state records; social impact of telecommunications; socioeconomic, demographic, computerized mapping; equity access to Cable TV;

There was general agreement among those interviewed that the need for S&T information and analysis has increased greatly over the past decade. One legislator explained, "Most of the growth of S&T information and the management of that information has been exponential almost on an annual basis for some time now. This is driving the need to have some meaningful way for legislators to be able to know how to set policy by having access to that information."

Five primary reasons were cited for the increase in need: (1) the complexity of science and technology issues before the legislature; (2) the amount of technical information available through computer technology; (3) the importance of technology to the state economy; (4) competition from other states and foreign countries; and (5) the sophistication of the public.

"With IBM leading the way, there is an understanding that New York's economy is directly tied to technology development and that the legislature must support policies to encourage its growth," said a legislator. "Telecommunications, computer technology, [and] biotechnology are all keys to New York's economic growth. For the legislature to understand and regulate those industries requires a great deal of technical skill that wasn't needed ten years ago," declared a key staff member. "The same answers that were good enough 10–15 years ago aren't good enough today. And that is pushing members up against the wall, and they are reaching out for scientific knowledge," a staff director explained. "Also with the democratization of society, new constituencies are becoming increasingly active participants in the political process. Therefore, issues such as the ethical and equitable distribution of impacts of certain kinds of technology advances become very pressing and important in the legislative decision-making process."

2. Internal and External Sources of S&T Policy Support

There are four interrelated features of the New York legislature to keep in mind when examining legislative S&T policy support. The first is that the legislative branch has 4,500 legislative employees—the largest number in the country—divided into numerous and highly specialized support mechanisms. The factors responsible for the large staff are, first, the desire of the legislature to maintain an equal position with the executive branch, which has had a long history of powerful, proactive governors. The second factor is a competitive, partisan environment within the legislature, with the Assembly traditionally controlled by Democrats and the Senate by Republicans. With the exception of the legislative library, all policy support programs are divided along party lines in both chambers. The third factor is strong leadership control over legislative process and staffing, and the fourth is the rivalry between New York City and the rural communities of upstate New York, which one legislator described as more influential than all other issues.

Internal Sources

Assembly

At the present time, both majority and minority members of the Assembly use committee staff as their fundamental source of technical information. The Speaker and minority leader's central Program and Policy Offices provide most of the staffing. As an official of the Speaker's office explained, the role of staff is "to provide members not with an opinion but with options. We must be very careful because the more developed and advanced the staff gets, there is risk that they effectively use their expertise to make policy, but it is the members who are to make the decisions." Referring to the influence of legislative staff, a key legislative leader who once had been a staff director commented only somewhat in jest that he had lost power when he got elected.

Another source of technical information which may become an increasingly significant internal mechanism for the Assembly is the Legislative Commission on Science and Technology. New York is one of the few states with a legislative mechanism specifically for science and technology. Created in 1979 to support the work of committees by producing background and option papers and to provide a service function to legislators on technical issues, it was modeled on the federal statute that created the congressional Office of Technology Assessment but tailored to New York.

New York legislative commissions are nominally joint, but in practice, their control is divided between the chambers.

The Legislative Commission on Science and Technology operates under the jurisdiction of the Assembly, and the Speaker appoints its chair and executive director. In spite of its original mission, respondents reported that the commission eventually became the tool of its chairs to support their own agendas, and it lost touch with its mission as a source of technical information for the general membership. Recently, however, the commission was moved to the jurisdiction of the Speaker's Program and Policy Office, which in 1993 reorganized its Program Development Group to coordinate the agendas of the legislative commissions and develop the Commission on Science and Technology as a research center for the rest of the Assembly. The commission chair, the development group, and the Speaker jointly set the agenda after listening to members to determine their interests. Respondents hope that this new governing structure will allow the commission to serve the interests of the entire state and not just the majority conference and to use the commission's technical skills for both short-term responses (the salt mine collapse and federal laboratory closings) and long-term research (the recently released report on DNA testing and its impact on public policy). According to Development Group staff, "Ideally, if we do our job right, by the time an issue hits the front pages and a legislator needs an answer, we will have done six months worth of work anticipating it."

The Speaker has appointed a new executive director of the Commission on Science and Technology, who has a technical background in engineering and atmospheric physics as well as legislative staff management experience. There are seven professionals on the commission staff who hold degrees in science (5) or public policy (2) at either the master's or doctoral level. Also affiliated with the commission staff is an American Society of Mechanical Engineers (ASME) fellow and an intern. The commission has a budget of approximately $300,000, which must be approved annually in the appropriations bill. In the opinion of the executive director, the commission needs both scientists and nonscientists, for example, a good mix would include a physicist, a chemist, a biologist, an engineer, a mathematician/statistician, an economist or MBA, and a person with technical writing skills.

There have been three chairs of the Commission on Science and Technology in the past two years, an unstable situation resulting in some altered priorities and operating styles, but not an altered mission. For example, all three chairs have supported a DNA study, and they are jointly supporting the three bills filed as a result of the report's recommendations. Assembly member Robert Sweeney, the present chair, considers stability important, and he hopes to stay "for a while." He is refocusing the agenda and trying to avoid "an issue de jour" approach. He will concentrate on the science and technology aspects of the treatment of breast and prostate cancer, biotechnology, environmental technology, and telecommunications. Commission staff are assigned to the different topics, but it is "difficult to stay ahead of the curve," and there may be a need to get advice from the outside. Assembly member Sweeney is planning to hold round-table discussions with experts across the state to bring attention to the issues and get their input.

The primary focus of the somewhat reduced commission staff will be on providing the legislature with early indications of the probable beneficial and adverse impacts of pending or proposed applications of technology and identifying, for legislative consideration, opportunities and other consequences that may flow from new scientific developments. Staff will continue to answer individual legislators' requests for technical information, but as a lower priority.

Another unique source of technical information for the Assembly is the Ways and Means Economic Research Office. It was established in 1987 to provide an in-house capability to the Ways and Means Committee for economic and revenue forecasting, eliminating reliance solely on the executive branch for information. The office employs seven professionals, four of whom have doctorates, including the chief economist who serves as director. Reviewed by an outside board of economic advisors from academia, business, and labor, the Office publishes the highly regarded biennial *New York State Economic and Revenue Report* based on extensive technical information. In 1993, it began publishing *Economic Update,* which tracks national and New York state economic trends. Both documents are available to the public. It also responds to requests from members for both short- and long-term economic information. The office is now beginning to look at the complex issue of forecasting expenditures and expects this study to take about five years.

In keeping with the partisan nature of the New York legislature, the minority members of the Assembly also have a program and policy office, although significantly smaller than its majority counterpart. Under the direction of the minority leader, it includes Ways and Means, Counsel, and Research and Program Development Office staff, who operate as a team to provide policy support. The research and program staff consists of 11 legislative analysts who provide both a service and research function. They respond to requests for information from both ranking minority committee members and individual minority legislators, prepare reports, monitor legislation, and assist in drafting legislation. Describing themselves as a "MASH" unit, they do whatever is helpful for the 56 minority members. The Research and Program Development Office does not have specific scientific expertise, but staff are able to access technical information from a variety of sources, including the Senate Research Office. They also get constituents with special expertise to help on a pro bono basis but "have to be careful to avoid bias."

The control of central staff by the leadership does not allow for a great deal of independent, entrepreneurial action on the part of legislators and their staff. New members of the Assembly are allotted only one personal staff member, but the number increases with seniority and leadership approval. Personal staff are typically appointed for political skills and not scientific training. However, one legislator—who himself has a technical background—has hired a technically trained person to serve as his one personal staff person and considers him his most important source of S&T policy support. "The day-to-day crush of citizens and lobbyists with a need for an immediate response limits my time, so the most efficient and effective way to brief me is verbally," says the legislator. With his strong scientific background, I know when he tells me something that it is accurate, and that he has the ability to analyze technical information and boil it down to 25 words or less," he explained. "If there are topic areas outside his particular expertise, he knows how to access those people. He also anticipates issues, and while he is not as tuned in as somebody who is doing research in a field, he stays in contact with them so he keeps me informed."

Senate

Majority senators have access to many policy support mechanisms, although none is specifically designated for science and technology. A senior majority senator explained that his most effective method for getting S&T policy support is to create teams composed of staff from the Program and Policy Office, the Finance Committee, legislative committees, and his own office. The team would also include staff from the Majority Counsel Office if it needs to draft legislation. When needed, external sources that the legislator knows and trusts will be used. The senator considers his personal staff the key since "everything filters through them." Commented a former staffer, "Majority senators get all the resources they need."

For senators without these well-developed networks, the Senate Research Office (SRO) responds to legislative requests from individual senators for information and analysis. With an annual budget of $2 million, 30 professionals with bachelor's or master's degrees respond to an estimated 10,000 requests a year. They are organized into 37 different function areas, but there is no specific responsibility for science and technology because it "straddles everything."

Under the control of the Senate majority leader, the Senate Research Office serves mostly majority members, although its 6- to 8-page briefing papers (called *Issues in Focus*) and its quarterly *Highlight Books* on major legislation are available to the entire legislature and the public. The office was originally established in 1955 as a bicameral agency. In 1975, when party control of the two houses split, the office was divided. The Assembly Research Office was not adequately funded and eventually was abolished. The SRO has also undergone change. Formerly, it also focused on long-term research through its Task Force on Critical Choices. A key staff member reported that SRO no longer has the luxury of spending six months on a project and has eliminated the critical choices function.

Minority senators have access to their own minority Program and Policy Office. On staff are 30 professionals, most with master's degrees. One staff specialist has a background in science and serves as an informal science advisor. The staff responds to approximately 2,500 requests a year and also serve as committee staff for minority members. A minority senator states that majority committee staff technically serve both parties, but "we have never gotten anything from them." Therefore, they have their own, albeit fewer, staff to assist with committee work.

Legislators themselves who have developed an expertise in certain fields can also be valuable sources of advice to their colleagues. A respondent commented, "We have a number of brilliant members who, once they bite into a topic and do their research on it, become a primary source." Another stated, "A lot of what legislators know comes from talking to colleagues they trust. It might be right or wrong, but when legislators develop a reputation as knowledgeable, members treat their opinion almost like gospel."

External Sources

The most important external sources of technical information and analysis for legislators are personal contacts whom they can trust. A staffer commented that sometimes these contacts can be too important, "sending members off on a crusade about an issue that has been misrepresented." Important institutional sources cited were academia, state agencies, and lobbyists.

Legislators often develop close ties with colleges and universities in their districts, especially those in the State University of New York (SUNY) system. Most of these contacts are on an informal basis, although the legislature once had a contractual relationship with SUNY Research Foundation in Albany. A former staffer commented that Cornell, which is both a private and a land grant college, has always provided technical support on agricultural matters and is now trying to reestablish its once strong tradition of service to the legislature in other areas. Other academic institutions cited were Rensselaer Polytechnic Institute (RPI), the Maxwell School at Syracuse University, and the 13 Centers for Advanced Technology (CATs). CATs are located at universities throughout the state and are under the jurisdiction of the New York Science and Technology Foundation, a quasi-public agency whose purpose is to strengthen technology development in the state. While the extensive resources of the state's universities and colleges are considered valuable sources of technical information for both legislators and staff, as one key staffer said, "the relationship between academia and the legislature needs improvement and is not what we would like."

Respondents cited problems with legislative reliance on the executive branch for policy support. "Some agencies have a high level of expertise, but we always have to worry about their agenda," commented a staff analyst. A legislator with a strong science background observed that "They are occasionally brilliant and occasionally disappointing. They have their own bias, driven in many cases by budgetary considerations. The statisticians and "number crunchers" tend to become de facto policymaking czars because the agencies don't want to get in a cross fire between the governor and his division of budget. The technical needs of the state are ultimately filtered through bookkeepers and accountants and lawyers, who are in many cases not technically adequate to make those decisions." Another key staffer stated bluntly, "The executive branch legislative liaison units are absolutely useless. The only information from the executive branch that is useful is through personal contacts that are trustworthy."

There are about 460 lobbyists listed in the *New York Political Handbook* who provide a great deal of information to legislators, but "the difficulty," said a member of the Assembly, "is sorting out the bias from the good information." One legislative analyst explained, "For a lobbyist to be useful, he has to have technical expertise. But there is still a problem whether he is snowing you or not. In addition, it is often not so much a case of inaccurate as incomplete information. You can't expect them to tell you something that hurts their case." The National Conference of State Legislatures (NCSL) and federal agencies such as the Congressional Budget Office, the Office of Management and Budget, the Census Bureau, the Office of Technology Assessment, the Environmental Protection Agency, and some federal laboratories were cited as useful sources of technical information. NCSL staff was singled out as "being particularly good at putting you in touch with people. If they don't have the information, they will know who does. They are very good at information sharing."

3. Characteristics of Useful S&T Policy Support

Legislators and staff agreed that for S&T policy support to be useful, it should come from a trusted source and be reliable, accurate, up-to-date, goal-oriented, objective, timely, and accessible. It should also provide options and be presented in understandable, nontechnical language and in a user-friendly format. "The sources most important to me are those that I can trust, that are reliable. In a profession in which reliability and trust are the most important variables, known quantities control your ability to succeed," explained a member of the Assembly. "It's also important that my technical advisors have the ability to evaluate their sources and understand whatever bias there may be."

A senator said that "technical information has to be very goal-oriented to be useful. It must focus on an existing solvable problem. It's not people going off and doing papers because someone thinks it is a good idea and it just sits there." A staff director thought it was important to present options and not just information. "What members are looking for is not just being able to go to somebody with expertise. What they are looking for is setting out what the various options are. There are very few issues where it is just cold hard facts." Other staff members thought a key to useful technical information was "to make it understandable to someone who hasn't much time." It was very important for staff "to have the ability to translate the jargon, and you can only do that if you understand it yourself."

In terms of accuracy and objectivity, partisan staff observed that "we have an obligation to the people we are working for to lay things out in a straightforward fashion. If you put out things that are factually correct, then legislators are going to know more about the issue. And with better information, legislators are going to make better policies, and then better politics. Then, they win and the institution clearly wins."

4. Legislative Use of Technology

Many of the staff felt that the New York legislature "has been tremendously empowered by computer technology. We can spin 300 times more information per hour than we did five years ago," reported a key staff member. "This has allowed analysts to provide more information and to have more checks in the check-and-balance system between the legislature and the executive branch and lobbyists. We now have to think and rethink how to harness that energy most effectively," he said. Both Senate and Assembly central staff use computer technology extensively and selected staff have access to the Internet and on-line services such as Lexis/ Nexis, Westlaw, Dialog, NYSERNET, and those of state universities. Staff also use computer technology for internal staff operations. For example, one manager has purchased a computer program which tracks members' requests. Every morning, he checks the tracking system to make sure that requests are fulfilled in a timely manner.

Computers are also available to legislators, but only senators have access to the Internet through the recent opening of the New York State Senate On-line Public Exchange Network, which was sponsored by Senate President Pro-tem and Senate Majority Leader Joseph Bruno. Called "Open Senate," it provides information about the Senate to anyone who has access to the Internet, including the e-mail addresses of the 42 senators who have chosen to post one. In addition, every Senate district office has computer access by modem to Albany and to the Senate mainframe.

The Assembly is still discussing questions about access, security, cost, and the implications of the New York Freedom of Information Law before it makes the Internet available to its members. "Part of the problem," said a staff member, "is that once you go on-line, there is really wide access to get out, but it means people can also get in. There is no problem if the public is asking for information, but how can the system stop being flooded by huge amounts of special interest e-mail?" Cost is also an issue. On-line services can cost $150 an hour. They also require training to use them effectively. Until these issues have been resolved, Assembly members and their staffs can access the Internet and on-line services at the legislative library. Perhaps the experience of the Senate will provide some answers.

5. Technical Information in a Political Environment

The proper balance between scientific validity and political viability is a complicated issue and frequently a major source of conflict. There is no doubt that technical information can play a significant role in political decision making as it did in the passage of the bottle bill in the early 1980s, when technical arguments successfully refuted the bottle industry's claims on environmental and energy costs, or in the case of analyzing soil conditions in the successful rescue of New York's wine industry from collapse. On the other hand, technical information can ultimately be irrelevant when deeply held opinions exist on such issues as the opening of the Shoreham nuclear plant, the storage of low-level nuclear waste in West Valley, or the regulation of food irradiation.

Often technical information and analysis is just part of the mix in the decision-making process. A legislator explained that no matter how "neutral" the technical information is, a certain coloration is always required to make it fit the political context. In New York, this means additional negotiating in an environment of great political differences, not only between parties but also between two very distinct geographical regions.

Respondents saw technical information as most important in preparing arguments in support or opposition to legislation and in bill drafting. It was less important in deciding what issues are important and deserve attention in the current session, and even less so in deciding what issues to focus on in the future. Agenda-setting was seen more as a function of leadership and reflected the view that technical information is frequently used to bolster an already fixed opinion rather than as a decisive factor in reaching that position. On the other hand, respondents acknowledged that technical information was important "to ensure that we are heading in the right direction and that basic facts are needed first before reaching a conclusion."

Technical information was least important in deciding how to vote on legislation, since respondents generally agreed that such information had to be available earlier in the decision-making process to be effective. Indeed, the timing of technical information in the legislative process is a key issue: if it is too early, no one is interested; if it is too late, positions have hardened and the information may seem irrelevant.

Another fundamental issue involving technical information in a political environment is the role of legislator. Is it to represent or to lead constituents? One legislator said he saw his role as educator and that in his view

> the role of a good legislator is to repackage complicated issues involving science and technology and put them into very stark, human terms so that they can be understood by everyone. You look for metaphors and motifs that can be understood by your constituents. For example, genetic testing is probably best crystallized in a short phrase, "Are you guilty for the sins of your father?" If he had heart disease, should you be precluded from getting health insurance? I try to talk to as many people as possible and educate them about the public policy issues that affect them.

Another legislator expressed the other point of view, saying, "It is a mistake to underestimate the electorate in understanding a particular issue. In the end, you need to represent the people who elected you. Nothing is more important than their opinions."

Two-year terms are also a problem. As one staffer commented, "Members of the Assembly and Senate are always running for office, trying to nudge their way to the front to get media attention. This is not a good match with S&T issues, which require a greater attention span."

Respondents agreed that access to internal sources of science and technology support had given more power to the legislature to deal with other political actors, such as the executive branch and lobbyists, and that this support is helping to preserve the constitutional balance of power between the legislative branch and the traditionally powerful New York governors, as well as "the fourth branch of government—over 500 registered lobbyists."

6. Legislative Satisfaction

The members of the Assembly and their staffs who were interviewed generally felt that there was a need for improvement in providing technical information in a "manageable fashion." Said one legislator, "Looking at all resources, it could be better. It's not terrible and I don't feel debilitated, but I do think there is much room for growth and improvement. There is a tremendous amount of information, but the veracity of the information or the determination of whether there is a bias to the information is a significant problem for legislators. At the present time there is no meaningful 'sniff test.'" In terms of the Commission on Science and Technology, a former chair expressed great satisfaction with both its responsiveness to his requests and its ability to anticipate issues. Other legislators felt that the policy support of the Commission on Science and Technology should be more available to all legislators, not just the chair and other commission members.

On the Senate side, respondents generally agreed that majority senators are "very satisfied with the science and technology information they ask for and get." Those senators who had established a team approach were particularly pleased with this approach. Respondents also expressed satisfaction with SRO and the legislative library.

In both the Assembly and Senate, minority respondents of both parties expressed concern over inequities in the distribution of resources among majority and minority members. A Democratic senator ranked his satisfaction with all sources of technical policy support fairly low and said that most of his information comes from his own reading. "Committee staff technically serves both parties, but we have never gotten anything from the majority staff," he said. From the perspective of a staff member, the greatest handicap was not the lack of availability of legislative resources but the lack of time and knowledge on the part of legislators. "The resources are there. The question is whether legislators avail themselves of them."

7. Recommendations

In discussing the possibility for improvement, a legislator described the broad problem as follows:

> There is room for improvement, but the big issue is how do you inform 211 people with widely divergent interests and how do you give them enough information so that they can make the right decision? My fear is overpopulating government with new committees and responsibilities. I would rather fit it into an existing pattern and use the discipline-specific committees to deal with the problem. They should be given the expertise to help legislators do their job and figure out what the public interest is. Too often we define that from competing special interests. That is, if we balance off the special interests and they're all not unreasonably unhappy, we think we have served the public interest. It is seems to me that is a pretty minimal definition of the public interest. The other interest out there is the public—the broad interests of 18 million people—and we have to figure out how they fit into the puzzle.

There was general agreement that any recommended changes that challenged the basic structure of partisan and leadership control were unlikely to happen. One long-term legislative observer commented, "Changes of the legislative culture won't happen incrementally. There would have to be a big blowup for fundamental reform." On the other hand, a key staff member felt that it was "a great time for change. Clearly, leadership has always been interested in information that they can use to their advantage, but now there is a need to think in longer terms. With the reorganization of the Program Development Group, Assembly leadership is putting more emphasis on longer-term planning, and clearly technology will be driven through almost everything we do in the future. Good politics is a long-term endeavor."

Legislative S&T Commission

A respondent with a long background in the affairs of the Commission on Science and Technology recommended that technical policy support to individual legislators be increased. "The Commission statute and goal of providing S&T policy support to legislators is a good model, but it doesn't work that way in practice. Members who get to be chairs want to use it for policy purposes, not for service to legislators," he said. He suggested that a way to avoid this problem was to have the chair of the Commission on Science and Technology also chair a standing committee to pursue his/her policy interests and leave the Commission on Science and Technology free to fulfill its original service function. He thought that changing the commission's name to Legislative Office of Technology Analysis might be a way to emphasize that mission. Respondents also cited the importance of stability for the commission and suggested that statutory authorization should come through separate legislation instead of through the annual appropriation bill, as is presently the case. Allowing the commission chair to also a chair a standing committee, or alternatively, making the compensation equal to committee chairs, might increase stability in the commission's leadership.

Other recommendations were: (1) to expand the commission's resources, possibly by hiring consultants with specific areas of expertise on a short-term basis, (2) to orient the

commission's work towards specific bills that are important
to the state rather than "just preparing research reports as
an end in itself," and (3) to make the commission presentations less academic. A member of the Assembly said,
"Presentation of basic information should be adjusted to
more fit legislators' needs. This doesn't mean that it has to
be reduced to one page, but there is a time factor for
legislators."

Senate Research Office

A long-term senate staff member recommended restoring
the Senate Research Office's Critical Choices Program but
doubts "if there is a call for it from across the street [the
Legislature]." He said that it would need "[support] for the
level of work necessary to produce a quality product and the
patience to wait for an answer that might take four to six
months." For example, the SRO wine industry report took
eight months to complete. "It [was] an involved process. It
took a lot of traveling, a lot of communication with legislators and industry representatives. It didn't just happen in a
week. And yet it had a great impact on keeping New York's
wine industry from 'dying on the vine,'" he said.

Standing Committee on S&T

Respondents generally opposed the creation of a standing
committee on science and technology as an unnecessary
interference with the functions of existing standing committees. A majority legislator commented that "in New York,
there is a legislative political dynamic where certain issues
have settled in certain committees which each new chair will
make sure remains within its jurisdiction." A minority
legislator agreed with using the discipline-specific committees, but said that they "must have staff expertise and it
should be available to all members." A former key staffer,
however, would support a science and technology committee

to develop state S&T policy and deal with other states, regions, and the federal government on S&T issues. "Having the congressional House Committee on Science and Technology has been very useful in Washington and could be in Albany," he said.

Joint, Nonpartisan Legislative Research Council

While there was some support for a joint, nonpartisan legislative research council in theory, in practice respondents felt that the New York legislature was too partisan for such a mechanism to succeed unless one party controlled both houses. One respondent with a long institutional memory commented that, having been tried once before and failing, it should be established by statute to ensure permanence, similar to the Wisconsin model. "At present there is little continuity in New York," he said. "Innovative programs disappear and then they get recreated and are thought to be new." As a former partisan staff person, he did not see an agency like the Congressional Research Service (CRS) at the Library of Congress as a threat and thought it could be very helpful in providing basic information which partisan staff could then use for their own legislative purposes.

Personal Staff

One member of the Assembly called for allowing more than one personal staff to legislators to work on technical issues. He explained that they need technically trained personal staff "because legislators suffer from information overload and the weight of so many responsibilities, and one is not enough." Deeply interested in technical issues himself, he said he ideally could use three additional staff with the quality of scientific training that his present staff person has.

Legislative Use of Computer Technology

Some of the recommendations for increased public access to on-line legislative information are in the process of being implemented through the State Senate On-line Public Exchange Network. However, Senate voting records are not yet available on-line to the public. An Assembly on-line network is still in the discussion stage. One respondent recommended the creation of an electronically accessible technical information clearinghouse that organizes information so that it is easily retrievable for both minority and majority program offices. Another respondent suggested the computerization of bill storage. "We don't need to store a thousand copies of every bill in a cubbyhole. When someone wants a bill, just print it. It could save all the printing costs of those extra copies," said a legislator.

Universities

One legislator recommended that greater interaction between state agencies and research laboratories be developed throughout the SUNY system. "For example, the Department of Environmental Conservation has excellent data on ground water quality but it is not stored or handled so as to be accessible to research scientists in a meaningful way. Almost all regulatory agencies are completely severed from academia. They are both on the public payroll and should be working together to serve the common good." He also suggested that there be a higher level of expectation for the utilization and better integration of human resources found throughout state government. As a good model, he singled out the Bio-Diversity Institute, staffed by Department of Environmental Conservation, staff of the Biological Survey of the state museum, staff scientists from the nonprofit Nature Conservancy, and legislators.

A technical staff member commented that, in his efforts to develop expenditure forecasting models, there was, at present, no one place where the necessary information resides. "We are trying to collect it," he said, "and it would be helpful if some academics could donate their time or some foundation would want to underwrite the effort. It will take about 5–7 years, but then we should be able to forecast both revenues at the same time (as we are already doing) and spending at a good level of detail."

Science Advisory Council

One respondent recommended the creation of a state science advisory council with legislative representation—similar to the one Governor James Hunt established in North Carolina—to focus on the importance of science and technology for New York and to bring its expertise to bear on public policy decisions.

NORTH CAROLINA
STATE PROFILE

ENTERED UNION:
November 21, 1789 (12th admitted)[1]
LAND AREA:
48,718; U.S. rank #29
POPULATION:
6.9 m (1993 est.)
U.S. rank #10[2]
Density per sq. mi. 140.5
DEMOGRAPHICS:
White 5 m; Black 1.5 m; Hispanic .08 m;
Native American .08 m; Asian .05 m
ECONOMY:
GSP: $141.1 b (1990); U.S. rank #12[3]
Agriculture (net farm income): U.S. rank #6
Manufacturing (total income): U.S. rank #13[4]
Mining (total income): U.S. rank #29
Per capita personal income: $18,702 (1993)[5]
Unemployment: 4.9% (1993)
Number of patents: 980 (1991); U.S. rank #16[6]
Number of SBIR awards: 244 (1983-91);
    U.S. rank #22
State technology development agency:
    No central agency; all programs are independent;
      budget: $37.5 m
EDUCATION:
High school graduation rate: 68%; U.S. rank #40[7]
State and local government expenditures on higher
    education: $2.4 b (1989-90); U.S. rank #7
    (by % of total expenditures)

Academic R&D expenditures: $502 m; U.S. rank #10[6]

POLITICAL:

U.S. Senators: 2 Republicans

Congressional Representatives: 12 (4 Democrats, 8 Republicans)

Governor—4-year term

 Since statehood: 71 (35 Democrats, 6 Republicans)

 Since 1970: 5 (3 Democrats, 2 Republicans)[8]

 Current Governor: Jim Hunt (D), 1st term[5]

State Legislators: 170[1]

 State Senators: 50; 2-year term

  1994: 39 Democrats, 11 Republicans

  1995: 26 Democrats, 23 Republicans[9]

 State Representatives: 120; 2-year term

  1994: 78 Democrats, 42 Republicans[1]

  1995: 53 Democrats, 67 Republicans[9]

 Length of session: no limitation

 Annual salary: $13.02; per diem living expenses, $92 subsistence allowance plus $522/month expense allowance; Senate president pro tem receives an additional $35,622/year plus $1,320/ month expense allowance; House speaker receives an additional $22,596/year; Speaker pro tem receives an additional $7,272/year

State budget: FY '93 $16.9 b; FY '92 $16 b; FY '91 $15 b[10]

Legislative budget: FY '92 $17.1 m[11]

Total staff: 485; U.S. rank #23[12]

[1] *CSG Book of the States*, 1994-1995.
[2] *World Almanac*, 1995.
[3] *State Rankings*, 1994.
[4] *Gale State Rankings Reporter*, 1994.
[5] *Almanac of the 50 States*, 1995.
[6] *Partnerships: A Compendium*, 1995.
[7] *CQ's State Fact Finder*, 1993.

[8] *Encyclopedia Americana*, 1992.
[9] *State Yellow Book*, Spring 1995.
[10] U.S. Dept. of Commerce World Wide Web census page <www.doc.gov/ CommerceHomePage.html>.
[11] *State Government Finances*, 1992.
[12] NCSL, 1988.

NORTH CAROLINA
STATE REPORT

Interview Profile

Legislature: 19 (3 senators, 2 representatives, 14 legislative staff)

Findings

1. Need for Science and Technology Policy Support

A strong consensus exists among respondents in North Carolina that technical information and analysis is necessary in the legislative process, but there is considerable skepticism as to whether the need for it has increased over time. Some respondents assert unequivocally that the need has increased, for example, one senior staffer who points to some increased staffing to handle the nonlegal issues faced by the legislature. Others acknowledge an increased need only in particular issue areas, for example, in science and technology for economic development. Still others suggest that there is an increased need only in parts of the legislative process, increasing for committee work but not for bill drafting. Even though the complex issues involved in bill drafting might imply a greater need for technical information and analysis, "the general rule is to draft legislation . . . and then the specifics come through the rule-making process."

Some staff believe that the need has not increased, but rather it has always been there: "I think we could use testimony from people with a scientific or technical background more than we do have. I think there's always been a need for it; I don't think there's necessarily been an increased need for it"; and, "I don't know if I've sensed an increased need, but there's always been a need for technical information." One legislator attributes his own increased need for technical information and analysis not from the environment but from his assumption of a leadership position, in which he finds himself "expected to provide that type of support and background information," because he is a more senior legislator. One senior staffer also discerns a greater willingness on the part of legislators to involve themselves and "to ask the difficult questions."

The chief issues identified by respondents as requiring technical information and analysis include: environmental issues such as low-level radioactive waste, solid waste, air and water quality, and underground storage tanks; agriculture and livestock issues; marine resources and fisheries issues; engineering data for management of historic sites; education reform; alternative energy and conservation; transportation; telecommunications; health care reform; tax reform; procurement of computer systems; economic development; emergency management; and social services.

2. Internal and External Sources of S&T Policy Support

Internal Sources

The staff of the Legislative Services Office (LSO) are the most important of all sources of technical information and analysis to the North Carolina legislature. LSO currently has five divisions: fiscal research, research, bill drafting, general administration, and automated systems.

The legislature created LSO in the late 1960s; prior to that, the state Office of the Attorney General drafted legislation and the Institute of Government at the University of North Carolina provided some staff support to some standing committees and interim study commissions. In 1969, the legislature created a fiscal research division because it was unwilling to trust the executive branch's management of President Nixon's revenue sharing program. The primary duties of the fiscal division are performing an analysis of the governor's budget and writing fiscal notes to estimate the cost of proposed legislation for five years. In 1993, the division also inaugurated the use of an expenditure and revenue forecasting model that has "changed the debate" by allowing legislatures to focus beyond the current biennium to a five-year horizon.

The legislature established the research division a year or two later, which grew with the perceived need to staff the (non-money) standing committees. Now, the research division has approximately 18 attorneys, three other analysts with advanced degrees (including one doctorate in education), and several paralegals. In 1978, a separate bill-drafting division was created, which currently has about a dozen attorneys. The functions of staffing committees and drafting bills are now almost entirely separated into the two divisions, and the Institute of Government no longer plays a role in staffing standing committees, although it does still contribute to study commissions. The automated services division largely provides technical support, although its director also provides significant policy support. Over time, the research division staff have become somewhat more specialized through new hires.

All five staff divisions are governed by the joint Legislative Services Commission (LSC), which is co-chaired by the Speaker of the House and president pro tem of the Senate. LSC used to have direct control over personnel issues, but now operates through a personnel committee for hiring, although staff continue to work at the pleasure of LSC. There is additional staffing for the offices of the Speaker and president pro tem. There have been significant tensions between the North Carolina House and Senate over staff issues and some sentiment to split the currently unitary staff.

Legislators themselves are not a particularly important source of technical information and analysis in the North Carolina legislature, although, according to one staffer, "if you trust a member who is a physician and an issue comes up, then it's very important." Another staffer points to particular members whom other members respect as "being knowledgeable and a source of information," regardless of their political leanings. Because a member may have "carried the political ball" on a tough technical issue, "he's respected when he stands up and says something; people listen to him."

One staffer describes the strategy of the Speaker "to try to identify and cultivate a knowledge level and experience level among our members, so that you [can] have members who others turn to on health care, on finance, or environmental issues." The strategy was exemplified by the creation, in 1991, of the Committee on Science and Technology. The hope was that the committee would be "an opportunity . . . to develop expertise and a whole cadre of legislators" who could deal with emerging technical issues, perhaps to take "a bigger view" of policy and "pick up these blips on the horizon, identify them, categorize them, and then be an information resource for the rest of us" in the legislature. The Speaker also created the new committee for reasons of political inclusion.

One issue the committee took up was a report to the 1992 session, entitled "Bridging the Gap between Science and Policy." The report recommended creating a state Environmental Research and Policy Center, in part to give North Carolina "a leg up on attracting" the planned federal National Institutes for the Environment (which never materialized). The proposed center received a great deal of opposition from the business community, and a low priority score from the Appropriations Committee ensured it would not be funded. The committee accomplished little else during its term—perhaps because "the legislature is not always adept" at this role and the committee represented "a highfalutin notion," and perhaps because the House leadership was too generous in allowing the committee to set its own goals. When the House organized in 1993 with one of the largest incoming classes of new legislators in state history, the Speaker did not renew the committee.

External Sources

Executive agencies are the most important external source of technical information and analysis to the legislature in North Carolina. The (legislatively chartered) Board of Science and Technology operates in the executive branch, and the director of the board also serves as the governor's science advisor. But there is minimal interaction between the board and the legislature. Personal contacts are also important sources of technical information and analysis, as are lobbyists.

State colleges and universities are an important source of technical information and analysis, particularly the Institute of Government (IG) at the University of North Carolina, Chapel Hill, which has a long-standing relationship with the legislature. IG was created in the 1930s to assist state and local government, and until the 1970s, it regularly provided staff support to the legislature. One legislator characterized IG as "very helpful in alerting us to topics, and also in doing in-depth research."

But much of the contact with the state universities is ad hoc at best. "We don't have professors come in and testify," reports one staffer. This staffer has spoken to university liaison offices and deans "to have access to some expertise," because he recognizes that "they just didn't have the contacts" to find the right experts on their own. Another legislator has "never used them," although North Carolina State University "said we should call on them for information. I don't know if they've got anything about things that I'm doing, but they're going to compile a directory of names with the subjects in which they are expert." Another staffer thinks that "it would be very good if there were a stronger link between the universities and the legislature. . . . If I had a ready directory, I would call those people up, but it's a big effort right now to figure out who to try to contact."

3. Characteristics of Useful S&T Policy Support

Respondents in North Carolina are articulate about what they find useful in sources of technical information and analysis. One staffer says what's important is "reliability, timeliness, a slightly different shading, accuracy. . . . I think all the analysts here, including me, depend on people in the executive branch a great deal, for example, but [the dependence is] carefully built on relationships over the years, and they're based on mutual respect and trust. And out of that comes accuracy, timeliness, reliability, all those other things." One legislator suggests that the trust of staff has the same characteristic of repeated play: "I trust my own research staff probably the most, because I can keep going back and digging."

Another staffer declares, "The information has got to be quick, it's got to be to the point, it's got to be short, it's got to address specific issues." Recognizing that many players in the legislative process are interested, respondents also valued "neutral" or "objective" information, by which they primarily meant not patently biased and "broad based" in origin. According to a senior staffer, good sources seem to be those which would fare well responding to "several questions that would probably come to mind: 'Who's paying for that study?' . . . 'Who is he or she beholden to?' . . . 'What is his [or her] intellectual bent?' . . . 'Is he [or she] on a glory trip?'"

That important sources of technical information and analysis had a "depth of knowledge" was only mentioned by one respondent. As a senior staff member said, the information "might be above contest and may be perfect scientifically. The fact that it is . . . to a great extent is irrelevant I think in the legislative process." Another staffer adds, "It's the perception of the organization, not necessarily the quality of the information."

4. Legislative Use of Technology

Electronic information networks like the Internet were not at all important sources of technical information and analysis to respondents, in large part because the priority of the automated services division of the LSO has been primarily to put legislative records onto the Internet so the public can have access, and only secondarily to provide access to the Internet for legislators and staff. Staff who need to do electronic searches or need to use Lexis/Nexis, etc., usually go through the research librarian.

Ten years ago, the legislature had six word processors and ten terminals running only two programs, a bill-drafting program and a bill-tracking program. By the summer of 1994, there were seven minicomputers networked with approximately 500 personal computers and 250 laser printers. One of the most heavily used applications (10,000–14,000 inquiry-sessions per month during session) is a bill-tracking program designed so that the public can use the telephone and get the current status of bills. Internal e-mail is another heavily used application, with approximately 100,000 messages every month in session. A senior staffer tells an excellent story of how a former Speaker learned of the importance of e-mail communication and set an example for its use as a communication and management tool. Some committee business is now done exclusively by e-mail.

The legislature has made available to individual legislators and the public a computerized redistricting map, and it is making available the Legislative Vote Reporting System (LVRS) to report all votes, and the Boards, Commissions, and Committees Information System to report the membership information of all boards and commissions in the state. LVRS is unique among the states. Although some members initially favored it, "the real motivating force was the press

. . . which really started to complain that they didn't have access to all these votes." The system is expected to be used for electoral politics as well. Indeed, symbolic politics is still very much alive in high tech: "Frankly, many people want [an Internet connection] because they want to put forth a high-tech image that's fashionable. So they would like to have the Internet. They want to be able to say they use the Internet. They want to print their Internet e-mail addresses on their business cards." There is also some suggestion that, at least for some of the substantive uses of the Internet, state-based sites will reduce the reliance of states on centralized clearinghouses like the National Conference of State Legislatures (NCSL).

It is not clear whether technical advances like the Internet and laptop computers, which are also just coming into their own in terms of legislative use, will allow the citizen legislature to live longer or kill it more quickly. One senior staff was equivocal: "I don't know. I would like to say, and I guess if I had to really take a guess I would say, it allows it to live longer. But again, the fact of the matter is, dialing in from home or on the road, it's just more work at home. It makes you a legislator even when you're not in Raleigh." Another staffer was just as hesitant: "There are a lot of people who seem to think that [computers] are going to be the bright new tomorrow, and I don't think that's going to happen. . . . In this arena, I don't think we'll ever get away or should get away from direct personal contact."

5. Technical Information in a Political Environment

Technical information and analysis is obviously only one part of legislative decision making, and respondents in North Carolina often articulated fairly sophisticated strategies for synthesizing technical information with the political process. Although there was no apparent consensus over whether technical information and analysis is more or less important than the opinions of constituents, leadership, fellow legislators, or lobbyists, respondents articulated clearly how they used technical information in the legislative process. One legislator, to whom "the opinions of my constituents are far more important than the information I receive," used his constituents' opinions to "more clearly direct what information I need to respond to." But he still found technical information useful "to clarify any misinformation by the constituents." One example of the priority of his constituents was a large infrastructure project to which this legislator's constituents were unalterably opposed. With "no way to logically communicate out there to these folks . . . the staff could provide me with every possible analyzation with information that could be right, and it wouldn't make any difference in terms of the position I take." This legislator also uses technical information very strategically when it comes to dealing with fellow legislators. It is important, he says, "if it helps me convince my fellow legislators to vote for what I want them to vote for, [and it is not important in that], regardless of the analysis of the information, I will then have to make an adjustment in the ultimate results to accommodate what will persuade my fellow legislators to come around."

Some respondents distinguish between technical issues, such as environmental issues or revenue, and other issues, such as abortion. In some "emotional" issues, such as a recent conflict over foul air from industrial hog farms affecting residential areas, "you've got to balance the equities there between two very powerful groups of constituents, and the only way that is going to be done is to have very good and very accurate technical information."

As in most other states, the stage of the legislative process in which technical information and analysis from staff is most important is in drafting bills. The information was also important—again, as in other states—in helping legislators respond to legislation introduced by other legislators and in evaluating previously passed legislation or administrative actions. It was less important in voting or short- or long-term agenda setting. The responses for North Carolina, however, were all slightly higher in all categories than the average responses.

As in other legislatures, the biggest barrier to the provision of technical information and analysis in the legislative context seems to be time and time management in the context of the legislative calendar. As one staffer described, "I think time is a barrier in the legislative process, and we tend to move very, very fast. And when we're not moving, the problem is we don't know necessarily what we're going to move on next or when we're going to move on it. . . . And so it makes it a lot harder on us to put together a real good analysis for them, as detailed an analysis as we could." Related to this time-management barrier is the volume of work and other aspects of the citizen-legislature, such as not always being in good contact with the legislators. Part of the barrier of time also manifests itself in the desire by some staff for greater clerical support: "I could produce a more useful work product if I had adequate clerical resources."

The supply of technical information and analysis to staff was also mentioned as a barrier. "The problem you always have in giving technical advice, . . . remembering that we are a staff that is primarily lawyers, . . . is we're always going out of the house . . . for assistance. . . . The difficulty is to make sure you're getting objective and accurate advice." Another staffer is "aware of . . . a universe of potential information out there, and to do a truly authoritative, exhaustive search like you'd want to do in the perfect world would require a much larger time commitment than you normally have." One staffer, a bill drafter, also explained that access to technical information and analysis was harder to come by in bill drafting than in committee work, because drafters are more generalist and because drafting is more confidential.

The issue of whether technical information and analysis provided by staff helps to strengthen the legislature vis-à-vis the executive branch is somewhat muddled in North

Carolina because legislative-executive relations in the state are unique: North Carolina is the only state with no executive veto, and the legislature has historically felt at less of a disadvantage than legislatures elsewhere. So, the technical information and analysis "has given [the legislature] a useful tool . . . because it's good to have numbers to back you up, but numbers can always be interpreted in several ways. [That] it makes a more sophisticated legislative process, I believe very strongly. . . . So vis-à-vis the executive branch, it's been an extremely useful tool." But another senior staff member is more impressed with the increased independence of the legislature because "now the legislators feel like they really can hold their own [and] that they will wield their power to get the information they need."

There is a strong consensus among respondents that the technical information and analysis provided by staff has given the legislature more power with respect to lobbyists. Although respondents easily acknowledge that "lobbyists still wield considerable influence," one staff member claims to have "detected once in a while some resentment; [lobbyists] would rather not have a competing voice, and that's some measure of our effectiveness." Or as one legislator said, "Anything the lobbyist told me I would check back with the staff. I guess I always would feel whatever the staff told me, I could trust that better than anything else." Legislators rely on staff to arm them with questions for lobbyists as well, and staff suggest that their work with lobbyists "helps [the lobbyists] globalize their position [and see] how it all fits together."

One long-serving member summarized the situation in North Carolina well: "Without question the staff does provide greater avenues of technical assistance and that, I think, helps the member to be better informed and make better-informed decisions. That's not to say, [however, that a legislator's] judgmental decision is any better or worse."

6. Legislative Satisfaction

Respondents feel that the provision of technical information and analysis to the legislature is satisfactory, both from the LSO in particular and all sources in general, although there remain some distinct problems. Of primary importance (at least during the summer of 1994) seemed to be pressure to split the staff into House and Senate staff, although according to one staffer, the demand really seemed to be for personal staff and that found expression only in a proposal to split the staff. One legislator seemed to agree: "We just don't have enough staff to really help us, and especially during the session, they're so pushed. . . . It would be better if our staff was divided so the Senate had one staff and the House had another staff."

Also influencing the level of satisfaction was the recognition that, in the words of one staffer, "the more information they get that causes them to think more long term, the more information they need. And it's not so much the quantity. The biggest problem we have is getting around the quality of it." Similarly, one legislator commented, "We have volumes of information which are thrown at us. We do not have the time and, in many instances, the skill to analyze that data thoroughly."

One staffer suggests that, as generalists, the staff is competent to satisfy legislators who are themselves generalists or not technically inclined, but that staff is not expert enough to satisfy legislators who are themselves specialists.

7. Recommendations

Given the turmoil about the possibility of dividing the staff into House and Senate staffs, there are many opinions about staff structure. Respondents seemed divided about the wisdom of separating the staff, but some saw it as an opportunity for greater specialization on the part of committee staff in particular. In general, staff seemed hostile to the idea, but legislators seemed more in favor of it.

Some respondents also suggested the hiring of more technically trained staffers to work with committees and the creation of staff teams that could join specialists with generalists on specific bills. However, one long-time legislator suggested that extreme specialization leads to the possibility of staffers becoming policymakers; this legislator suggested preventing that by rotating staffers among committee assignments, a kind of term limit for staffers. Staffers would also like to see more lower-level research support staff to whom short tasks could be delegated in the hope of better meeting demands for timeliness and responsiveness.

Many respondents suggest that more intensive computer training is also needed, because there are significant differences among the skill levels of legislators and staff. Staffers also would like a better system for time management, especially around the beginning of sessions.

Legislators want better directions to access the information they suspect is available but difficult to get to. Better directories of both internal and external resources—"that if you want to know about this, this is who you call"—would be helpful. Legislators also want more "clear and concise" information, including, as one suggested, more face-to-face exchange of information with staff rather than printed information. One staffer also suggested that the legislature make more intensive use of expert public members of study commissions, and another suggested that committee assignments for legislators be held more constant to enable the development of legislative expertise, especially with turnover as high as it has been.

One staffer also would like to see a person or organization somewhere in state government "to get money for the state to do some of the initiatives they want to do" and to help communicate with other state interests such as the congressional delegation and the executive branch.

OHIO
STATE PROFILE

ENTERED UNION:
March 1, 1803 (17th admitted)[1]
LAND AREA:
40,953 sq. mi.; U.S. rank #35
POPULATION:
11.1 m (1993 est.)
U.S. rank #7
Density per sq. mi. 269[2]
DEMOGRAPHICS:
White 9.5 m; Black 1.2 m; Hispanic .1 m;
Asian .09 m; Native American .02 m
ECONOMY:
GSP: $222.1 b (1990); U.S. rank #7[3]
Agriculture (net farm income): U.S. rank #15
Manufacturing (total income): U.S. rank #3[4]
Mining (total income): U.S. rank #12
Per capita personal income: $19,688 (1993)[5]
Unemployment: 6.5% (1993)
Number of patents: 2,930 (1991); U.S. rank #8[6]
Number of SBIR awards: 635 (1983-91); U.S. rank #9
State technology development agency:
Ohio Science and Technology Council (provides
overall guidance), includes Thomas Edison Pro-
gram and Ohio Coal Development Office;
budget: FY '94: $27.5 m (Edison Program and Coal
Development Office)
EDUCATION:
High school graduation rate: 74%; U.S. rank #27[7]
State and local government expenditures for higher
education: FY '89-90 $3 b; U.S. rank #29
(by % of total expenditures)

Academic R&D expenditures: FY '91 $504 m;
     U.S. rank #9[6]
POLITICAL:
U.S. Senators: 1 Democrat, 1 Republican[5]
Congressional Representatives: 19 (6 Democrats, 13
     Republicans)
Governor—4-year term
     Since statehood: 64 (22 Democrats, 23 Republicans)
     Since 1970: 5 (2 Democrats, 3 Republicans)[8]
Current Governor: George Voinvovich (R), 2nd term
State Legislators: 132[1]
     State Senators: 33; 4-year term
          1994: 13 Democrats, 20 Republicans
          1995: 13 Democrats, 20 Republicans[9]
     State Representatives: 99; 2-year terms[1]
          1994: 53 Democrats, 46 Republicans
          1995: 43 Democrats, 56 Republicans[9]
     Length of session: no limitation[1]
     Annual salary: $42,426.90; no per diem living ex-
          penses; Senate president receives an additional
          $23,706.83/year; Senate president pro tem an
          additional $17,913.80/year; House Speaker an
          additional $23,706.83/year
State budget: FY '93 $31.6 b; FY '92 $30.4 b;
     FY '91 $27.8 b[10]
Legislative budget: FY '92 $33.1 m[11]
Total staff: 524; U.S. rank #21[12]

---

[1] CSG Book of the States, 1994-1995.
[2] World Almanac, 1995.
[3] State Rankings, 1994.
[4] Gale State Rankings Reporter, 1994.
[5] Almanac of the 50 States, 1995.
[6] Partnerships: A Compendium, 1995.
[7] CQ's State Fact Finder.

[8] Encyclopedia Americana, 1992.
[9] State Yellow Book, Spring 1995.
[10] U.S. Dept. of Commerce World Wide
     Web census page <www.doc.gov/
     CommerceHomePage.html>.
[11] State Government Finances, 1992.
[12] NCSL, 1988.

OHIO
STATE REPORT

Interview Profile

Legislature: 9 (3 senators, 2 representatives, 4 legislative
staff)
External: 3

Findings

1. Need for Science and Technology Policy Support

There was general agreement from legislators and
legislative staff alike that a need for legislative science and
technology support exists. "Absolutely, there is a need,"
declared a key staff official. "There are an overwhelming
number of science and technology issues which need
technical information and advice, but unfortunately we don't
have it. It is a glaring weakness. Your study is something
that needs to be done, and we need to learn from it and
make changes," he said. A senator agreed: "We have a wide
range of issues, all the way from defense conversion to the
impact of chickens on windshields. We are struggling with
how to get this kind of technical information."

A legislative leader of the House said that at the top of the
agenda are low-level radioactive waste disposal and telecommunications, "but we also need more information on
distance learning and whether we should rewire every
school. I'm not sure that we are ready. I'm not sure that we
understand what's involved. The infrastructure is not in
place. It cannot be done by a quick fix," she explained. In

terms of low-level nuclear waste, a senator asked, "How are legislators to know what are the dangerous agents? How do we deal with them? Where do we find waste disposal sites? What are the criteria for selecting them?" In reference to tax information, a committee chair said, "We are basing decisions on things that happened forty or fifty years ago when we were a manufacturing state. Now, we're moving onto technology and we need to have a lot of updated information."

Additional examples of science and technology issues before the Ohio legislature are telecommunications; removal of hazardous wastes from industrial sites; federal mandates, including Superfund and clean water; privatization of waste cleanup; recycled products by state agencies; energy conversion; auto emission inspection; infectious waste incineration; clean air permits; power line siting; sustainable agriculture; municipal water supplies; mammography equipment; HIV testing; lead screening; commercialization of technology; funding and evaluation of Edison Technology Centers; administrative services agreement on standards; means to further improve the business climate in Ohio; questions about commercialization processes; banking and insurance issues; and the impact of technology on workers' compensation.

Respondents generally agreed that the need for technical policy support had increased over the past decade, primarily because of the growing importance of technology to the state economy, the increase in the complexity of issues before the legislature, and the need for educational reform. Ranked next were executive branch initiatives requiring legislative response and federal mandates requiring state implementation. Cited as less important were the end of the Cold War and the influence of lobbyists. Of least significance was competition from other states and abroad. An additional reason one respondent mentioned was that the "knowledge of citizens' groups has increased, and they are holding the legislators' feet to the fire."

In terms of the state economy, Ohio has been actively involved in developing technology as a cornerstone to its economy since the early 1980s. In 1983, Governor Richard Celeste created the Thomas Edison Program, which now includes nine Edison Technology Centers, a seed development fund, and technology incubators. In 1989, the state established the Ohio Science and Technology Commission, composed of industry, academic, and government leaders, to develop a science and technology policy for Ohio for the 1990s and beyond. Governor George Voinovich's strategy of improving the "climate of growth and development" has resulted in Ohio's being the state with the highest number of new and expanded corporate facilities.

This economic activity has been reflected in the legislature where many issues involving technology development and its requirement for improved education and training have increased the need for technical information and analysis. "We can't expect Ohio to move forward unless we have got an educated work force," said a key staff official. "Unfortunately there is not very great support for higher education among Ohioans in general. That has been shown by all the polls that we have done, so if you are going to get people to understand why it is important, you have to make that a priority."

Respondents deemed educational issues "very important," and a major educational reform bill for education sponsored by Senate President Stanley Aronoff had recently been enacted into law. It called for the creation of an educational management information system to gather the kind of information "we need to make decisions for the future and to introduce more accountability." The Senate had also increased the appropriations to higher education beyond requests of the Governor and the House of Representatives. "We get the last crack at the budgets and have been able to hold those increases in conference. I am pretty proud of that, and obviously that is a component of what your study is all about," declared a Senate staff member. The legislature has also been discussing the equalization of educational opportunity through the geographical distribution of information systems in order to facilitate distance learning. Respondents also mentioned retraining as particularly necessary, not only because of defense conversion but also because of technological changes worldwide.

Regarding executive branch science and technology initiatives requiring legislative response, a staff member said that this was probably true when Governor Celeste was in office and had "a science and technology advisor to help him work in that area." However, he thought it was less important under Governor Voinovich, "simply because he has been a very frugal administrator and has basically cut back the budget for his own office and I am not sure if they have an executive scientist."

2. Internal and External Sources of S&T Policy Support

Ohio has traditionally been a low-tax state, and spending for state government reflects this tradition. According to a 1992 National Conference of State Legislatures (NCSL) report, Ohio ranks 49th, ahead of only North Carolina, in total per capita expenditures for general state government and 47th in per capita spending for the legislature.

Internal Sources

The most important policy support mechanism identified was the Legislative Service Commission (LSC), a centralized, nonpartisan agency that serves both houses. The "professional backbone of the legislature," LSC is responsible for staffing committees, drafting legislation and amendments, preparing bill analyses, and doing nonpartisan, short- and long-term research in response to legislative requests. In 1993, LSC responded to 1,700 requests, drafted 2,500 bills, provided 1,300 analyses of bills, and prepared 35,000 resolutions and letters of commendation.

The commission has a staff of 55 professionals, 30–35 of whom are attorneys; the others have master's or doctoral degrees. A few have science backgrounds, "but are not hired for that purpose." In the late 1970s and early 1980s, LSC had a science and technology advisor on staff as part of the National Science Foundation's (NSF) State Science, Engineering and Technology program, but the position no longer exists. The staff is divided based on subject matter which match committee jurisdictions.

The primary committee dealing with science and technology is the Senate Economic Development, Technology and Aerospace Committee which, like all committees, is assigned one LSC staff member. "If technical legislation is referred to this committee, an effort will be made to become informed, but the committee does not have a large enough staff to include someone who is technically trained," explained a LSC official. However, they have 4–5 technically capable analysts who "know how to access the necessary information and/or who have become very knowledgeable after years of experience working on these issues." The chair of the committee, Senator Charles Horn, is recognized as the leader on science and technology issues in the legislature. He is both an attorney and an engineer, and "it is his personality that drives the issue in the Senate and there is no comparable person in the house," observed a respondent.

LSC is operated by the leadership of both chambers. There are seven senators and seven house members on the commission, and the leadership rotates every two years between the Senate president and the Speaker of the House. The commission appoints the director, who appoints the staff. The work of the LSC is always nonpartisan regardless of party control, and it does no constituent work. The budget is $6 million.

Under the administrative control of the LSC but functionally independent is the Legislative Budget Office. It is responsible for staffing the separate finance committees of the House and Senate, reviewing the executive budget, conducting fiscal studies of programs and revenue proposals, monitoring agency expenditures, drafting fiscal notes, and providing liaison to the four partisan caucuses. Its budget is approximately $700,000 with a total staff of 34. Most professional staff hold master's degrees and two have doctorates, "although doctorates are not necessary or even possibly a positive requirement," commented a staff member. The staff are primarily economists who were cited by one legislator for "providing very important tax information on determining legislation," and for their analysis of the fiscal impacts of long-term health care. "However, we are not equipped to respond to overall science and technology issues," explained staff members.

Another important source of policy support is the majority and minority caucus partisan staff who "are very important in researching issues for more in-depth and politically sensitive responses," said a legislator. The caucus staff "help their own members formulate policy, develop legislation, and get it passed," explained a caucus official. The staff is roughly proportionate to the size of the legislative membership. In the Senate, for example, the Republican Senate Caucus had 15 staff (13 professionals and 2 support persons) and the Democratic Caucus about 8 or 9. The minority is allowed to do its own staff hiring but staff can be removed by the CEO of the Senate "if they are doing a bad job." Partisan caucus staffs do not work across party lines. Caucus staff who are assigned to do policy research and analysis have no specific S&T expertise. "We don't have any technically trained people per se on our caucus staffs. The closest we get would be our research budget people who are assigned to the caucuses, and none of them are scientists," said the official. Having spent three years as an undergraduate in physics, this official commented that he is "the closest thing to a scientist that we have here" and that his academic background and legislative experience had convinced him that technical expertise was "something we need more of."

Legislators viewed other technically trained legislators as very important sources of information and advice. For example, Senator Horn, who represents the district that includes Wright-Patterson Air Force Base in Dayton, is "the guy that people talk to on science and technology." As part of his mentor role, he has invited the whole legislature to tour Wright-Patterson and become acquainted with its activities.

Personal staff is also important. "To the extent that technical policy support is done at all, a legislator's personal staff is the real key," observed a staff official. "Unfortunately, I don't think a lot of them are really tuned in to that. And they are really overwhelmed by constituent work and work-a-day realities of life here. Having only one staff person and a secretary for a senator with a 300,000-person district is just unbelievable. But you get a good aide who has an interest in technical issues, they can be extraordinarily important," he said. A senator agreed that his personal staff was the best source for getting information from public interest seminars, conferences, NCSL, and national media, as well as alerting him to the political ramifications of science and technology issues. Personal staff, however, are generally not technically trained. "They are barely paid and not expert in anything."

External Sources

The most important external resources in Ohio were the executive branch, state universities, NCSL, and personal contacts. Next in importance were trade association reports, lobbyists, and private universities. Least important were federal agencies with the exception of Wright-Patterson, and electronic networks. Some respondents also mentioned the private sector as an additional important resource.

Since the legislature does not have extensive technical expertise of its own, it is not surprising that it relies on the executive branch for support. Mentioned as particularly helpful to legislators were the Department of Development, the state EPA, the Thomas Edison Program, the Governor's Science and Technology Council, and the Public Utilities Commission. "I think that most executive agencies, not all but most, have been pretty good at providing information regardless of party. Now it might take longer to get it if you are in the minority, because initially they might let some of their own people go first, but I think they have been pretty evenhanded," said a staff official. A senator observed that "there is a good relationship with the executive branch. It is a good balance with neither dominating the other."

Respondents ranked state universities and colleges equally with the executive branch, and also mentioned private academic institutions, such as Case Western University and the University of Dayton as sources. The role of universities is a relatively recent development. "In 1977," explained a long-term legislative staff official, "there probably were only one or two state institutions that really understood the importance of working with the legislature on anything. It is amazing since they are the state universities and this is the state legislature and that is where their money comes from. But around that time, both the president of Ohio University, Charlie King, who is just stepping down after 18 years as president, and the previous president of Ohio State University, Ed Jennings, and his successor, really took the relationship between the universities and the legislature to the next level. They have come down here and testified before committees. They have also worked with members individually to explain to them what the needs for higher education really are. And they have tried to work out a relationship with the administration that allows them to do more in the way of research and to help the legislature out with its programs."

Respondents also mentioned the Thomas Edison Centers located at universities around the state, as useful sources of technical information for those legislators who are familiar with them—estimated to be less than 50 percent of members of the legislature. Ohio created these centers to be on the cutting edge of science and technology research. However, there is no clearinghouse function to disseminate information, and respondents stated that the centers vary in responsiveness. Another legislator commented on working with the Technology Research Institute at the University of Dayton and the technicians at Wright-Patterson Air Force

Base. "We have a contract with Wright-Patterson to help us with the windshield problem. We are learning how to work together, but it isn't easy. We need to learn what each institution does best."

Several respondents recognized lobbyists as "very powerful in Ohio." However, respondents generally agreed that information from lobbyists needed verification by the LSC and/or the LBO. A staff official made a distinction between the "old-time lobbyists," whose knowledge on technical issues is "probably not as sophisticated as it should be, and independent, contract lobbyists, who are a lot brighter and more aggressive. Rather than trying to become masters of the issues themselves, they will bring in a spokesman from the affected industry or group and let them provide the information. There are about a half dozen of these contract lobbyists, and I think they are becoming more important."

Additional useful sources of policy support are trade associations, NCSL, and the Council of State Governments (CSG) and, depending on the legislator, individual personal contacts, particularly at Wright-Patterson Air Force Base and private industry such as Battelle and Xerox. Use of electronic networks is still "in its infancy," but respondents predicted that as legislators and their staffs became more comfortable with them, their significance as a source of technical information would grow.

3. Characteristics of Useful S&T Policy Support

Legislators agreed that useful policy support on technical issues has to be supplied by a familiar source. It has to be easily accessible, accurate, credible, presented in a useful format in nontechnical language, nonpartisan, and available in a timely fashion to meet legislative needs. The "comfort level has to be high," said one legislator. Another legislator identified "quick responses" as another top priority. Respondents cited the LSC and LBO as generally meeting these standards, although they rated timeliness a little lower than the other criteria. In terms of in-depth analysis, external sources, such as state universities and Thomas Edison Centers were mentioned as providing useful technical policy support. "It is usually not possible to find in-depth analysis and quick turnaround responses from the same source," said a legislator.

Respondents also cited partisan caucus staff for their accessibility and credibility, particularly their efforts to maintain accuracy on technical issues in spite of their partisan role. "We certainly wouldn't put anything out there that was not factually correct. That is a prescription for losing, maybe not in the short run, but certainly in the long run. We wouldn't have lasted as long as we have if we had done that, so I would say that in terms of accuracy, we are very good," said a caucus staff member.

4. Legislative Use of Technology

Centralized staff agencies are computerized and linked to databases through services such as Lexis/Nexis, Legisnet, On-line, Ohio Link, Dialogue, and the Internet. Computer use by legislators, however, is minimal, and a staff member estimated at the time of the interviews that "only 3 out of 132 legislators have any computer capability." The Senate was in the process of creating an interconnected computer system and providing e-mail, with the expectation that legislators would have their own information system in the next few years. Respondents mentioned that the legislature has not been using the Ohio Data Network, which links state agencies, libraries, universities, and schools and provides access to the Internet. "Although they should be using it, they don't," said an administration official. "It is important that they become involved and learn about existing technologies and are trained in their use."

Legislative staff have used computers on the controversial issue of redistricting. In 1990, for the first time, the State Reapportionment Board used computer resources to map districts and "to do it right and to allow us to withstand board challenges." First, it created a data base that merged census data and the election data by ward and precincts. The Board decided instead of "hiring an out-of-state vendor to come in and do it, they would split the job between two of our state universities, Ohio U and Cleveland State." Funded by a $800,000 appropriation, the institutions bought the necessary hardware and software and trained their graduate students in geographic information systems. "And now we have two of the best programs in the country," declared a staff official.

5. Technical Information in a Political Environment

In response to questions about the importance of technical information in the legislative decision-making process, legislators indicated that the most important stages were bill drafting, evaluating the impact of enacted legislation or administrative action, and providing information to assist in deciding how to vote, but "obviously not how to vote [since] staff are very careful not to respond [to such queries]." Less important were responding to legislation filed by others and deciding what issues to focus on during the current or next session.

Caucus staff responses indicated a greater involvement in deciding future issues. "We anticipate two years ahead," a key caucus official said, "and with term limits coming in the year 2000, the staff will be even more important in this as well as the other stages of the policymaking process." He explained that because the margin of party control in the Senate has been relatively close and elections occur every two years, he tries to anticipate the most important issues during this two-year period, such as economic development, education, and health care. "Part of what each side is trying to do is create a legislative agenda that they can go to the voters on and say, 'Here are our programs.' It is not like what the term 'partisanship' in an election contest means, where basically you are out there kicking the other guys in the butt or something like that. This is part of the essence of the legislative process, which is to formulate policy choices for the voters. So, I would say the information that we provide is, to the best of our ability, 100 percent accurate." Another key staff official agreed that term limits will have a major impact on the legislature, requiring staff to play a bigger role in preserving the institutional memory. "I don't know which way it will go—either the nonpartisan staff will become very important or the partisan staff will become very important."

Respondents saw technical information as only one of many factors in political decision making. Opinions of constituents can play an important role, especially "if they are enlightened," said a legislator, "but you still have to inquire into the background of their opinions." He saw his role as educator as well as representative and explained that "generally we go on the philosophy that you are elected to use your best judgment. We take the time to educate the constituents and do not base decisions on political nose-counting." Another legislator declared that the problem with constituent opinion was that "on only five percent of the votes do I really know what my constituents think, so 95 percent of my votes are based on my knowledge." A staff member concurred that it was hard to reach constituents, especially in senatorial districts with populations of 330,000 each, where "TV costs too much money." Staff also observed that knowledgeable constituents are "less politically important than those with political clout" and that "all the rational arguments may not be very important." On low-level radioactive wastes, for example, "often facts don't matter or turn out not to be true."

In terms of the relative value of the opinions of other legislators and legislative leadership versus technical policy support, respondents generally agreed that colleagues' support was important, but that technical information could be overriding, especially since "the legislature is often misinformed," said a legislator. Respondents credited technical policy support, when available, with giving more power to the legislature in dealing with lobbyists. "The problem," explained a caucus official, "is we don't have the staff to independently generate our own information. That is one of the things that is hard to explain to people when they talk about keeping taxes down and, at the same time, they bitch about special interests and how powerful they are. Well, if we don't have the ability to generate our own research, then we have to depend on other people," he said. In terms of power relative to the executive branch, some thought that internal resources had increased the legislature's independence, but one respondent observed that "most of the power is in the hands of the governor. Proactive mechanisms in the legislature are almost nonexistent."

6. Legislative Satisfaction

In general, respondents agreed that there was need for improvement in providing technical policy support to legislators. "Parts are satisfactory, but legislators need to improve their access to technical information," said a senator. "LSC has good technical people and some have become very effective, but there's always room for improvement." Other legislators' comments ranged from "pretty satisfied" to "it's pretty weak." A key staff member explained,

> There are an overwhelming number of science and technology issues which need technical information and advice, but unfortunately we don't have it. We have traditionally been a very low-tax state and according to NCSL, the 49th or 50th in per capita spending on the legislature. The consequence of that is that while we have some very excellent staff members, we don't have nearly as many as we should have. In the legislature here, all we had for ten years was one scientific person, and now we have none. It is a glaring weakness.

Other staff members commented that, in their opinion, "Legislators are satisfied, but they need more technical information and analysis and don't know they need it. They don't know what they don't know."

7. Recommendations

Legislative Service Commission/Legislative Budget Office

Legislators and staff recommended that the Legislative Service Commission "could use more scientific and technology expertise." It was their opinion that additional personnel was needed to be able to evaluate the science and technology content of bills before they are passed and to strengthen LSC's audit and oversight function on administrative actions after passage. This was seen as particularly important with the coming of term limits in 2000, because "this will reduce the effectiveness of legislators and lobbyists will take over on technical issues if the staffs are not given more resources."

A legislator specifically recommended that LSC improve its data collection and management. "They have delays in gathering data from outside sources and don't seem to have a good central source. They need a more refined database to supply them with information from other states and local governments and cities. They need more management of the data." Another legislator recommended that LSC prepare an issue directory, "so that legislators know where they can go on different issues. It would be nice if they had a directory of every issue from A to Z which were assigned to a particular staff person." A legislator also suggested that they increase their computer capability. "I think they should be on-line," he said. "They should have more computers. The Legislative Budget Office should do more cost-benefit analyses. Now they don't anticipate the growth, only the losses."

While there was general agreement that more scientific expertise was needed, staff cautioned that because of the wide range of technical issues only one technically trained staff person "would be worse than none." A legislator made the similar observation that a single technical advisor might not be very useful, since "today's expert can be tomorrow's has-been." Another question raised was that while there was need for additional research on science and technology issues, it would be difficult to explain the need without an immediate crisis. "So with our penny-wise, pound-foolish policy, we get behind in the learning curve," said a staff official. However, there was a comment that "now with the state budget looking better, it might be a good time for LSC director Bob Shapiro to ask for additional resources. He has enough credibility. If there are going to be more technical resources, LSC would be a good place to locate it."

Legislative Science and Technology Committee

There was little support for creating a new science and technology standing committee. Rather, respondents recommended that the existing Committee on Economic Development, Aerospace and Technology receive additional support. "It is difficult to establish new committees," said a key Senate staff member. "There are already too many committees for the 33 senators, who now serve on four committees as it is. And who are you going to put on a new S&T committee? It is not easy to find people with a science and technology background. It would be much easier to strengthen Senator Horn's committee by giving him additional personal, partisan staff and increasing the nonpartisan LSC staff with technical expertise," he recommended.

Other legislators and staff supported this recommendation, although some respondents mentioned that an advantage of a legislative committee devoted to science and technology would be an undiluted focus on technical issues, as is not now the case. A science and technology committee could travel around the state, hold hearings, talk to editorial boards, and explain and sell issues to voters. The likelihood of strengthening the present committee was not considered high, however. "Politically, technology development is not as appealing as other more short-term projects, even if it will be more productive in the long run," explained a legislator. However, changes might be made if more attention "could be paid to identifying the need." He suggested that "perhaps the

Kennedy School project will be the beginning of this process."

Central Legislative Clearinghouse

A state representative recommended creating a central clearinghouse of technical information with direct access for legislators. "The House is just starting to get computers, and we need to be sure that we are coordinating technological equipment," he said. The House leadership just purchased a new system this year and found that it was not compatible or transferrable. A new legislative arm could help make these decisions on how the legislature should use technology. The representative also said that the legislature needs easier accessibility to information on the federal level. "We get some from NCSL but we need more feedback, especially on federal mandates that states are required to implement." A senator agreed that it would be helpful to have "one specific place to call."

Legislative-University Partnership

A long-time staff member recommended the creation of a new partnership between the universities and the legislature. Ohio is "building on its academic strengths by creating selective world-class technology centers around the state. In order to do this, the relationship between universities and the state legislature needs nurturing. We are beginning to see those ties built district by district, and I think it is something that will continue." It was his belief that these ties will not only help the academic institutions provide education and training, but will also enable them to offer technical expertise to the legislature in deciding on the best public policies for the state.

Executive Branch

A legislative leader recommended that the legislature strengthen its ties to the Governor's Science and Technology Council, which was created to provide guidance to the state on technical issues. Since the interviews, a liaison relationship between the Governor's Council and the Legislative Service Commission has been formally established through a memorandum of understanding. As part of its outreach program, the council is considering the publication of a regular science and technology newsletter, which will be available to the legislature.

Midwestern Technology Network

A senator recommended that Ohio support the development of a consortium of midwestern universities located at Wright-Patterson Air Force Base to utilize its research facilities, provide advanced degree instruction and applied technology training for graduate students, and create a technology network center to commercialize Wright-Patterson technology. Such a consortium could also serve as a resource to midwestern state legislatures in accessing technical information.

WISCONSIN
STATE PROFILE

ENTERED UNION:
May 29, 1848 (30th admitted)[1]
LAND AREA:
54,314 sq. mi.; U.S. rank #25
POPULATION:
5 m (1993 est.)
U.S. rank #18
Density per sq. mi. 92[2]
DEMOGRAPHIC:
White 4.5 m; Black .2 m; Hispanic .09 m;
Asian .05 m; Native American .04 m
ECONOMY:
GSP: $1 b (1990); U.S. rank #18[3]
Agriculture (net farm income): U.S. rank #23
Manufacturing (total income): U.S. rank #10[4]
Mining (total income): U.S. rank #37
Per capita personal income: $19,811 (1993)[5]
Unemployment: 4.7% (1993)
Number of patents: 1,265 (1991); U.S. rank #3[6]
Number of SBIR awards: 106 (1983-91); U.S. rank #27
State technology development agency:
Department of Development (several programs are
housed in various units); budget: FY '94 $1.6 m
EDUCATION:
High school graduation rate: 84.2%; U.S. rank #7[7]
State and local government expenditure for higher
education: $1.9 b (1989-90); U.S. rank #15
(% of total expenditures)

Academic R&D expenditures: FY '91 $388 m;
    U.S. rank #13[6]

POLITICAL:

U.S. Senators: 2 Democrats[5]

Congressional Representatives: 9 (3 Democrats,
    6 Republicans)

Governor—4-year term
    Since statehood: 41 (9 Democrats, 29 Republicans)
    Since 1970: 6 (3 Democrats, 3 Republicans)[8]
    Current Governor: Tommy Thompson (R), 2nd term

State Legislators: 132[1]
    State Senators: 33; 4-year term
        1994: 16 Democrats, 17 Republicans
        1995: 16 Democrats, 17 Republicans[19]
    State Assemblymen: 99; 2-year term
        1994: 52 Democrats, 47 Republicans
        1995: 48 Democrats, 51 Republicans
    Length of session: no limitation
    Annual salary: $35,070; per diem living expenses
        $75; Assembly Speaker receives an additional
        $25/month

State budget: FY '93 $14.6 b; FY '92 $13.6 b;
    FY '91 $12.4 b[10]

Legislative budget: FY '92 40.7 m[11]

Total staff: 688; U.S. rank #14[12]

[1] *CSG Book of the States,* 1994-1995.
[2] *World Almanac,* 1995.
[3] *State Rankings,* 1994.
[4] *Gale State Rankings Reporter ,* 1994.
[5] *Almanac of the 50 States,* 1995.
[6] *Partnership: A Compendium,* 1995.
[7] *CQ's State Fact Finder,* 1993.

[8] *Encyclopedia Americana,* 1992.
[9] *State Yellow Book,* Spring 1995.
[10] U.S. Dept. of Commerce World Wide
    Web census page <www.doc.gov/
    CommerceHomePage.html>.
[11] *State Government Finances,* 1992.
[12] NCSL, 1988.

WISCONSIN
STATE REPORT

Interview Profile

Legislature: 13 (4 representatives, 9 legislative staff)
External: 2

Findings

1. Need for Science and Technology Policy Support

There was unanimous agreement among respondents that legislators need science and technology policy support. "Clearly, there is a need for a synthesizing role, and a digestive role because there is no shortage of information out there, be it from interest groups or other organizations," said a senior staff member, "and as more legislatures are wired into advanced information systems, there will be even more access to unlimited sources of information." As one example, during the floor debate on pesticide regulation, a senator held up a bibliography of about 60 studies on the issue for which there was no summary of findings and, therefore, no way to utilize the information.

Other examples of science and technology issues before the legislature included: information technology and its impact on privacy and other constitutional rights; the information superhighway; interactive gambling; environmental protection; hazardous materials handling; high-level nuclear waste disposal; air pollution; Federal Clean Air Act implementation; ozone layer depletion; electromagnetic fields

(EMF); recycling; mining laws; renewable and alternative energies; utilities regulation and deregulation; biotechnology; genetically engineered organisms; bovine growth hormone (bovine somatotropin—BST); biological diversity; transportation; and state planning.

Respondents generally agreed that the need for technical policy support had increased over the past decade and cited as the most important reasons the complexity of issues and the importance of technology to the state economy. "Biotechnology is nothing that my father, when he was in government, ever dreamed of, whereas now it is a big deal," said a legislator. They also identified telecommunications as a complex new technology of great importance to the economy of the state.

Next in importance was the influence of lobbyists and interest groups, "reflecting the increase in interest in science and technology issues by the public." Advocacy groups are increasingly going to the legislature with their concerns about dealing with the "sins of the past" and also because "it is cheaper to settle differences through the legislature instead of lobbying the executive branch or going to court." Legislators require technical knowledge not only to be able to vote properly but also "to keep these groups honest," commented a staff member.

Respondents also ranked highly the use of technology for educational reform, followed closely by state implementation of federal mandates. Of lesser importance were state and international competition and responding to executive branch initiatives, although recently "the legislature has gotten more involved in what used to be primarily executive branch functions, including science and technology policy. As time has gone by, it has assumed more oversight and greater professional responsibility." Reflecting the state's lack of defense facilities, the end of the Cold War has played little or no role in increasing the need for technical policy support.

2. Internal and External Sources of S&T Policy Support

Wisconsin has a long tradition of progressive government going back to the beginning of the century under the leadership of Governor Robert LaFollette. The Progressives believed in "democracy, the educated citizen, and reform," and this tradition carries on today in a political environment which has been characterized in a recent book by Tom Loftus, former Speaker of the House, as the "politics of fair play."

At the turn of the century, the progressive reform movement recognized that legislators needed policy support in order to be able to represent the people and counteract the influence of special interests. In 1901, Wisconsin established the first legislative reference bureau in the nation to provide professional services, such as research and bill drafting, to all legislators and "to bring democracy into the legislative branch. So, while our agency is strictly nonpartisan, our creation and existence was very much a political statement," explained a bureau official. "It means that a representative who is an auto worker on the assembly line who comes up here will get just as good services as a rich businessman or some lawyer, somebody with a lot of education or somebody with access to the special interest groups." In 1914, LaFollette, then a U.S. senator, created the Congressional Research Service (CRS) based on the Wisconsin model and, after almost a century, both agencies are still providing support services to members of their respective legislative bodies.

Internal Sources

Wisconsin now provides its 132 legislators (33 Senate; 99 Assembly) with three primary nonpartisan professional staff offices to provide policy support services. There is "great reliance on these staffs." In the opinion of a staff director, nonpartisanship is one of the main reasons for their credibility.

> Leaders of both houses and both parties have done whatever they can to insure that nonpartisanship or bipartisanship survives. We know that it is in neither of our interests if we move to a partisan bent on any subjects, because once we are there, we can never get ourselves back. It also means we are able to hire good people who don't feel coerced into a partisan position, don't feel coerced into fund raising, don't feel coerced into campaigns, all of the things that we are not interested in doing. But, in fact, we are able to hire people who are interested in government and public policy and in seeing that issues are handled with professional caring.

The central agency that provides the primary source of science and technical policy support to legislators is the Legislative Council. Co-chaired by a Senate and an Assembly member, its 22-member committee is evenly balanced between the houses and parties. The staff is comprised of 18 lawyers and two people with technical backgrounds, including the staff scientist who has a master's degree in chemical engineering and a doctorate in environmental studies. Together with the staff scientist, attorneys with long legislative council careers have developed a "tremendous amount of scientific expertise," said a committee chair. Compensation ranges from $36,000 to over $85,000, which "allows this to be a career option rather than just passing through, as in many other states," stated a staff member. Recognizing the importance of qualified, professional staff, they are generally paid more than legislators, who all receive the same amount, including the Speaker. The council's annual budget for 1994 fiscal year was $2,159,000.

Council staff provide policy support to legislators by staffing all 48 standing committees except finance and retirement, interpreting and evaluating materials from advocacy groups and lobbyists, and responding to legislative requests. They also staff the Legislative Council study committees that are set up during the interim in the second year of the biennium to examine topics that require in-depth analysis and from which legislation often results. The study committees, the membership of which is divided between legislators and the public, have a great deal of credibility. "They tend to set the legislative agenda," explained a state representative. Legislative Council staff are permitted to sit next to the chairs during committee hearings and give advice. Their reports on hearings often include policy recommendations. At the time of the interviews, the staff scientist was developing legislation on information systems policy based on extensive research for a legislative study committee. A legislator, when asked about her use of the staff of the Legislative Council, said they "make it possible for me to excel."

The second of the three legislative service agencies is the Legislative Fiscal Bureau. It serves both chambers and both parties, and the Joint Committee on Legislative Organizations appoints the director. The Fiscal Bureau has a staff of 31 professionals, including two doctorates, two attorneys, and master's degrees in public policy, public administration, and economics. Compensation and budget levels are similar to those of the Legislative Council. Their mission is "to provide whatever fiscal and policy information and analysis that the legislature either individually or as a body asks us to provide to them in the context of their legislative responsibilities," said a bureau official. "Our analysts are encouraged to understand programs. How do the programs work? How many clients are served? What are the policy implications? What is the government trying to do? Who manages them? How do we manage them? Then we fix the dollars after we understand that."

The Fiscal Bureau is highly regarded in Wisconsin. A legislator observed, "Their people are really good. They deal with fiscal issues, and they provide information on the way the situation is now and a brief history of what has been done. They will say here are some possible alternatives that you might find to reach your goal of doing whatever it is that you first asked them for and here are the consequences of each of those alternatives. I mean they are just so good."

A major part of the work of the Fiscal Bureau is to review any bill that affects revenues or expenditures for the legislative finance committee. It works cooperatively with the Legislative Council on reviewing these bills, including those involving science and technology issues. Many legislators, including the Speaker, cited the importance of the Fiscal Bureau as part of the legislative team that provides technical support to the Wisconsin legislature.

The third part of the policy support team is the Legislative Reference Bureau, which is divided into the legal bill-drafting department and the reference and library section. In bill drafting, there are 24 professionals who draft the final versions of all bills, including those sent over from the Legislative Council, prepare amendments and substitutes, and produce the session law volume of all legislation enacted annually and a drafting manual every two years. They write memoranda, letters of legal opinion and ad hoc opinion, and attend committee meetings, if requested, in cooperation with the Legislative Council staff.

Compensation levels are similar to the other two service agencies with whom they work very closely. Particularly "on really tough, very politically charged issues where responses are demanded in a very short time, a Legislative Council attorney, a Fiscal Bureau analyst, and an attorney from the Reference Bureau will work together," said a Reference Bureau official. "To be able to accomplish it, you need to do away with all of your egos very quickly and sit down and divvy up the work load and do it. And that interaction can be a very big plus. You get somebody that is as smart as you are, who knows a lot in their area and who is boned up on it, and you are not talking to someone that doesn't know anything. People on my staff say that it is one of their most rewarding experiences." He explained further that "in some states, it is the same attorney who would draft the bill and would staff the committee, so you have one staffer who would have all the knowledge on that draft. I don't think in Wisconsin that the legislature would stand for that. It is kind of a check-and-balance system that really gives a lot of different information and keeps everybody on their toes."

The second part of the Legislative Reference Bureau is the reference and library section. Twelve professionals respond to approximately 2,000 requests per month for information from the legislature, other government members, and the public. The staff prepare short, objective informational briefs and longer information bulletins. "We will present both sides of the issue, or all sides of the issue as best we can identify them, but we will never make a policy recommendation, because that isn't our role," said a staff member. A large reference library containing both historical and technical information is available to support staff research. Typically, a brief does not go into much technical detail other than defining what the problem is. Bulletins go into much greater detail on issues of wide applicability and ideally attempt to anticipate an issue before it becomes a full-fledged policy debate. They maintain a clipping service and also prepare the *Wisconsin Blue Book*, a biennial publication concerning Wisconsin state government.

Many of the staff have been at the library for a long period of time and have built up specialties and expertise which make it possible for them to translate technical information into nontechnical language. However, in terms of keeping abreast of science and technology issues, although there is a good deal of in-house training and staff are able to take courses, a library official said that "there is only so much you can do with that. You are not going to train an historian to be a chemist by sending him or her to a seminar on recent advances in chemical engineering or whatever, so there are limits to what you can do."

In general, personal staff are not used directly as sources of technical information but more as liaisons to the extensively used legislative service bureaus. Legislators themselves were not seen as a major resource. "It really is a mixed bag," said a personal staff member, "especially in the science and technology area. We have what I would call extremists on both sides of an issue, and some legislators do consult them. It depends on where they are coming from, but, generally, legislators depend on staff more."

External Sources

In general, respondents did not rank external resources for technical policy support very highly, perhaps because the internal sources fill the need. However, in response to survey questions, they cited universities, executive branch agencies, and lobbyists among the most useful.

It is interesting and somewhat surprising that the Wisconsin Idea, which historically stood for the commitment of the land-grant university to solve public sector problems, seems no longer to exist. While useful personal contacts between individual faculty members and legislators and central staff remain, "to the extent that academic institutions have gotten involved in supplying policy support to legislatures, it is pretty poor," was the opinion of a key state legislator. And yet only a mile-long street separates the state capitol and the main campus, many legislators are university graduates, and public service is part of the university charter. Respondents mentioned that academia is often not sufficiently aware of legislative needs and only interested in "their wants."

The relationship between the executive branch and the legislature is affected by the much-used governor's item veto. Considered the strongest in the country, the governor has the power to veto bills in whole or in part, including words or numbers in bills which contain an appropriation. This veto power has resulted in a "weakened legislature," according to many of those interviewed. "We have about the weakest legislature in the country in Wisconsin, and the bureaucrats generally just laugh at us. They see us, in my view, as an impediment to the smooth operation of government," stated a long-term legislator. However, some respondents cited their use of state agencies. For example, drafts of reports prepared by the Fiscal Bureau, especially on technical issues such as the Clean Water Act or the Clean Air Act, were circulated to the state agencies for their comment. "People are very good about doing that. They know we are going to get a lot of play on these, and so it's good for us and good for them and it helps us keep up with their programs."

An aide to a Republican senator finds state agencies very helpful because "they know how the legislature functions and so they know how necessary it is to get the information quickly, and it is often in their best interest to do so. I think that they also appreciate what types of time constraints the legislature faces so they do not too often overwhelm either in terms of the technical nature of the information or just the quantity. They will sometimes provide good executive summaries of two- or three-page articles on some problem or some proposed solution."

A Democratic legislator also uses executive agencies but "always with a grain of salt. We get the information from them, but you have to remember where it is coming from. They are extremely political," she said. "Yes, we rely on them, but we have to verify their information through other sources," explained a senator's aide.

Respondents mentioned lobbyists as important sources of technical information almost on a par with universities and executive agencies. Perhaps because they are so strictly regulated and must operate in an environment of high political standards, lobbyists were referred to with considerable respect. A legislator commented that she finds lobbyists "very helpful, granted that they have an agenda of their own." An aide commented that "we have a pretty good personal knowledge of the lobbyists and generally they are all pretty good. There are some lobbyists that just want to make points by getting things passed and building their businesses, and I would say we are extremely skeptical of them." A key staff official explained that he was "not a big fan of getting the lobbyists in here a lot. But when we do need assistance from lobbyists, we will directly call corporations or companies and talk to their technical people. Those are the people we are going to be talking to, not their political people."

Other external sources that legislators make some use of are the National Conference of State Legislatures (NCSL), the Council of State Governments (CSG), trade journals, and national news magazines. Ranked least useful were federal executive agencies and national electronic networks, such as the Internet, which at the time of the interviews were little used by legislators.

3. Characteristics of Useful S&T Policy Support

Respondents agreed that in order for it to be useful, S&T policy support must be credible, objective, accessible, concise, understandable, timely, and nonpartisan. Accessibility and objectivity were of key importance. "You can pick up the phone and ask the council a question and get an answer almost immediately," said a legislator. "Also they are really nonpolitical, and they do give pretty objective answers. If you delve into the political, they don't become political, but they can give you the political implications." Nonpartisan staff has a long tradition in Wisconsin. In 1901, the first director of the Legislative Reference Bureau stated that "given the choice between a partisan staff or no staff at all, take the later." He was convinced that information and advice must to be free from "partisan taint to be credible." That policy has prevailed to the present time among the central staffs.

A legislator explained the importance of understandable language. "Legislators like myself are not technicians, and some of the things we have to do get into language that scares legislators away. So they ignore the issue rather than have to grapple with DNA or megabytes or whatever, and as a result, it is very difficult to get them interested and involved in the issues," he said. A staff member agreed. "It's very difficult for someone to sit down and read a journal on, say, telecommunications, talking about all of the things that you could do, without any real focus on how policy affects that technology and how that policy is going to affect constituents. I think that oftentimes the presentation is too focused on the technical and not enough on the applications or policy."

A central staff member emphasized the importance of accessibility and timeliness. "The legislature is a reactive institution, and information has to be available easily. One of the reasons that lobbyists are so effective is because their information is very easily accessible," he said. To be useful, information must also be available on a timely basis. "This can be within ten minutes to three hours to two weeks," he continued. "If there are some problems in getting the information, you have to know the constraints that you are operating under, but legislators are reasonable people by and large."

4. Legislative Use of Technology

Central staff offices are computerized and have access to a variety of databases such as Internet and Lexis/Nexis. At the time of the interviews, computer use by legislators was minimal, a situation of extreme frustration for a computer-literate legislator who complained that he had been trying for one month to get the Wisconsin Legislative Information System (WILLIS) to hook up his computer so he could access data on his system. "Obviously, the state cannot afford to buy each new bell and whistle every time it comes along, but if they bought a computer system at the outset that allows expansion and flexibility, then you wouldn't have to spend a fortune. If something comes up, you just upgrade."

As more legislative offices go on-line, the central staff offices will not be the only "holders of the keys to access to advanced information system databases. Individual personal staff, caucus staff, as well as the library central service agency staff will all have access," said a key staff member. "However, the usefulness of this kind of information is going to vary," he explained. "Legislators are not just going to plug into some specialized research network on who knows what subject and just start understanding that literature and that discussion. But that typically is not what the legislators need anyway. They want the more distilled approach, and so it depends on where you go on the network and how critical and how central the information is to the policy debate."

At the time of the interviews, Wisconsin was putting considerable resources into updating its internal networking communications system, including connecting legislators' offices to an internal e-mail system. In 1995, the legislature went on-line through the Internet. Presently, the legislature is connected through the Department of Administration gopher server, but plans are to move to a legislative server in the future.

5. Technical Information in a Political Environment

A major question in the discussion of legislative science and technology policy support is how critical technical information is in the public policy debate. A technical legislative expert said, "Sometimes, it is in the forefront—for example, fluorocarbon ozone depletion, mercury in water, or public drinking water standards, or something similar—then the science is at the nub of the policy issue. But most of the time, science is just one of many factors in a wide constellation of factors."

Recognizing that it is only one of many factors, we asked when in the process of political decision making was technical information most useful. The legislators considered it most helpful during the time of bill drafting. In some cases, it was important in responding to legislation drafted by others and evaluating previously enacted legislation and administrative actions. It was not important in deciding how to vote or in determining issues for the current session. Those issues were more likely to be determined by executive branch initiatives or constituent interests. In terms of future sessions, respondents felt technical information might play more of a role either through the Council Interim study committees' or council staff's alerting legislators to impending technical issues.

Respondents mentioned that technical information was most helpful early in the decision-making process before political sides had been drawn. "I think science applied to an issue before it heats up can do some good. Once some of these other political considerations begin to play up, I think that science will get pushed out of the process," said a faculty member. He explained:

> On volatile issues such as the use of bovine growth hormones, technical expertise might never have much influence. You could get into a legislator's office and sit down and the legislator would look right at you and say, "I know this isn't a human health threat, but I have got to deal with farmers back home and I have to deal with mothers with young children who are concerned about this. Quite frankly, they don't believe your research, they don't believe the technology is harmless, and so all of your technology isn't helping me out of the difficult political situation in which I find myself." And so I think the politics of this issue drove it much harder than any of the science and technology that was there. In fact, the legislators didn't find science to be terribly useful to them as they wrestled with this problem with their constituents. Even though they did tell you "I believe your science," my folks don't believe it back home.

A faculty member graphically described the added problem of legislators coping with "science for hire":

> Legislators were put in difficult positions because some advocacy groups were very careless in how they used

science. They used science to scare the begeebers out of people in the state. You go down the list, cancer and x number of diseases were being associated with the potential use of bovine somatotropin (BST). It was almost a perversion of science. It is an interesting thing that is happening in science. Maybe it has always been there, but it is sort of a new wrinkle on "my lawyer can beat your lawyer." Now it is, "my scientist can beat your scientist." Ninety-five percent of the scientific community can come to consensus or even maybe 99.9 percent can come to consensus on something, and yet one scientist who has probably done little work or has no research published, nothing on this, can raise very serious charges. And so it just struck me in the BST thing that you can have such a body of scientific evidence on one side of it and it can be stood on its head.

A representative agreed that "under the pressure of politics," legislators generally view their constituents' opinions as more important than technical information, although he himself, because it is his field, would be more influenced by the science and then would try to educate his constituents to his point of view. Another legislator said that "it depended on who the constituent was and how much confidence I had in the constituent's knowledge." On the other hand, other respondents, particularly from central staff, felt that technical information strengthened the role of the legislature in relation to the executive branch and lobbyists.

The greatest barrier to providing legislators with technical information was seen as "the many competing demands for attention. Those who want to know will give you the time and get it, but by and large, if they aren't interested, you aren't going to force it on them," said a staff analyst. A legislative aide reported that when his senator wanted to get the attention of his colleagues on a pesticide bill, he printed the information on blaze orange paper so he could watch them reading it on the floor of the Senate. In terms of competence, one legislator said that one change he has seen during his tenure is that "more and more legislators are what I would call scientifically literate. They have grown up with these issues, and these terms are not foreign to them . . . although the interest level varies tremendously from legislator to legislator."

On the wider issue of technology and democracy, one legislator issued a strong warning about the threat of the information revolution eroding the liberties of the American people:

> It occurs in all these little ways, and the government sits here and pays little attention because each technology is sold on the basis of access or efficiency, or getting rid of fraud or ending speeding on our highways or making our neighborhoods safer. But all of those things in combination are a slippery slope which is sliding towards a technological hell. You know when you start to talk about this, you come across as a Luddite, that you are anti-technology, and I'm not. These technologies can do marvelous things to help people, to cure disease and save them time and effort and money. But they also have a major, major propensity for evil. And that part is generally overlooked by those whose simple desire for more and more money overwhelms their thoughts of protecting an individual's rights and privacy.

6. Legislative Satisfaction

Legislative satisfaction with technical support received from the central legislative service agencies was universally very high. Comments included "excellent," "very professional," "resourceful," "can trust them," and "scrupulously nonpartisan." Said one legislator, "I think they must get together every Monday morning and recite their nonpartisan oath. None of them have any kind of hidden agenda or push their own ideas." An indication of the confidence legislators have in the Legislative Council, for example, is that although the agency keeps detailed logs of its work, it has never once been asked for them. In terms of science and technology policy support, the legislators interviewed were highly complimentary, especially in regard to the staff scientist and the council attorneys with technical expertise. A legislative staff director commented that there are two sides to satisfaction, one from the legislative side and the other from the staff side. "Good legislators know how to use good staff. Fortunately, we have some very good legislators who want to be there, put in their time, and are able to lead their committees in debate."

The only suggestions for improvement from legislators were greater legislative availability and use of computer technology, which may already have been put in place, and restricting the influence of lobbyists on the council study committees. "Compared to other states, we are going to look very good. But if you compare us with when I started ten years ago, I think we have some real problems," commented a committee chair. "In Wisconsin, the Legislative Council process has been insulated from the political system, which is itself somewhat insulated from the special interests [and] the big money, but I fear the whole center is shifting."

In terms of outside resources, a legislator was less complimentary, particularly regarding technical support from the university. "The university has a tremendous number of people who deal with scientific issues," he said, "but the difficulty is that they are more likely to investigate Micronesia than problems here in Wisconsin. Basically, there is scorn for such activity. My understanding is that if something is pragmatic, it is less valued academically. In addition, there is the problem of science for hire, which makes it even more important that the in-house staff be technically trained so they can sort out what is fact and what isn't, and that is a very key issue." Another legislator observed that "one of the difficulties is that academics often have a problem coming to the point. They go off on a tangent that is either too wide or too narrow."

A faculty member agreed that in spite of Wisconsin's long tradition of a rich relationship of exchange of scientifically based information between the university and state government, "there is a feeling today that maybe things aren't working as well as they did at some earlier point. The Wisconsin Idea is a little bit tattered and worn out in the elbows. The academic reward system is not as much oriented towards public service as it once was. Scientific knowledge was once less questioned than it is today, and universities are beginning to be viewed as yet another advocacy group and don't hold quite the perch in the pecking order that they once did," he said. Nevertheless, he felt that the university has an obligation to improve their support to the legislature:

> There's a real feeling that those of us in the university haven't worked hard enough at sharing knowledge. Although the faculty has a good deal of expertise to apply, we don't apply it very well, very coherently, very effectively at the other end of the street. We have trouble understanding the legislative process, the pressures, the deadlines, the need not to mull something on and on, the need to come to a decision and to do it within a time frame that makes political sense to those you have elected to public office. We haven't been thoughtful enough about anticipating issues that are likely to be before the legislature and gotten our own people together to do adequate reviews of the scientific evidence that may relate to some of these issues. Because we haven't gotten together, we often speak with not one or two or three voices, but we speak with 30 different voices and eventually nobody downtown knows what we are talking about or whom to believe.

7. Recommendations

There is a high level of satisfaction with the technical information and analysis of Wisconsin legislative service agencies and, therefore, respondents made only a few recommendations.

S&T Literacy of Legislators

A member of the Assembly recommended that at the beginning of every session, there should be in-service, hands-on training for legislators on the use of technology. He also thought it important that the ethical implications of technology be part of the course. "You can get a lot of the technical expertise and that's fine, but you remember that while the Nazis were great technicians, they were a little short on ethics," he said.

In terms of encouraging scientists to run for the legislature, another member of the Assembly thought that scientific backgrounds (which he himself has) could be helpful but that the specialization that a doctorate requires results in narrowly defined areas of expertise. "What you really want is scientific literacy so that legislators feel comfortable with concepts and can understand basic scientific principles. I think that comes from 101-level science classes as an undergraduate and perhaps from reading even what is available at newsstands, so a legislator can separate what's reasonable from what's unreasonable."

Central/Personal Staff

One legislator commented that as legislative technical issues become more and more complex, the staff scientist might become "overwhelmed" and the time might come when the legislature might feel a need for "technically trained personal staff like Congress, but not at present." Staff agreed that while it was impossible for one person to be an expert on all technical issues, technical training and long experience with issues made it possible to understand basic scientific principles and technical terminology well enough to serve as a translator for legislators. A senior legislative staffer felt that more critical than technical credentials were research and analytical skills and the ability to think independently. As he explained:

Maybe the best qualification is to take all of the 101 courses, across the board, a wide spectrum. We have had interns here that have had specialized training and came out of a Ph.D. program, and they have been disappointed and frustrated because there are very few issues that typically fit neat and tidy into any one discipline. If you're the Congressional Research Service, maybe you can afford that specialization, but at the state level, especially a state the size of Wisconsin, we can't afford that large a staff. The other important caveat is that lots of times the science is not the center point of the public controversy; it is a contributing actor that has only a supporting role.

S&T Legislative Committee

There is little support for a separate science and technology committee; the general opinion was that technical issues covered so many areas, they should be dealt with by the subject committees, for example, the natural resources, environment, energy, health, and telecommunications committees. In fact, at the time of the interviews, there was an Assembly Committee on Science and Technology, but it had received so few bills and met so seldom that it was likely to be disbanded.

Legislative Access to University Expertise

Legislators expressed interest in improving access to the tremendous amount of scientific expertise that exists at the University of Wisconsin, although they were skeptical about the willingness of academics to understand legislators' needs. A faculty member agreed that the university had to improve its efforts. "I think there's a feeling in the faculty that we really have to be a little more organized on our end, and, yes, we all have academic freedom and, yes, anybody can approach the legislature whenever they want with whatever they want, and that is at is should be, but we as an institution have some obligation to get together and to work things out."

Possible institutional mechanisms mentioned for improving legislative access to university expertise were the Division of University Outreach and the University Extension Program. A faculty member cited the Water Resources Center as a university department that is interested in a closer working relationship with the legislature. A specific suggestion from a committee chair was to formalize the relationship between certain faculty members and relevant legislative committees. At the time of the interviews, he was exploring the development of such a relationship with the College of Agriculture and Life Sciences. Another suggestion was to involve the LaFollette Institute in holding a conference to examine the ramifications of the technology revolution on the Bill of Rights.

State Science and Technology Policy

The Governor's Commission for the Study of Administrative Value and Efficiency (SAVE) has recently issued its report on goals and strategies for Wisconsin in the twenty-first century. This ambitious effort on the part of government, industry, labor, and academia to redirect the state's future includes developing a new Wisconsin Idea "using the knowledge of the university, private colleges, and business to develop science and technology policy." "The governor and the legislature need to tap the state's knowledge in a nationally distinctive way in drafting policies, laws, and programs" states the final report. As part of the 1995 Wisconsin Act 27, the legislature has now enacted into law specific legislation to implement SAVE recommendations, including the establishment of an information technology fund.

WYOMING
STATE PROFILE

ENTERED UNION:
July 10, 1890 (44th admitted)[1]
LAND AREA:
97,105 sq. mi.; U.S. rank #9
POPULATION:
470,242 (1993 est.)
U.S. rank #50
Density per sq. mi. 4.8[2]
DEMOGRAPHICS:
White .4 m; Hispanic .03 m; Native American .01 m;
Black .004 m; Asian .003 m
ECONOMY:
GSP: $12.6 b (1990); U.S. rank #48[3]
Agriculture (net farm income): U.S. rank #38
Manufacturing (total income); U.S. rank #50[4]
Mining (total income); U.S. rank #11
Per capita personal income: $19,539 (1993)[5]
Unemployment: 5.4%
Number of patents: 51 (1991); U.S. rank #49[6]
Number of SBIR awards: 4 (1983-91); U.S. rank #50
State technology development agency:
    The Science, Technology, and Energy Authority;
        budget: FY '94: $350,000; FY '95: $600,000
EDUCATION:
High school graduation rate: 78.6%; U.S. rank #15[7]
State and local government expenditures for higher
    education: $223 m (1989-90); U.S. rank #26
    (by % of total expenditures)

Academic R&D expenditures: FY '91 $23 m;
U.S. rank #49[6]

POLITICAL:

U.S. Senators: 2 Republicans[5]

Congressional Representatives: 1 Republican

Governor—4-year term

Since statehood: 22 (10 Democrats,
12 Republicans)[8]

Since 1970: 4 (2 Democrats, 2 Republicans)

Current Governor: Jim Geringer (R), 1st term[5]

State Legislators: 90[1]

State Senators: 30; 4-year term

1994: 10 Democrats, 20 Republicans

1995: 10 Democrats, 20 Republicans[9]

State Representatives: 60; 2-year term[1]

1994: 19 Democrats, 41 Republicans

1995: 13 Democrats, 47 Republicans[9]

Length of session: odd years, 40 legislative days;
even years, 20 legislative days[1]

Annual salary: $75; per diem living expenses $60
(not to exceed 40 legislative days during an odd
year or a total of 60 over two years); Senate president receives an additional $78/day; House
Speaker receives an additional $78/day

State budget: FY '93 $1.9 b; FY '92 $1.9 b;
FY '91 $1.8 b[10]

Legislative budget: $3.1 m[11]

Total staff: 113; U.S. rank #48[12]

---

[1] *CSG Book of the States*, 1994-1995.
[2] *World Almanac*, 1995.
[3] *State Rankings*, 1994.
[4] *Gale State Rankings Reporter*, 1994.
[5] *Almanac of the 50 States*, 1995.
[6] *Partnerships: A Compendium*, 1995.
[7] *CQ's State Fact Finder*, 1993.

[8] *Encyclopedia Americana*, 1992.
[9] *State Yellow Book*, Spring 1995.
[10] U.S. Dept. of Commerce World Wide
Web census page <www.doc.gov/
CommerceHomePage.html>.
[11] *State Government Finances*, 1992.
[12] NCSL, 1988.

WYOMING
STATE REPORT

Interview Profile

Legislature: 16 (5 senators, 4 representatives, 7 legislative
    staff)

Findings

1. Need for Science and Technology Policy Support

There is no consensus among respondents in Wyoming about whether the need for technical information and analysis has increased in recent years. Those who say it has increased cite, for example, the increasing complexity of governing in a highly regulated world. Others suggest a more nuanced perspective that although the need for technical information or analysis as such has remained constant, the demand for better quality data has increased; that is, "as the regulations from the federal government, the mandates, get more stringent and specific the need is increasing for more accurate data and good data." Still others see a stasis or even a backtracking: "It's amazing, [but] no. I see things getting less. It's simply kind of spooky. I think the caliber of legislators is changing, especially with term limits. . . . Their interim work is not as thorough as it once was. It's more that it covers a . . . broader scope of issues, but by the same token, it's not as in-depth as it once was."

Despite this apparent dissension about change over time, the respondents recognize a number of issues before the legislature that do require technical information and analysis, particularly issues in energy and the environment such as hazardous waste disposal, storage of spent nuclear fuel, and oil production and other resource extraction concerns (mine safety, severance taxes, etc.). Other important issues with technical content are in areas of game management and agriculture, education and health care reform, workers' compensation, state and federal land use, telecommunications, and transportation.

There is some sense—especially in a comparative context—that technical information and analysis is not particularly important in Wyoming politics, in large part because—as one respondent paraphrased U.S. Senator Alan Simpson—Wyoming is a small town with unusually long streets. Some respondents almost had to stretch to find examples of issues in which technical information and analysis was important. One legislator guessed, "In my six years in the Wyoming legislature, I don't think I've ever seen anything that I would call real in-depth research analysis. The time and interest span don't allow for it. You do an awful lot of things on a gut reaction to either a superficial or a moderate amount of research and analysis."

2. Internal and External Sources of S&T Policy Support

Internal Sources

The most important source of technical information and analysis for the Wyoming legislature is its Legislative Service Organization (LSO), a centralized, nonpartisan staff agency. LSO has a director and 12 professional staff divided among a legal services division, a budget and fiscal division, and a program evaluation division. The latter group is also associated with the Management Audit Committee and began as a financial audit group. The legislature created the LSO in 1971 in response to outside criticism of its low level of professionalization and the high level of influence of lobbyists. LSO grew to 19 full-time equivalents, including support staff, by 1979, and with the planned addition of more program evaluation staff, will increase to more than 20 full-time employees. LSO's primary task is bill drafting; it performs only secondary research, generating one- and two-page work products.

The relationship between staff and legislators is "close and friendly and informal." Each staff member is responsible for two or three committees. When, for example, an interim committee meets, the LSO staffer will be responsible for all aspects of committee support from taking the minutes to answering specific questions about the statute to plugging in the coffee pot. At times, LSO gets involved in procedural matters as well. Staff generally describe their role as that of a "conduit" or a "bridge" from the real sources of information to the legislators.

Many of the respondents, particularly the legislators themselves, agreed that legislators are also important sources of technical information and analysis. There are two Wyoming legislators with doctoral degrees, and others with professional background in many of the issue areas, such as ranching, with which the legislature deals. One legislator claimed to be a very important source: "I go to the library and do my own research." Nevertheless, there is much skepticism about the extent that the citizen-legislators in Wyoming are or can be informed about technical issues other than those with which they might deal professionally.

External Sources

The external sources of technical information and analysis in Wyoming seem to be important in large part because of their unique status. State executive agencies are the most important external source, followed by the National Conference of State Legislatures (NCSL) and other organizations to support state government, the University of Wyoming, and finally lobbyists.

Wyoming has had a durably divided government, and there is significant skepticism of the expertise in the executive agencies. But respondents recognize the unique position of agency experts as administrators of the programs in question. In some instances, agencies perform analyses that are legislative prerogative in other states, such as estimating the fiscal impact of proposed legislation on programs (known as "fiscal notes"). Nevertheless, respondents indicate that the agencies are less politicized than the lobbyists and trade associations because the their sources are a matter of public record. On the integrity of information from state executive agencies, one legislator indicated that, in ten years, "there's only been one or two cases where I've felt that the administrators . . . were trying to pull the wool over our eyes. There's been a few more cases where they've omitted facts because the facts were not asked for."

NCSL and other organizations supporting state government loom large in Wyoming, according to one legislator, because they are "Johnny-on-the-spot." For a small staff, the clearinghouse functions of NCSL are very important and the publications are accessible and useful, although some of the analysis might have an "Eastern" or more urban/ suburban bias. Another clearinghouse mentioned was the American Legislative Exchange Council (ALEC), an organization with conservative affiliation.

The University of Wyoming—the only four-year institution of higher education in the state—is also an important source of technical information and analysis, although, as in other states, there are some indications of dissatisfaction and tension between the university's roles as supplier of information and recipient of funds. One legislator describes a method of accessing information from the university as picking up the phone and calling the university's lobbyist. Another staffer describes university research: "By the time it gets to this level, probably the true and pure research has been filtered to the point of becoming . . . how the university wants to present itself, which is technically . . . correct but in need of more funding."

There are two organizations at the university dealing with issues related to technical information and analysis: the Center for Policy Research, which maintains a library of policy-relevant reports, and the Science, Technology and Energy Authority (STEA), which is a tool for technology-based economic development in the state. STEA received a legislative charter after the legislature itself tried to engage in economic development projects and ended up with a "boondoggle."

Lobbyists are important sources of technical information and analysis in Wyoming, especially because they are very responsive, but respondents suggest that their importance is limited by recognition of their partiality. One legislator describes a strategy to deal with lobbyists: "As we leave the chambers at noon and I've got a question on a bill coming up that afternoon, I try to find a pro and a con lobbyist and say, 'Tell me why I should or shouldn't support this." And when I get back from lunch, on my desk are the pros and the cons."

3. Characteristics of Useful S&T Policy Support

Despite its divergence from most other states, the characteristics of useful scientific and technical support described by Wyoming's respondents are generally the same as in other states: accessibility, reliability, and responsiveness. No one has "more one-on-one contact than we have. We know the individuals. You tend to trust those that you know, and you can judge whether you value or don't value their information," says one legislator. As elsewhere, this familiarity and trustworthiness was associated with a sense of possession: "I think it's our own contacts, our own things that we're more comfortable with," whether the source is the staff at the LSO, personal contacts, or the Wyoming congressional delegation.

There is some sense, however, that the executive agencies in the state are, in the words of one long-time staff member of LSO, "the sole experts I think everybody recognizes on certain issues." In the intimate political environment of Wyoming, there is little room for redundancy, and useful sources seem to useful because they are often unique. In the same way, the University of Wyoming is the lone four-year institution of higher education in the state, and "they are important to use because they're the only source of that kind in the state."

4. Legislative Use of Technology

The Wyoming legislature has had a computerized bill- and amendment-drafting tracking system since 1977. LSO became fully computerized about three years ago, and the staff makes use of an internal e-mail system. The computer system is used primarily for bill-tracking, word processing, and "number-crunching." The Internet and on-line databases are not very important sources of technical information and analysis, in part because staff members do not have access at their desks but must go to the library. Since the bulk of staff work is bill drafting, the primary sources are Westlaw and Lexis.

Wyoming is the only state legislature in the nation not to have electronic voting in either of its chambers. (There are two explanations for not moving to electronic voting: it is just as quick if not quicker to show hands, and electronic voting means more recorded votes, which some legislators want to avoid.) Bills for electronic voting have passed the House in previous years, but not the Senate.

5. Technical Information in a Political Environment

Technical information and analysis is obviously only one part of legislative decision making, and in Wyoming it seems not to be a particularly large part. There is no apparent consensus among the respondents that technical information and analysis is more or less important than the opinions of constituents, leadership, or fellow legislators, although legislators seem to weigh it more heavily than staff expect. In many cases, respondents attribute the relative weight of technical information versus constituent opinion to the character of the issue; technical information would not be very important in one with high emotional content, for example, gun control.

The political environment in Wyoming is not conducive to the development of a great deal of technical information or expertise. The state is not populous, has a relatively homogeneous population and minimal human services problems, consequently there are few demands on the citizen-legislature, which is only slightly staffed. Beyond the short sessions, the joint interim committees usually meet only one or two days per interim. The incentives for legislators to specialize and do committee work are minimal, because floor procedures in both chambers make floor debate and amendments plentiful. Furthermore, turnover is increasing and the number of legislators with technical expertise acquired through long service is dwindling.

As one might expect, the stage of the legislative process at which LSO had the greatest importance was in drafting legislation. Information and analysis from LSO was also important for legislators in responding to legislation introduced by others and in evaluating previously enacted legislation. It was less important in long- and short-term agenda setting and least important in helping legislators decide how to vote. LSO is primarily reactive in its work mode, and respondents do not want staff to be any more proactive.

The primary barrier to the provision of technical information and analysis identified by respondents was time: respondents felt that time constraints—which overlap with staffing constraints—impair LSO somewhat in its ability to provide useful information. Some of the time constraints are also derived from the ability of the sources of staff, such as NCSL, to perform quickly. Other barriers include the ability of staff to extract information from the agencies or find unbiased outside sources, and the ability of citizen-legislators (with not much seniority) to understand the technical information and its complexities and uncertainties. In some sense, technical information encounters a barrier in the state's dominant political culture that minimizes its importance through an informal approach to governance and a laissez faire preference. As one respondent related, "If I hear one more time, 'If it ain't broke, don't fix it,' I think I'll gag. Yet, that does seem to be the watchword."

There is general agreement that the technical information and analysis provided by LSO staff has helped make the legislature more powerful or authoritative with respect to the executive branch and nearly unanimous agreement with respect to lobbyists. In the words of one legislator, "We'd just be whipped without them," especially considering the part-time nature of the legislature. As in some other legislatures, respondents recall times, for example, when lobbyists wrote bills directly for the legislators.

6. Legislative Satisfaction

There is a good deal of satisfaction in Wyoming with LSO and its role in the provision of technical information and analysis, but less satisfaction with the overall provision of technical information and analysis. Legislators seemed marginally more satisfied than staff believe they are. Respondents suggest that a great variance in terms of quality exists among the external sources of information and that they are sometimes satisfied with products and sometimes not.

7. Recommendations

There is some skepticism in Wyoming about how long the relatively informal style of government can endure. As one respondent said, "I think it's appalling that this state runs itself with so little research. . . . It seems to me we're used to legislating by anecdote." But there are as of yet few concrete proposals or recommendations for improvement. LSO has been looking to increase its program evaluation function, and there have been some proposals to revamp the process of writing fiscal notes. There is some sentiment to increase the number of LSO staff, particularly in technical areas that might include, for example, the collection of data to compete with executive and lobbyist data. But there are also budgetary and space constraints to new hiring, as well as the possibility of going well over capacity during interims.

Respondents would like to see greater computer and Internet access. Staff also mentioned the desire for greater funding—not just for staff but also for legislators—to support increased professional interaction with their counterparts in other states. The idea of increasing the ability is not unique to the proposal to increase funding for out-of-state travel. One legislator counselled that the "best way to [increase the technical capacity of the legislature] is to elect a spectrum [of legislators who] have the expertise." Staff also suggest that more, or more expert, staff are not justified, because their current capacity is not sufficiently tapped by the legislators.

LIST OF
ACRONYMS

AIDS	acquired immune deficiency syndrome
ALEC	American Legislative Exchange Council
ASME	American Society of Mechanical Engineers
BOP	Business Organizations and Professionals
CATs	University Centers of Advanced Technology
CEO	chief executive officer
CQ	*Congressional Quarterly*
CRS	Congressional Research Service
CSG	Council of State Governments
DWI	driving while intoxicated
EDR	Economic and Demographic Research
EMF	electromagnetic field
EPA	Environmental Protection Agency
EPSCoR	Experimental Program to Stimulate Competitive Research
GPS	Global Positioning System
GRA	Georgia Research Alliance
GSP	gross state product
GTEC	Governor's Technical Excellence Committee
HLS	House Legislative Service
HRO	House Research Office
IG	Institute of Government at the University of North Carolina
K-12	kindergarten through 12th grade
KLTPRC	Kentucky Long-Term Policy Research Center
KSG	Kennedy School of Government
KSTC	Kentucky Science and Technology Council
LAN	local area network
LRC	Legislative Research Commission

LSC	Legislative Services Commission
LSO	Legislative Services Office
LSO	Legislative Service Organization
LSU	Louisiana State University
LVR	Legislative Vote Reporting System
MTI	Minnesota Technology, Inc.
NAFTA	North American Free Trade Agreement
NCSL	National Conference of State Legislatures
NMERI	New Mexico Engineering Research Institute
NMTEC	New Mexico Technology Excellence Committee
NSF	National Science Foundation
OTA	Office of Technology Assessment
OTP	Office of Technology Policy
PC	personal computer
PRISM	Partnership in Reform Initiatives in Science and Mathematics
R&D	research and development
RPI	Rensselaer Polytechnic Institute
REC	Revenue Estimating Conference
S&T	science and technology
SAVE	Study of Administrative Value and Efficiency
SBIR	Small Business Innovative Research
SERVE	South-Eastern Regional Vision for Education
SREB	Southern Regional Exchange Board
SRO	Senate Research Office
SRS	Senate Research Service
SSI	Systemic Science Initiative
STEA	Science, Technology and Energy Authority
SUNY	State University of New York
TRP	Technology Reinvestment Program
UNM	University of New Mexico
WILLIS	Wisconsin Legislative Information System
WIPP	Waste Isolation Pilot Project
WWW	World Wide Web